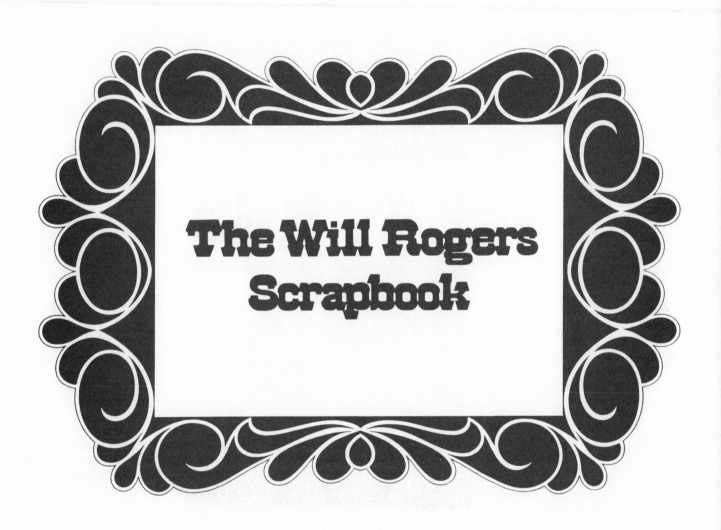

The Will Rogers Scrapbook

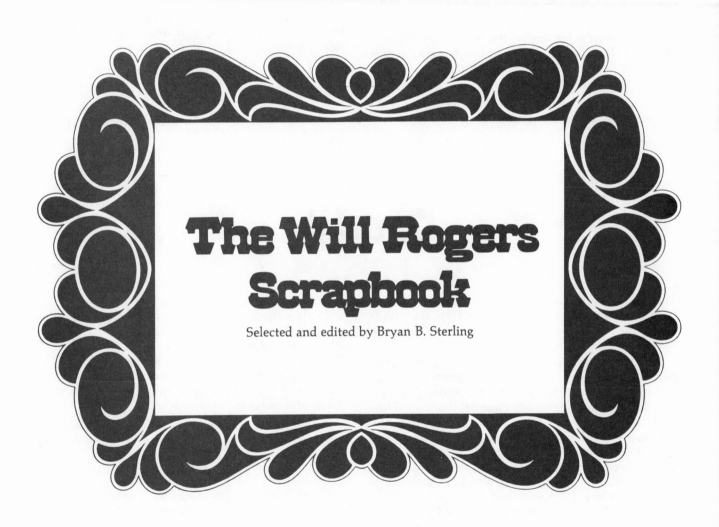

The Will Rogers Scrapbook

Selected and edited by Bryan B. Sterling

BONANZA BOOKS
New York

Acknowledgments

This book is based not only on personal efforts made over many years, but also the dedicated work of others who deserve to be most prominently cited:

Paula M. and Robert W. Love, curator and manager, respectively, of the Will Rogers Memorial, Claremore, Oklahoma. Devoted and noble guardians, my mentors and my friends,

Will, Jr., Mary and Jim Rogers, the children of Will and Betty Rogers, who have allowed me to immerse myself in the treasures they have preserved,

The Will Rogers Memorial Commission, those conscientious custodians, who under their chairman, Dr. Raymond W. Knight, encouraged my efforts,

May Poole, Helen Eaton and Irene Milam, nieces of Will Rogers, who shared with me their treasured memories,

Friends, associates and coworkers of Will Rogers, who told me facts and anecdotes which otherwise might have been lost,

Newspaper editors, librarians, collectors and fans, who have, in so many cases, provided valuable additional information,

Frances N. Sterling, my wife, last only because of decorum. She slaved valiantly, far beyond the requirements of the marriage vow.

My thanks to all of you. You have enriched my life.

Credits

The material and pictures in this book have been drawn from a number of sources, primarily from the collection of the Rogers Company and from the Will Rogers Memorial, Claremore, Oklahoma.

Specific credit must be given for the following photographs, courtesy of Twentieth Century-Fox: page 87, *State Fair,* © 1933, Twentieth Century-Fox Corporation. All rights reserved. Page 88, (bottom), *They Had to See Paris,* © 1929, Twentieth Century-Fox Corporation. All rights reserved. Page 89, (bottom), page 90, *A Connecticut Yankee,* © 1931, Twentieth Century-Fox Corporation. All rights reserved. Page 91, *Dr. Bull,* © 1933, Twentieth Century-Fox Corporation. All rights reserved. Page 92, page 93, page 153, *David Harum,* © 1934, Twentieth Century-Fox Corporation. All rights reserved. Page 93, *The County Chairman,* © 1935, Twentieth Century-Fox Corporation. All rights reserved. Page 95, *In Old Kentucky,* © 1935, Twentieth Century-Fox Corporation. All rights reserved. Page 119, *Lightnin',* © 1930, Twentieth Century-Fox Corporation. All rights reserved. Page 125, *Handy Andy,* © 1934, Twentieth Century-Fox Corporation. All rights reserved.

Credit must also be given to the Museum of Modern Art, New York, N.Y., for supplying the following photographs: pages 124, 142, 148, 166, 170, 174.

Photograph on page 130 by Chidnoff.

The photograph appearing on pages 54–55 courtesy of NBC-TV, Project XX, "The Story of Will Rogers."

Library of Congress Cataloging in Publication Data

Rogers, Will, 1879-1935.
    The Will Rogers scrapbook.

    Reprint of the ed. published by Grosset & Dunlap, New York.
    Includes index.
    1. Rogers, Will, 1879-1935. 2. Entertainers—United States—
Biography. 3. Humorists, American—Biography. I. Sterling,
Bryan B. II. Title.
[PN2287.R74A37 1980]   792.7'028'0924 [B]
    ISBN 0-517-33458-5   80-25832

Contents

Foreword

When Bryan Sterling asked me to write a foreword for this book, I told him that I would be glad to try but that I didn't know just what would be appropriate. He suggested some personal recollection or, perhaps, an evaluation of Dad's importance, as seen in retrospect.

Now, it may seem odd but as the years have rolled by, the Will Rogers whose daily article was read by millions — the star of stage, screen and radio known as the Cherokee Kid, the Poet Lariat, the Cowboy Philosopher, or America's Good Will Ambassador — has become almost a separate person from the Will Rogers I knew as Dad, Pop, Pa Willie, and the Old Man.

You see, I remember a fellow who used to wrestle with Big Boy Williams alongside the polo field, and who, in a Sunday game at the Riveria Polo Club, reached out and bulldogged Big off his horse so that the two fell rolling on the grass in front of the grandstand. I'll never forget the day I bumped him so hard it knocked his horse down and he landed on the sideboards. He lay there motionless and as I jumped from my horse and ran to him, all I could think of was that I had killed him. As I got to his side, he moved and tried to sit up. Still stunned and groggy, the first words he said were, "Is Rowdy all right?"

Oh, I remember a man who loved to rope. Mother used to say that Dad would rather rope than eat. We had a little mouse-colored calf that could kick you in the chin with any foot. Dad called him the visitor's calf. One day when Ed Vail, a rancher friend, stopped by, nothing would do but we would pen the calves and rope a few. Now, Dad loved a practical joke and it wasn't long before he had talked Ed into tying down a couple. Dad, of course, pointed out the little mouse-colored calf and Ed roped him. As he stepped off his horse and went down, the roped calf met him halfway. It was quite a battle. One minute Ed would be on top and the next minute the calf, but he finally got him tied. Dad was laughing so hard he almost fell off his horse, and when Ed — with his shirt all ripped, his nose bloody, and his pants torn — walked up to Dad and said that he figured it was his turn to try the calf, Dad said, "Oh no, he's restricted to visitors only."

My recollections are too full of a man comforting an eight-year-old boy when his pony was killed by a Pacific Electric train, and I remember that same Dad, with tears in his eyes, trying to console three children when our little Sealyham terrier died from a snake bite.

I think I'll just have to leave an evaluation of his importance to others, for, you see, the Will Rogers I knew best was the Will Rogers I saw for the last time: squatted down on his heels, a tin plate piled high with fried beef, beans, and sour-dough biscuits, drinking coffee so strong it would eat the filling right out of your teeth, and visiting with us cowboys around the "Mashed O" chuck wagon about ten miles northeast of Muleshoe, Texas.

— James Blake Rogers

Introduction

Late on a summer's evening in 1935, Will Rogers died. One man, the Eskimo Clare Okpeaha, saw the small plane fall into the Alaskan inlet. He waded far into the shallow water and called out. But his was the only voice piercing the Arctic stillness. There was no answer.

Many hours would pass before America learned the news. Then, special radio broadcasts and extra editions of newspapers brought fragments of additional information to a stricken people. To a country in the midst of a deep depression and rapidly approaching a war, the loss of its single most reassuring voice was calamitous. Men and women cried openly, without shame. Motion picture houses remained dark, and both NBC and CBS radio networks were silent for thirty minutes. Never has a private citizen thus been mourned.

A quarter of a century later, almost to the day, I met Will Rogers. My assignment was to produce a phonograph recording of America's foremost humorist. In the luxurious comfort of a four-engined jet airliner taking me from New York to Los Angeles, I devoured a biography, to give me some background knowledge. It only whetted my curiosity. I wanted to learn more, much more, about this man I had never known. And then, in an office in the heart of Beverly Hills, I listened for the first time to the voice of Will Rogers. It reached across the years, years of many changes, of crises and triumphs, and it captivated me as surely as it did millions in the days of early radio. The spell of this Oklahoman, so unpretentious, has held me all the years since. I never grow tired to read or hear that chronicler of a bygone era, when all was so different.

And always there is Will Rogers, his blue eyes twinkling in their wise way, showing me that nothing has really changed at all. That everything had been so similar, and man, as man will, has managed to live through it all, to emerge triumphant. And then, man, as man will, stumbles headlong once more into precisely the same abyss. Will Rogers, the cowboy philosopher, must surely look down on us and chuckle. And anyone within earshot will probably hear him drawl: "Don't take yourself so serious! Just live your life so you wouldent be ashamed to sell your family parrot to the town gossip."

B.B.S.

Chronology

1879
November 4, Will Rogers born on his father's ranch, near Oologah, I.T. (Indian Territory), now Oklahoma.

1887
[–1892] Attends schools (Drumgoole, near Chelsea; Presbyterian Mission School, Tahlequah, I.T.; Harrell Institute, Muskogee, I.T.).

1890
Mary America Rogers (mother) dies.

1892
Willie Halsell College, Vinita, I.T. (approximately 4 years).

1896
Scarritt College Institute, Neosho, Missouri.

1897
[–1898] Kemper Military School, Boonville, Missouri.

1898
Begins work as cowboy on the Ewing Ranch, Higgins, Texas.

1899
[–1902] Manages Rogers ranch, attends roping contests.

1902
Leaves for South America, via England; works for about 5 months with Gauchos, then leaves for South Africa.

1903
South Africa, joins "Texas Jack's Wild West Show," billed as the Cherokee Kid. Leaves to tour Australia and New Zealand with Wirth Brothers Circus.

1904
With Colonel Zach Mulhall Show at St. Louis, Missouri (World's Fair). A few vaudeville bookings in Chicago.

1905
With Mulhall Show at New York's Madison Square Garden as part of Horse Show. First New York vaudeville appearance. Vaudeville career begins, lasts to 1915, including 3 trips to Europe.

1908
November 25, marries Betty Blake, at Rogers, Arkansas.

1911
Clem Vann Rogers (father) dies. Birth of first son, Will, Jr. in New York City.

1912
[–1913] Specialty act in Broadway show "The Wall Street Girl" starring Blanche Ring.

1913
Birth of only daughter, Mary Amelia, at Rogers, Arkansas.

1914
London, England, in show "Merry-Go-Round." Vaudeville in America.

1915
First airplane flight at Atlantic City, N.J. Appears in musical "Hands Up"; Ned Wayburn's "Town Topics"; and Ziegfeld's "Midnight Frolic." Birth of second son, James Blake, on Long Island, N.Y.

1916
[–1925] Ziegfeld Follies.

1918
Birth of third son, Fred Stone Rogers. While working in "Follies" at night, makes first motion picture (made at Ft. Lee, N.J.) "Laughing Bill Hyde."

1919
Published *The Cowboy Philosopher on the Peace Conference* and *The Cowboy Philosopher on Prohibition*. Moves to California to begin two-year contract with Goldwyn Studio.

1920
Fred Stone Rogers, age 20 months, dies during diphtheria epidemic.

1922
First radio broadcast (Pittsburgh, Pa.). Produces and stars in his own motion pictures. Begins series of weekly, syndicated articles (McNaught Syndicate), which continue to 1935.

1923
[–1924] Stars in two-reel comedies for Hal Roach. Publishes *Illiterate Digest*.

1925
[–1928] Travels all over America on lecture tour.
[–1927] Writes daily article "Worst Story I've Heard Today."

1926
London, England, appears for four weeks in the Charles Cochran Review. Writes *Letters of a Self-Made Diplomat to his President*. Benefit for Florida hurricane victims. Made honorary Mayor of Beverly Hills. Trip to Russia.
[–1935] Begins series of "Daily Telegrams," syndicated to over 400 newspapers.

1927
First civilian to fly from coast to coast with mail pilots. Publishes *There's Not a Bathing Suit in Russia*. Made "Ambassador at Large of U.S." by National Press Club, Washington, D.C. Visits Mexico with Charles A. Lindbergh, as guest of Ambassador Dwight Morrow. Benefit tour for Mississippi flood sufferers.

1928
[–1929] Substitutes for friend Fred Stone in musical comedy "Three Cheers," with Dorothy Stone.

1929
First sound film for Fox Film Corporation *They Had To See Paris*, with Irene Rich. Publishes *Ether and Me*.
[–1935] 21 films for Fox.

1930
Radio broadcasts for E. R. Squibb & Sons.

1931
To London to observe Disarmament Conference. Benefit for drought victims in Southwest. Appears on national radio broadcast on unemployment with President Hoover, Calvin Coolidge, Al Smith, and others. To Managua, Nicaragua for benefit of earthquake and fire victims.
[–1932] To the Orient.

1932
Central and South America tour.

1933
[–1935] Radio broadcasts for Gulf Oil.

1934
Trip around the world. Stars in Eugene O'Neill's stage play "Ah Wilderness" in San Francisco and Los Angeles, California.

1935
August 15, dies in plane crash with Wiley Post, famous pilot, near Point Barrow, Alaska.

Will's Own Story

1. The Early Days in the Indian Territory

Memoirs is an old Cherokee word which means that you put down the good things you ought to have done, and leave out the bad ones you did do.

Anyhow, this story opens on the banks of the Verdigris River in the good old Indian Territory, four miles east of a town called Oologah, and twelve miles north of a town called Claremore. The plot of the story is a youth who was prowling up, down, in and across said Verdigris River.

I was born at our old ranch. It was a big, two-story house, but on the back we had three rooms made of frame. Just before my birth, my mother, being in one of those frame rooms, had them remove her into the log part of the house. She wanted me to be born in a log house. She had read the life of Lincoln. So I got the log house end of it OK. All I need now is the other qualifications.

Rutherford B. Hayes was President at the time of my birth. I was the youngest and last of eight children. My folks looked me over, and, instead of the usual drowning procedure, they said, "This thing has gone far enough! If they are going to look like this, we will stop."

I was born because it was a habit in those days, people dident know anything else. Nowadays the income tax allows you $200 for each child. Just removing his adenoids cost more than that, to say nothing about his food, tonsils and fraternity pins. In those days, a doctor would bring you into the world for two dollars a visit, and make good money at it. Everything you were born with was supposed to be buried with you. But nowadays, when you die, all you have left at the funeral is scars and stitches. If you had the stomachache, the doctor cured it; if you have it nowadays, they remove it.

So I just figured out, I was born as a martyr to the ignorance of the old-time doctors. It was the law of averages that put me there. I arrived when childbirth was not grounds for divorce. If a family dident have at least eight children in those days, the father was either in jail, or deceased. "Mother and Baby doing well!" was our national yell.

It falls to the lot of few to be born on national holidays. I claim November 4th as my birthday. That was election day, but I was never able to get elected to anything. I am going to jump out some day and be indefinite enough about everything, so they will call me a politician; then I'll run on a platform of question marks and be elected unanimously, then reach in the Treasury and bring back my district a new bridge, or tunnel, or dam, and I will be a statesman.

As I say, all I got to do is get muddled up enough on public affairs. Anyhow, I was born on election day. Women couldent vote in those days, so my mother thought she would do something, so she stayed home and gave birth to me. The men were all away. I decided to get even with the government. That's why I have always had it in for politicians. Being born on election day, it kinder gave me the advantage of seeing the bunk of it all. I arrived amid a day of crooked ballots. The next year, 1880, why, Garfield was elected President on my first birthday. I dident vote, but they voted my name every year up to 18.

Garfield was assassinated in a depot in Washington, waiting for the Baltimore & Ohio train. He is the first man ever assassinated waiting for one of those trains, but he is not the first casualty, as thousands have starved to death waiting for 'em. I can remember the day of the assassination. I cried that day — well, I cried the day before and the day after, too. But I remember that particular day well.

Darkies raised me. I wasent only raised among Darkies down in the Indian Territory, but I was raised by them. And Lord, I was five years old out on the ranch before I ever knew there was a white child. There wasent any others around there. The first one showed up there when I was about five years old. You see, I was raised with the Darky children. Then one white one showed up about the same time that Hereford cattle came in. I thought this white child and this bald-faced Hereford was the same breed.

My ancestors dident come over on the Mayflower, but they met the boat. My father was Clem V. Rogers. Claremore is the county seat of Rogers County, which was named for him. My father was one-eighth Cherokee Indian, and my mother was a quarter-blood Cherokee. I never got far enough in arithmetic to figure out just how much "Injun" that makes me, but there's nothing of which I am more proud than my Cherokee blood.

It was old Andy Jackson that run us Cherokees out of Georgia and North Carolina. Now to tell the truth, I am not so sweet on old Andy. You see, every time old Andy couldent find anyone to jump on, he would come back and pounce on us Indians. Course he licked the English down in New Orleans, but he dident do it till the war had been over two weeks, so he really just fought them as an encore. Then he would go to Florida and shoot up the Seminoles. Then he would have a row with the government, and they would take his command and his liquor away from him, and he would come back and sick himself onto us Cherokees again.

But old Andy made the White House. The Indians wanted him in the White House so he would let us alone for a while. Andy stayed two terms. The Indians were for a third term for Andy, but he had to get back to his regular business, which was shooting at the Indians. They sent the Indians to Oklahoma. They had a treaty that said: "You shall have this land as long as the grass grows and water flows." It was not only a good rhyme, but it looked like a good treaty, and it was — till they struck oil. Then the government took it away from us again. They said, "The treaty only refers to 'water and grass'; it dident say anything about oil." So the Indians lost another bet. The first one to Andrew Jackson and the second to the oil companies.

But after some of the Cherokees went back and saw where they used to live in Georgia and North Carolina, why, we always felt that Andy had unconsciously done us a favor. For Georgia never was heard of again till Ty Cobb, and North Carolina was in a rut till the cigarette companies pulled them out. So we Cherokees can always kinder forgive old Andy for not knowing what he was doing. Got to give old Andy credit. He fought duels when duels was duels, and not just the inconvenience of getting up before sunrise.

It was our tribe of Cherokees that sold the original old Cherokee Strip. I think the government only give us about a dollar an acre for it. We had it for hunting grounds, but we never knew enough to hunt oil on it. I can remember as a kid, the payment we had, when the government paid out the money to the Cherokees for it. There was something over three million dollars, as there was that many acres, and we got about $320 a piece, I think it was.

The Cherokees are supposed to be the highest civilized tribe there is, and yet, that's all we got in all our lifetime. We sold a fortune in oil and wonderful agricultural land to get that little $320 a piece. Yet there was the Osages, lived right by us, and they got that much before breakfast every morning, and they are supposed to be uncivilized. So it shows you, it kinder pays not to know too much. I would trade my so-called superior knowledge right now for an Osage Headright. If you had their payment, you wouldent need to know anything, only where the payment was going to be held.

My father was a senator in the tribe for years and was a member of the convention that drafted the Constitution of the State of Oklahoma. My father was a captain under Stand Waitie during the Civil War, but you couldent get much war news out of Papa. I

sho didnt inherit this continuous flow of blathering from him. He afterwards freighted from St. Joe, Missouri, to Dallas, Texas. He did that for years until he found out that St. Joe, Missouri, didnt have anything that Dallas, Texas didnt have — outside the James Boys. Under the circumstances, I think my father was pretty wise in quitting hauling from St. Joe to Dallas. He went into the cattle business and settled on a ranch we have in the family yet. They drove a bunch of cattle from down there, up to Kansas City. Well, when they got to Kansas City, they couldent sell them, so they said, "What other town have you got around here that want three thousand cattle?" They said, "Why, St. Louis!" So Papa and his gang lit out for there, only 590 miles.

Now if I wanted to make a scenario out of this, instead of the truth, I would tell you that they couldent sell in St. Louis and had to go on to Chicago, but such is not the truth. They only lost one steer. He jumped off the boat, crossing the Mississippi, going over to East St. Louis, and tried to swim back to Missouri. He really committed suicide rather than enter Illinois.

Then, they all had to ride back to the Indian Territory horseback. Papa rode a mule on the whole trip.

Mama's name was Mary, and if your mother was an old-fashioned woman, and named Mary, you don't need to say much, everybody knows already. What little humor I have came from her. I don't remember her humor, but I can remember her love and understanding of me.

In those days, that old kitchen stove was kept hot after supper. And not only the teakettle was filled, but other pots and pans, and the family washtub was dragged up by the fire, and you went out to the well and helped your Pa draw some water to mix with the hot. While you was doing that, your Ma, if you

With boyhood friend Charlie McClellan (right).

stayed lucky and had a Ma up to then, was getting out all the clean clothes and a-fixing the buttons and a-laying out the schedule of who was to be first. And she was the only one who could tell just how much hot water to put in to make it right. And if anybody had to feel of the hot water and get burned, it was her, not you, and she found dirt behind, and in, your ears that all the highfaluting fixtures in the world can't find today.

Now that was an event. It meant something. It brought you closer together. But now, bathing is so common, there's no kick to it. If two members of the same household have to use the same bath, it is referred to now as a community tub.

Now mind you, I am not against this modern accomplishment. I realize that these manufacturers of fixtures have advanced their art to the point where they are practically modern Michael Angelos. In the old days, an elephant hook was almost necessary for a wife to drag her husband toward anything that looked like water. Today, those interior bath decorators can almost make one of those things inviting. But in doing so, they have destroyed an American institution and ruined the only calendar that a child ever had. That was the Saturday Night Bath! Nowadays, a child grows up in ignorance. From the cradle to the altar, he don't know what day of the week it is. In those good old days, he knew that the next morning after that weekly earwashing, he was going to Sunday School. Now he has not only eliminated the bath on Saturday, but has practically eliminated Sunday School, for neither he nor his parents know when Sunday comes. If the father of our country was Tutankhamend tomorrow, and after being aroused from his tomb was told that the American people today spend two billion dollars yearly on bathing material, he would say, "What got 'em so dirty?"

As I think back on it, we were a primitive people in those days. There were only a mighty few known diseases. Gunshot wounds, broken legs, toothache, fits, and anything that hurt you from the lower end of your neck on down as far as your hips was known as bellyache. Appendicitis would have been considered the name of a new dance, or some new game with horseshoes. Gallstones would have struck us as something that the old-time Gauls would heave at the Philistines, or the Medes and the Persians.

Nervous indigestion was another unknown quantity. In order to have it, you had to be nervous, and in order to be nervous, you had to imagine you had some imaginary illness and that nobody understood you. Well, in those days, when you felt that way and couldent explain why you were queer, they had an asylum for you. There was no such thing as indigestion then, as everybody worked. Of course, when a bunch was talking, and there was quite a sprinkling of girls and women, why we did have such a parlor name for this plot as Cramp Colic; that was Latin for bellyache.

I sure do remember one of my dear old mother's remedies for it. They just built a fire in the old kitchen stove and heated one of the old round, flat kitchen stove lids — the thing you take off the stove if you want what you're cooking to burn. Well, they would heat it up — not exactly red hot, but it would be bright bay. They took it off, wrapped it up in something, and delivered it to your stomach with a pair of tongs. We didnt know what a hot-water bottle was, and the only thing made out of rubber then was boots, and the top of lead pencils, and gents' wearing collars. A drugstore had to get their money out of paregoric, Cheatam's Chilli Tonic and pills by prescription. There were no rubber goods, banana splits, steaks, lettuce sandwiches, flivvers and flasks.

Well, anyhow, the heat from one of those stove lids burned you, so you soon forgot where you were hurt-

14

Showing off for photographer, at family ranch.

ing. It not only cured you, but it branded you. You would walk stooped over for a week, to keep your shirt from knocking the scab off the parched place. Anybody that would look at you who was not familiar with a stove cap would think that an elephant had stepped on you. All it needed was the little scalloping around the edges to make it look like where his toes had sunk in.

Oh, yes, we did have chills, from what we afterwards learned was malaria. I used to have one every other day. Some people had them every day, but you can't expect in this world to have everything. Days when there were no chills billed, with me, I could get out and do a fair kid's day work; but on chill days I didn't punch the clock at all. My day's work was to chill, and I hope I am not egotistical in saying it, but I did a good job at it. I had it down pat.

This is the way you chill: First, you get cold and you shake, your teeth chatter and your body commences shimmying. City folks call it a dance, we call it a disease. Then, after the shaking is over, you get a fever and your head hurts like it is going to burst. When the head quits hurting and the fever goes away, why, that's all there is to the chill; it's over — that is, it's over for that day.

I used to try and have them two days running, so that would give me a few days off; but, no siree, you couldent do it. Those chills knew when they were going to happen. Quinine was a regular food, not a medicine. It set on the table, the same as sugar. The minute you would take it, you'd eat something right quick to take away the taste — but you never could do it quick enough. Well, I finally shook the chills off, and in years to come I never was bothered with them anymore.

My father was pretty well fixed, and being the only male son, he tried terribly hard to make something out of me. He sent me to about every school in that part of the country. In some of them I would last for three or four months. I got just as far as the Fourth Reader, when the teacher wouldent seem to be running the school right, and rather than having the school stop, I would generally leave. Then I would start in another school, tell them that I had just finished the Third Reader and was ready for the Fourth. Well, I knew all this Fourth Grade by heart, so the teacher would remark, "I never see you studying, yet you seem to know your lessons." I had that education thing figured down to a fine point. Three years in *McGuffey's Fourth Reader*, and I knew more about it than McGuffey did.

But I don't want any enterprising youth to get the idea that I had the right dope on it. I have regretted all my life that I did not at least take a chance on the fifth grade.

One of the first schools I went to was Drumgoole. It was a little one-room log cabin, four miles west of Chelsea, Indian Territory. It was all Indian kids went there, and I, being part Cherokee, had enough white in me to have my honesty questionable. There must have been thirty of us in that room that rode horseback and walked miles to get there. We graduated when we could print our full name and enumerate to the teacher the nationality of the last Democratic President.

Mind you, you wouldent believe it, but we dident even have a stadium. Think of that in this day and time! Thousands and thousands of acres surrounding us with not a thing on it but cows, and not a concrete seat for a spectator to sit on! Well, you see, as I look back on it now, a school like that dident have any license to exist. It had to perish.

As I say, the school went out of business. We wasent able to get games which was profitable. It seems that other schools grabbed off all the other good dates and got the breaks in the newspapers. We couldent seem to ever be accused of professionalism. I could see the finish, even as far back as when I was there, along in 1887. Why, I can remember when the coach couldent get enough of us 15 boys out to make a team. We got to running horse races instead. Why, there was just lots of days I dident go out for skull practice at all. I had a little chestnut mare that was beating everything that any of them could ride to school, and I was losing interest in what we were really there for. I was kinder forgetting that we was there to put the old school on a paying basis by seeing how many times we could get through that goal with that old pigskin.

I got to thinking, well, horse racing is the big game, that's where the money is, that's what the crowds pay to see. But as years went along, it showed that I was a lad of mighty poor foresight. Little did I dream that it was football that was to be the real McCoy. Course, we had no way of hardly telling it then, for we was paid practically nothing at all. In fact, we had what I would call a real Simon Pure amateur team. Course, we got our sideline (schooling) free.

Course, I will admit one of the alumni got me to go there. He had spent three weeks there and couldent get along with the teacher, and he wanted to do what he could for the old school, so he procured me. I looked like a promising "end." I could run pretty fast. In fact, my nickname was, and is to this day among some of the old-timers, "Rabbit." I could never figure out if that referred to my speed or my heart.

The rough way they was playing in those days, it dident hurt my feelings any not getting in the game often. I played what you might call a "wide end." I would play out so far that the other 21 would be pretty well piled up before I could possibly reach 'em. You see, when I picked this "wide end" job, I kinder figured that I would arrive a little late for most of the festivities. That's why to this day I don't carry any football scars or bruises. I was fast, but I never seemed to be fast enough to get there in time to get into one of those massacres.

As I said, the school stayed with books such as *Ray's Arithmetic* and *McGuffey's First, Second,* and two pupils in the *Third Reader*. We had even a Geography around there, but we just used it for the pictures of the cattle grazing in the Argentine and the wolves attacking the sleighs in Russia. Well, you see, they just couldent see what was the future in colleges. They just wore out the old books, instead of wearing out some football. We was a-printing our ABC's, when we ought to have been marking down "tackles back" and "lateral passes." We had Indian boys that could knock a squirrel out of a tree with a rock. But do you think the regents knew enough to get a coach like Pop Warner and teach 'em how to hide a ball under their jerseys? No. They just had the old-fashioned idea that the place must be self-sustaining by learning alone, and you see where their ignorance got them.

Now the weeds is higher there than the school house was, and that's what is happening in a few places in this country. We got those same "Drum-goole" ideas. They won't switch and get to the new ideas that it's open field running that gets your old

college somewhere, and not a pack of spectacled orators, or a mess of civil engineers. It's better to turn out one good coach than ten college presidents.

I studied art at Willie Halsell College. I also took elocution. I stopped just in time, or I would have been a Senator.

My old Daddy then packed me off to Kemper Military Academy, at Boonville, Missouri, in '96, thinking the discipline might tame me. I took a dozen of everything with me, but my education dident last long enough to wear them out. Me and Ben Johnson down at Chickasha, Oklahoma, were buddies together at Kemper, just a couple of ornery Indian boys. But the fact is that we were sent to the Missouri State Reformatory, which is located near the same town, and, through somebody's mistake, they enrolled us at the Kemper Military Academy, instead. It was one of the finest military schools anywhere. I was two years there, one year in the guard house and the other in the *Fourth Reader*. One was about as bad as the other. I was spending my third year in the fourth grade and wasent being appreciated, so I not only left 'em flat during a dark night, but quit the entire school business for life.

I could have gone to West Point, but I was too proud to speak to a Congressman.

Billy Johnson of Canadian, Texas, was also an inmate, and a ranch boy, like I had been in Oklahoma, so he advised me of a friend at Higgins, Texas. I, not wanting to face my father with what little I knew, lit out shuck for there.

There has always been some curiosity about how I left Kemper Military Academy in the winter of '98, whether I jumped or was I shoved. Well, I can't remember that far back. All I know is that it was a cold winter, and old man Ewing's ranch on the Canadian River at Higgins, Texas, wasent any too warm when I dragged in there.

Just a while back I was driving over the country where years before, as a boy 18 years old, I had helped drive a bunch of cattle from that very place to western Kansas, and there wasent a house or a chicken in a whole county. That plains was the prettiest country I ever saw in my life, as flat as a beauty contest winner's stomach, and prairie lakes scattered all over it. And mirages! You could see anything in the world — just ahead of you. I ate out of a chuck wagon and slept on the ground all that spring and summer of '98. Lots of folks went to the Klondike, but I couldent get any further away from my home in the Indian Territory than Texas. The limit of my "pay dirt" was, I think, 30 dollars a month.

Yes, Kemper was my last school, and I sure hate to admit it. But there is no use trying to bull it through that I have done much book reading, for I havent. But with the Senate operating six hours a day, and the House the same, all the investigations, and the robbers getting out of jails, the million-and-one things going on, and I read it all, I just got started wrong. All educated people started in reading good books; well, I dident. I seemed to have gone from Frank Merriwell and Nick Carter, right to the *Congressional Record*, just from one set of low fiction to another.

2. Wild West Shows and Vaudeville

y show career kinder dates from the time I first run into Colonel Zach Mulhall. It was in 1899 at the St. Louis Fair — not the World's Fair, just the big St. Louis Fair they hold every year. They had decided as an attraction that they would put on a roping and riding contest. They were not called rodeos or stampedes in those days. They were just what they are, a "Roping and Riding Contest." Well, I was pretty much of a kid, but I had just happened to have won the first, and about my only, contest at home in Claremore. Then we read about them wanting entries for this big contest in St. Louis. Well, someone sent in my name, and the first thing I knew, I was getting transportation for myself and pony to the affair. Well, I went, and Colonel Zach Mulhall had charge of it. He was then, and had been for years, the General Livestock Agent for the Frisco Railroad System. That was a very important job in those days, for it took in all the livestock shipments on their whole line. He knew every big cattleman in the Southwest, and almost everybody else.

I dident get very far in this St. Louis contest. I made the serious mistake of catching my steer, and he immediately jerked me and my pony down for our trouble. But it gave me a touch of "Show Business," in a way, so that meant I was ruined for life, as far as actual employment was concerned.

The Colonel had a couple of daughters, Miss "Bossy," and Lucille. Bossy was quite a good rider, but she never took it up in a professional way that little Lucille did. Lucille was just a little kid when we were in St. Louis that year, but she was riding and running her pony all over the place; that was, incidentally, her start too. It was not only her start, but it was the direct start of what has since come to be known as the "cowgirl." There was no such a thing, nor such a word, up to then, as "cowgirl." But as Colonel Mulhall from that date drifted into the professional end of the contest and show business, why, Lucille Mulhall gradually came to the front and was the first well-known cowgirl.

After that contest, and a few others around the country that the Colonel promoted, why, I drifted off to South America, South Africa, Australia, and around the rest of the universe for a while. I broke all records of sea sickness. I just landed on deck long enough to envy the Statue of Liberty for being in a permanent position and not having to rise and fall with the tide. I dident last even to see Sandy Hook. Oh, I sho was sick, and say, talk about doing things, our ship cut some capers a bucking horse couldent do. Why, this thing did everything but rare up and fall backwards.

I couldent have any luck eating, and I lay on my broad back the whole trip. My diet consisted of a small portion of two lemons, on the whole trip. When I came on deck the last day, they thought a new passenger got aboard. Well, after not having luck enough to die, we finally landed.

When I got back to America, it was the fall before the start of the World's Fair in St. Louis, in 1904. Well, I went out to Mulhall from Claremore a lot that fall and winter, rehearsing and practicing for the big show which the Colonel was to have at the Fair for the whole year.

His shows were of the very best. Neatness was one of his hobbies. His life was miserable, trying to keep me presentable. "Look at the Injun!" He always called me "Injun." "He won't wear a silk shirt, and I have bought him a dozen!" He was generous to a fault. When Colonel Mulhall had money, we were all rich. When he dident, well, you wouldent hardly know it. He never hollered; he never complained; he took misfortune with a smile.

We were in St. Louis during the whole summer of the Fair, with the "Cummings and Mulhall Wild West Show on the Pike." The following year he took a small, picked bunch of us to Madison Square Garden, to work as an added attraction with the Horse Show. I hope Tom Mix don't mind me telling that he was with us too. He has enough so that he don't have to worry about how old people might think he is. We got twenty dollars a week, and was both overpaid. Well, we wasent exactly overpaid, because we dident get the twenty. The show closed, and Tom went back to Oklahoma, and I dident have enough to get back on. But with my little roping act, I was lucky enough to get on the stage, direct from Madison Square Garden.

The old Colonel has long gone now, but I can still hear him say, "Come on, boys, let's give 'em a real show, a Mulhall show! Lucille, now, baby, rope like you never roped before! Injun, wake up and get in there!"

Keith's old Union Square on fourteenth street was the one where I made my first stage appearance. But it was the theatre where they sent me the second week where I made my best hit, and I stayed at it all summer. That was at the greatest vaudeville theatre of that and all times. That was Hammerstein's. I stayed on the roof one whole summer. We played on the roof at nights, and downstairs at matinee. We have never produced another showman like Willie Hammerstein, and the old man was living in those days and with what that theatre made, he was able to indulge in presenting opera.

I used a horse then and had a cowboy ride him across the stage at a run, and I made catches on him as he run by. Buck McKee was the cowboy that rode a little cowpony, Teddy. He trained the pony for the stage. It wasent a trick pony, he just worked on a smooth stage with felt-bottom boots buckled to his feet like galoshes and ran for my fancy roping catches. But Buck trained that pony to do on a slick stage, just what a good turning cowpony can do on the ground. We started the act in the spring of 1905. He was with me, I think it was four or five years. We made two trips to Europe together. That was in the spring of 1906. We went to the Winter Garten Theatre in Berlin; that was the premier vaudeville theatre of all of Europe. We played there a month. The act was

TEXAS JACK'S CIRCUS.
THE
CHEROKEE KID
THE WORLD'S
CHAMPION LASSOER.

He will perform the following feats with the Lasso:

Catching a Horse by One Leg, Two Legs and Four Legs.

Throwing the Rope with his Foot and Catching the Horse.

Forming a Loop in front of his body, carrying this behind him and catching the Horse.

Holding the Lasso by one end, Jerking the rope through the air
and tying single and double knots during its flight.

*Several Varieties of the "Crinoline," making It on Horseback, forming a circle
round the Horse with a Lasso 65 feet long,*

THE MOST WONDERFUL FEAT KNOWN.

Holding a Lasso in each hand, throwing both at the same time and catching Horse and Rider, each by
the neck, while going at full gallop.

19

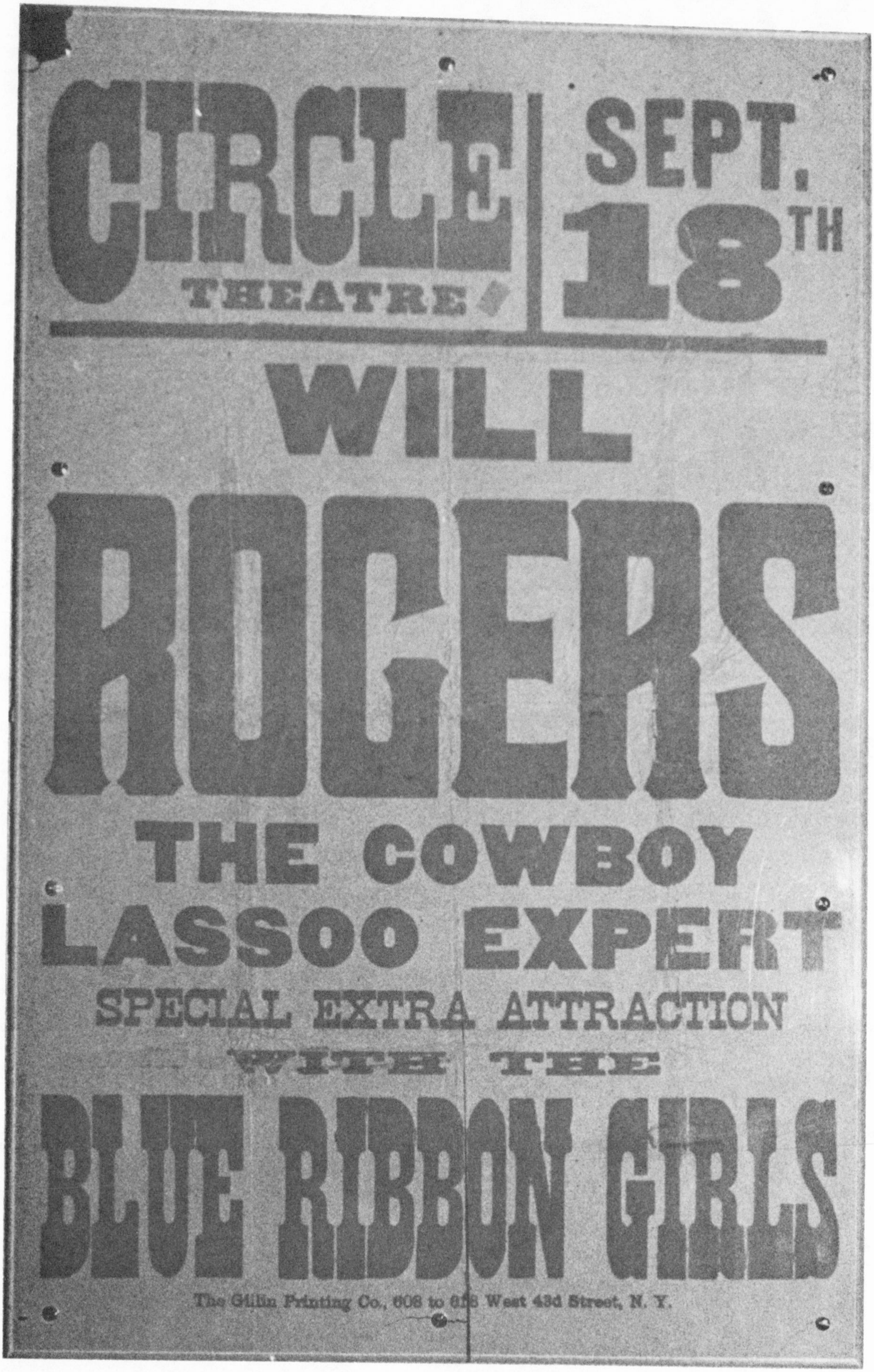

CIRCLE THEATRE SEPT. 18TH

WILL ROGERS

THE COWBOY LASSOO EXPERT

SPECIAL EXTRA ATTRACTION

WITH THE

BLUE RIBBON GIRLS

The Gillin Printing Co., 608 to 618 West 43d Street, N. Y.

20

MAJESTIC | WEEK OF JUNE 19

LOUISE DRESSER
THE COMIC OPERA FAVORITE

EDWARDS·DAVIS & CO.
IN A BRILLIANT NEW PLAY

HARRY FOX AND MILLERSHIP SISTERS
IN A CLASS BY THEMSELVES

THE FOUR HUNTINGS
WITH A RIOT OF FUN

TAYLOR-KRANZ-WHITE
GREAT RAGTIME SINGERS AND PLAYERS

THREE ESCARDOS
IN THEIR NOVELTY TRAMPALINE ACT

CORINNE FRANCIS
SINGING COMEDIENNE

NARROW BROS.
AND THEIR ENTERTAINING NOVELTY

RE-ENGAGED

WILL ROGERS
THE DROLL COWBOY

PRICES 15, 25, 50 AND 75 CTS.

WINTERBURN SHOW PRINTING CO. CHICAGO

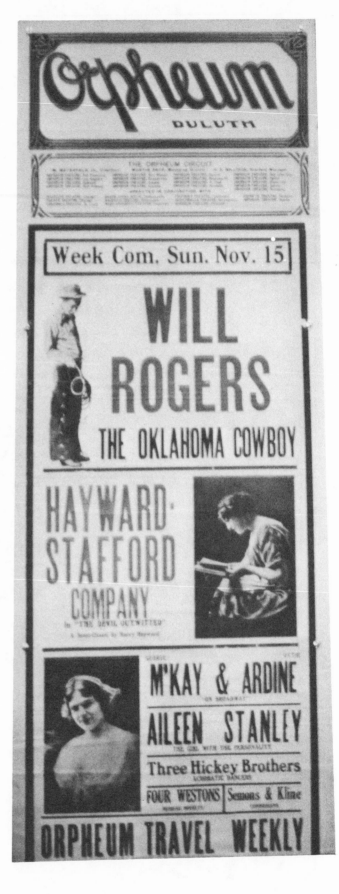

Orpheum
DULUTH

THE ORPHEUM CIRCUIT

Week Com. Sun. Nov. 15

WILL ROGERS
THE OKLAHOMA COWBOY

HAYWARD· STAFFORD COMPANY
In "THE DEVIL OUTWITTED"
A Stage Classic by Harry Hayward

GEORGE M'KAY & ARDINE VICTOR
ON BROADWAY

AILEEN STANLEY
THE GIRL WITH THE PERSONALITY

Three Hickey Brothers
ACROBATIC DANCERS

FOUR WESTONS | Semons & Kline
MUSICAL NOVELTY | COMEDIANS

ORPHEUM TRAVEL WEEKLY

21

CONTRACT.

Between the „**Wintergarten**" G. m. b. H., party of the first part and

party of the second part, the following engagement-contract has been agreed upon by both parties:

(1) The Wintergarten G. m. b. H. engages

W. Rogers, Trickespert (with Assistant and Horse

for a period commencing *April first* 1906 until *April 30th* 1906 inclusively, the party of the second part hereby undertaking to be on hand in Berlin in good time and to hold a complete dress rehearsal if the Wintergarten G. m. b. H. so desires.

The party of the second part *W. Rogers* is obliged and hereby agrees to appear in and act at every performance during the time of this agreement. Without a written permit of Wintergarten G. m. b. H. the party of the second part is prohibited from assisting at any public or private performance during the time of the contract and hereby expressly agrees not to accept any engagement in Berlin within one year after the termination of said contract.

(2) The party of the second part hereby agrees to furnish all necessary properties, fixtures and apparatus (the installation of which is at his own expense) as well as the necessary orchestral music and costumes required for *his* performance in faultless and perfect condition.

(3) The party of the second part hereby agrees to accept this engagement subject to the rules of the house as now in force at the Wintergarten G. m. b. H. which rules the party of the second part hereby expressly acknowledges and regards as a vital part of this contract. The party of the second part furthermore agrees to adhere to and follow all business of the Wintergarten G. m. b. H. or their autorised representative in every point. In case of *W. Roger*'s refusal to do so, Wintergarten G. m. b. H. is entitled to terminate and annul this agreement without further notice. Wintergarten G. m. b. H. is also entitled to terminate and annul the ~~~~ the first the salary of the engagement.

~~~~ the Wintergarten ~~~~ *W. Rogers* a salary of ~~~~ Frs. ~~~~ 60 Pf.) *Three Thousand ~~~~ hundred M.*

per month. The salary is postpayable on the 1st and 16th of each month; from this sum will be deducted *10*% Commission for the agency of *M. Shea* at *New York*. Salary will not be paid for days on which no performances take place. For the month of February two days salary will be deducted.

(5) In case of disputes between the contracting parties, the party of the second part hereby agrees to submit to the jurisdiction of the Berlin Courts, i. e. agrees to sue or be sued or accept service of writ or judgment by default, even if residing elsewhere in Germany or abroad.

With show girls in vaudeville finale, circa 1908.

quite a novelty, as it was the first one to ever use a running horse to be lassoed at on the stage.

We came from Berlin to London, and played the Palace Theatre there, then went back to London in 1907. When we stepped on the stage together, Buck was on horseback. He always said, "I can get away if anything happens, but the audience can get you."

Along about that time, Betty Blake, down in Rogers, Arkansas, had a mental relapse and said "yes," after several solid years of "no's." I was married in 1908. The day I roped Betty, I did the star performance of my life.

From cheap hotels to dark stage entrances, Betty trudged her way. And sometimes the salary wasent any too big to ship Buck and his wife, and Teddy and my wife and self to the next town. In fact, I think Buck rode Teddy on some of the short jumps. It was great fun, not a worry. I regret the loss of vaudeville more than any part of it. It was the greatest form of entertainment ever conceived. Nothing in the world ever gave the satisfaction of a good vaudeville show. We was mighty proud to be playing in it. It had class in those days.

In 1915 I went up on Mr. Ziegfeld's roof, in the Midnight Frolic show. It was the start of all the midnight and late style of entertainment, that has since degenerated into a drunken orgy of off-colored songs. The Frolic started right on the stroke of midnight and would have 50 or 75 people in the cast, bigger than all the modern-day musical shows given at regular hours. It had the most beautiful girls of any show Ziegfeld ever put on, for the beautiful ones wouldent work in the Follies; they wouldent work at a matinee, for they never got up that early. We used to have a time getting 'em up for the midnight show. I don't mean I did. I dident have to go round waking

any of 'em up, but somebody did.

The same bunch of folks, that is about 50 percent of the main ones, were up there at the Frolic every night. It was folks with lots of money and plenty of insomnia. It was the start of my doing topical things. Betty always used to ask me how I was doing. I told her, pretty good, but some of my jokes wasent going as good as they did, for folks couldent just keep laughing at 'em every night. So she said, why don't you read the papers. And I found that Congress was funnier three hundred and sixty days a year than I could ever be.

I stayed with Ziegfeld after that trial show for ten years, with one or two small intermissions for pictures. We never had a contract. I got two hundred and fifty a week, and got my first car, an Overland, and drove it out to Long Island every night about two thirty in the morning. It got to knocking so much, that one night the cop arrested me. "Hey, you can go down the road at night, Rogers," he said, "but you got to leave that thing. You're like an alarm clock at three A.M."

Rex Beach was responsible for my little toehold in the movies, this eighth science. I played by request of Mrs. Beach in one of his stories, called "Laughing Bill Hyde." The part was rather that of a crook who received money under false pretenses. Mrs. Beach had seen my little act in the Follies, so she decided that I was the one to do naturally this crook who obtained money under false pretenses.

I was just getting a good start in the movies, when they appointed Will Hayes to clean them up, and I had to get out. Now they are talking about cleaning up the spoken drama, and I will have to move again. I am going into politics! Nobody ever cleans that up, so I will be set for years.

[Right:]
In Follies skit, 1925.

OTTO R. KNAUER
Formerly FRED. H. HARTMANN
Bakery and Lunch Room
104 BERGENLINE AVENUE

PROGRAM—(Continued.)

EMILY GREENE & CO.
Presenting the Playlet,
"A Minnesota Romance,"
By Chas. Horwitz.

Cast of Characters

Robert Sibley, from Chicago .... George Casselberry
Ethel Burgess .... Miss Alma Stelard
Tilly Swanson .... EMILY GREENE
The Burgess Home in Minneapolis. October.

WILL ROGERS
Champion Lariat Thrower
Little Bill was born this week.

WILL "MUSH" RAWLS
Supported by
ELLA VON KAUFMAN,
In a Minstrel Comedy, **"The Willing Worker."**

(Program continued on next page.)

[Above:]
Program from the Hudson Theater, Union Hill, N.J., for week of October 16, 1911. Notice Will's handwritten entry.

ZIEGFELD ROOF

THE MEETING PLACE OF THE WORLD
ATOP NEW AMSTERDAM THEATRE, NEW YORK

FOLLIES-FROLIC BALL

OF 1918

THURSDAY EVENING, APRIL 25, 1918.

FLORENCE ZIEGFELD, Junior
OFFERS
A COMBINED PERFORMANCE OF THE
ZIEGFELD MIDNIGHT FROLIC
AND
ZIEGFELD FOLLIES OF 1917
Under the Stage Direction of
NED WAYBURN
Lyrics by GENE BUCK Music by DAVE STAMPER

NOTE—DANCING BEFORE AND AFTER THE PERFORMANCE ALSO DURING THE INTERMISSION.

PART I.

1 "WE ARE THE BRIGHT LIGHTS OF BROADWAY," Yvonne Shelton
Misses Margaret Morris, Pauline Hall, Marjorie Beverley, Agnes Jepson, Marie Wallace, Geraldine Alexander, Peggy Carter and Daisy De Witt.
2 "THE INEBRIATED CANINE"..........................Don
Officer, Russell Vokes
3 "THE MOTOR GIRLS"..........................Frank Carter
The "Stutz" Girl.......................... Eleanor Dell
The "Cadillac" Girl..................... Lillian Tashman
The "Packard" Twins......Marion and Madeline Fairbanks
The "Hudson" Girl .... Marjorie Cassidy
The "Ford" Girl .... Kathryn Perry
The "Rolls-Royce" .... Mlle. Dolores
4 "EGYPTIAN CARICATURE" .... Fanny Brice
5 "SWINGING ALONG" .... Lillian Lorraine
6 "I AIN'T MARRIED NO MORE"................Bert Williams
7 "ORIENTAL JAZZ" ....Ann Pennington
8 "THE SPRING DRIVE"..................... Lillian Lorraine
9 "TIMELY TOPICS" .... Will Rogers
(He is liable to talk about anything or anybody)
10 PATRIOTIC PICTURES
arranged by
MR. BEN ALI HAGGIN
(a) "THE SPIRIT OF THE RED CROSS"........Marjorie Cassidy
(b) "ENGLAND" .... Ethel Davies
(c) "BELGIUM" .... Martha Mansfield
A Victim..................Marie Wallace
An Orphan .... Kathryn Brewster
(d) "FRANCE" .... Marcelle Earle
(e) "AMERICA" .... Dolores

PART II.

11 "THE BROADWAY BLUES"................. Lillian Lorraine
Misses Perry, Beverley, Alexander, Carter, Johnson, Falconer, Marshalk, Brooks, Gleason, Smith, Eberts, Worth, Jepson, Butlin, Ellsworth and Stanley.
12 "THE CREATOR OF JAZZ DANCING"................Frisco
13 COMEDY JUGGLING ....W. C. Fields
14 "FRESH FROM THE BRONX"....................Eddie Cantor
15 "A SYNCOPATED FROLIC".................. Ann Pennington
16 "TRY A RING, DEAR!"......................Yvonne Shelton
Misses Carter, Johnson, Perry, Falconer, Johnson, Brooks, Beverley, Drange and Dell.
17 SONG AND DANCE........................... Frank Carter
18 "JUST YOU AND ME"..........Fannie Brice and Eddie Cantor
assisted by
Ned Wayburn's Triple Tappers
19 "QUEEN OF THE WIRE"......................Bird Millman
20 "VICTORY" .... Lillian Lorraine
(In the following order of entrance)
Emily Drange

[Preceding page:]
Will Rogers, fifth from right in front row, in The Wall Street Girl, *1912.*

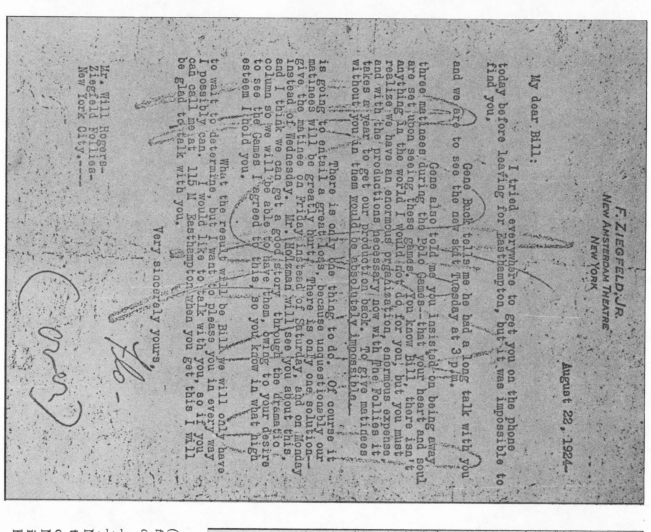

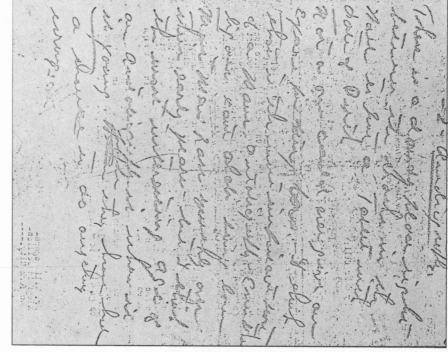

(Left:) Letter from Florenz Ziegfeld agreeing to change matinee days to accommodate his star. (Will Rogers noted content, crossed it out, marked (over) and wrote on the reverse side (above):

-2- Autobiography

There is a dandy place right between the cracks in the Wall to put a Tablet with date of Birth.

Not a one could ever give an excuse for being born. I think that is the most important part of a Mans autobiography. Even the big ones can't alibi being born.

Most men pass quickly over their early years—but I think the most interesting age of an Autobiography is when it is young. Before they have had a chance to do anything wrong.

3. Dopey

We both come from Oklahoma. I went to Madison Square Garden in New York with Colonel Zach Mulhall in 1905. Then went on the stage. He dident come till 1915, ten years later. I first saw him at a town in Connecticut. I think it was Westport. I liked him, and he come home with me, and I think he liked me. And the whole family liked him, and he lived with us all these years, up to a few days ago, when he left us, and it made us all sad, very sad. He was one of the family, he had helped raise our children. He come to our house the same time Jim, our youngest, did. I was working in Ziegfeld's famous Midnight Frolic. We were living in a little home we had rented across the road from Fred Stone's lovely summer home at Amityville, Long Island. We went there to be near Fred and his family. We had a wonderful time that summer.

Yes, Jim and Dopey came that summer. Jim was a baby boy, and Dopey was a little round-bodied, coal-black pony, with glass eyes, the gentlest and greatest pony for grown-ups or children anyone ever saw. I don't know why we called him Dopey. I guess

it was because he was always so gentle, and just the least bit lazy. Anyhow, we meant no disrespect to him.

Outside of a pony I had in the Indian Territory, when I was a boy, and that put me in the exhibition roping business, why along pretty near next to him in affection was Dopey. I remember "Chapel," a bay horse that I owned and used in all my movie chases down steep hills in the old silent days — and that I know saved my life many times. I still have him, he's a freelance. And "Bootlegger" another famous little Oklahoma black pony from the Osage Nation, he is also with us. He was a famous roping pony, and afterwards was with me on Long Island, where I used to try to play polo. He was little and had a long mane and tail, which is unknown in polo, but he became famous through his quick turning.

These, and various others that at different times I have become attached to, were all more of my own, individual ponies, but Dopey belonged to the family. Our children learned to ride at two, and during his lifetime, Dopey never did a wrong thing to throw one

From Ropin' Fool, *produced by Will Rogers (1922). Buck McKee*
rode Dopey. Rope was whitened with shoe polish.

off, or do a wrong thing after they had fallen off. He couldent pick 'em up, but he would stand there and look at 'em with a disgusted look for being so clumsy as to fall off. He never kicked or stepped on one of them in his life, and he was a young horse when I first got him, but he was always naturally gentle, and intelligent.

I used to sit on him by the hour — yes, by the year — and try new rope tricks, and he never batted an eye. Then I learned some trick riding, such as vaulting, and drags, and all that. In fact, he was the only one I could ever do it on. Then in 1919 we went to California to go in the movies. Dopey, and another bay pony we had acquired for Mary, they occupied the best palace horse car by express. Then I would come back to New York to work another year for Mr. Ziegfeld in his Follies, and the first thing loaded would be Dopey. Then after a year in New York, back to the movies again, and back would go Dopey.

One year I took Dopey in a Follies baggage car, on the whole tour with the show, and kept him in the riding academies and practiced roping every day with

him. Charley Aldrich, a cowboy, used to ride him and run by for my fancy roping tricks. He has been missed with a loop more times, and maybe caught more times than any horse living. In a little picture called *Ropin' Fool*, where I did all my little fancy catches in slow motion, he was the pony that run for them. He was coal black, and I had my ropes whitened and the catches showed up fine.

In a tan bark ring we had in our Beverly Hills home, all the children learned trick riding on him, standing up on him running, vaulting, and they would use him with Dodo, to ride Roman style. It was all allowed because I knew they were on gentle ponies.

Dopey has been set free for four or five years, hasent had a bridle on him. Fat as a pig. But when nineteen years of your and your children's life is linked so closely with a horse, you can sorter imagine our feelings. We still have quite a few old favorites left, but Dopey was different. He was one of the family. He raised our children. He learned 'em to ride. He never hurt one in his life. He did everything right. That's a reputation that no human can die with.

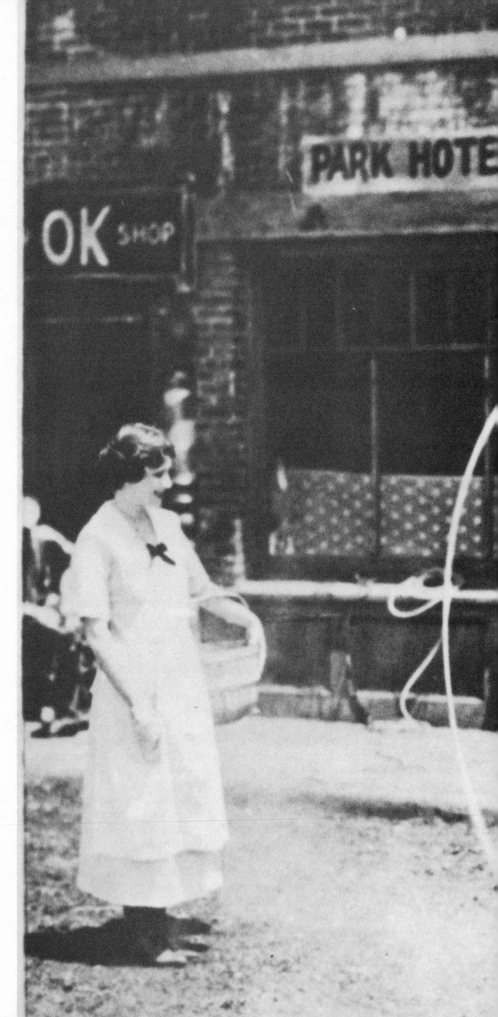

Doing the "Texas Skip" to impress Irene Rich in a scene from Ropin' Fool. For exercise Will often executed 1,000 "Skips" a day.

4. Looking Back, Forward and to Both Sides

The Best Joke I heard today was told to me by Jimmy Rogers, the
youngest of the Rogers clan, Old Jim is ten now and he is what is
known as a natural Comedian, He may never be a Comedian by purpose,
but he will always be funny unconsciously, Everybody that comes to
our house gets some kind of a kick out of Jim, The children like to
play show , and we *HAVE* them a little Theatre in the basement, with
Scenery and footlights and all, They were putting on a show there
the other day and Bill, the oldest, fourteen, was giving Jim some
jokes to tell, He was rehersing Jim They were
doing a double talking act and Bill was to ask Jim the questions,
Here is the 'old Boy they had as one of their rib ticklers, " Who was
that Lady I saw you walking down the street with" Then Jim was
supposed to knock us off the seats with," Why that wasnt any Lady,
that was my wife" Well all of us, and a few that had dropped in to
eat on us, went down to hear the show, They were going along
pretty good and when they got to " Who was that Lady I saw you
walking down the street with?" Jim kinder got stuck in his lines,
and Bill was waiting for his reply when Jim said," Why that was no
Lady that was MAMMA"
" Children, turn those lights off, its time to go to bed, Mother spoke
sharply, But old Jim had knocked 'em off the seats with a good gag,

*During the mid-twenties Rogers wrote a daily
column called "The Best Joke I Heard Today."
This is a sample of Will's typing.*

*A traveling father enjoys a special sojourn at home,
reading to young Jimmy and Mary.*

I have observed that any time a reporter takes down notes, it's just to show how different they can write a thing in the article from what you told them. The question that every guy asked who used to come to interview me was, "Did you really come from out West?" I got so tired of hearing it that I used to tell them, "No, I'm from New Jersey, but don't you tell anybody." The next question, invariably would be, "How did you get on the stage?" Say, anything can get on the stage. It's keeping them off that's hard. A fellow can be the champion soup eater, and if he can locate a manager that will set him up behind a bowl of soup and tell him to go to it — if he can keep the audience amused and the soup holds out — why, he's on the stage.

I am asked, "Who writes your stuff, and where do you get it?" And the surprising answer is: the newspapers write it! All I do is get all the papers I can carry, and then read all that is going on. I have found out that the more up-to-date a subject is, the more credit you are given for talking on it. The remarks you make must be founded on facts. You can exaggerate and make it ridiculous, but it must have the plain facts in it.

I have often said in answer to inquiries as to how I got away with kidding some of our public men, that it was because I liked all of them personally, and if there was no malice in your heart, there could be none in your gags, and I have always said I never met a man I dident like.

I have written on nothing but politics for years. It was always about national or international affairs. I have been in almost every country in the last few years. I have talked with prominent men in those countries, our ambassadors or ministers, and I would have to be pretty dumb to not soak up some information. Now I read politics, talk politics, know personally almost every prominent politician, like 'em, and they are my friends, but I can't help it if I have seen enough of it to know that there is some baloney in it. And I am going to call 'em like I see 'em. If I don't see things your way, well, why should I? I hope I never get so old that I can't peek behind the scenes and see the amount of politics that's mixed in this medicine before it's dished out to the people as "pure statesmanship." But I got no philosophy. I don't even know what the word means. The fourth reader — *McGuffey's* — is as far as I ever got in school. I am not bragging on it. I am thoroughly ashamed of it, for I had every opportunity. Everything I have done has been by luck, no move was premeditated. I just stumbled from one thing to another. I might have been down. I dident know at the time, and I don't know yet, for I don't know what "up" is. I may be lower than I ever was. I don't know. I may be making the wrong use of any little talent (if any) that I accidentally have. I don't know.

But those were great old days — but darn it, any old days are great old days. Even the tough ones, after they are over, you can look back on them with great memories.

Anyhow, life is a racket, so get a few laughs; do the best you can, take nothing serious, for nothing is certainly depending on this generation. Each one lives in spite of the previous one and not because of it. And don't have an ideal to work for. That's like riding towards a mirage. Believe in something for another world, but don't be too set on what it is, and then you won't start out that life with a disappointment. Live your life so that whenever you lose, you are ahead.

[Left:]
Left to right:
Jimmy, Mary,
Mrs. Rogers,
Will,
Will, Jr.

THE WHITE HOUSE
WASHINGTON

October 8, 1934.

Personal

Dear Will:

   We saw "Judge Priest" last night. It is a thoroughly good job and the Civil War pictures are very true to life as I remember the battles of that period!

   Also, I am very glad to see that you took my advice in regard to your leading lady---this time you have one who is good to look at and can also act.

   I suppose the next thing you will be doing is making application for an appointment on the Federal Bench. I might take you up on that!

                              Always sincerely,

                              Franklin D Roosevelt

Will Rogers, Esq.,
Beverly Hills,
California.

[Left:]
A great baseball
fan, Will visits with
pitcher Dizzy Dean.

[Below:]
One of the posters advertising Rogers'
series of travelogs made in Europe.

"In Paris"

They call
this the
Latin Quarter
because no
one can
speak latin
and no
one has
a quarter.

WESTERN UNION

ANYTHING—— EVERYTHING. RUSSIA.

WE USED TO BE WORRIED ABOUT X ONE OF OUR PUBLIC MEN WHEN WE HADENT
HEARD ANYTHING OF HIM IN A LOMG TIME. NOW WE DONE WORRY. WE KNOW
HE JUST BEEN WRITING A BOOK.

NO WONDER OUR EXPORTS TO THE REST OF THE WPRLD FELL OFF, WE STARTED
WRAPPING EVERYTHING IN CELOPHANE AND THE KEX NOBODY KNOWS HOW TO
OPEAN XXKXGXKGKXGX ANYTHING.

THE RUSSIANS FIGURED OUT EVERYTHING IN THEIR COMMUNISTIC SYSTEM
EXCEPT HOW TO GET ENOUGH TO EAT.

RUSSIA IS GOING ALONG FINE THEY ONLY SHORT OF THREE THINGS' THATS
FOOD, ROOMS. AND CLOTHES. THEY AINT SHORT OF WORK. THEY GOT PLANTY
OF THAT.

~~AND IF YOU WOMEN THAT THINK YOU HAVENT GOT EQUALITY WITH MEN
LIKE THEY HAVE IN RUSSIA. THE ONLY DIFFERENCE IS A PICK AND SHOVEL.~~

RUSSIA RUNS EVERYTHING COCKEYED FROM WHAT WE DO, IF A BIG MAN IN ANY
OF OUR PARTYS LIKE TAMMANY, OR THE REPUBLICANS, OR DEMOCRATS, THEY KINDE
GET TOGEATHER AND SQUARET UP. IN RUSSIA THE BIGGER THE MAN OF THE PATY
THAT GETS INTO SOMETHING WHY THE FURTHER HE GOES INTO SIBERAIA.

[Above:]
Will would type his notes on any available piece
of paper but preferred telegram forms.

[Right:]
Asked to help his home town, Will sent this
letter. A shipment of fish arrived shortly.

DEPARTMENT OF COMMERCE.

FISHERIES DEPARTMENT.

DEAR SIRS. I HAVE WRITTEN AND ASKED FOR EVERYTHING IN MY
LIFE, XX(NOT THE GOVERNMNET) THEY ALWAYS BEEN THE ONE •
WRITING TO ME TO SEND EM SOMETHING• BUT I TELL YOU THIS IS
THE FIRST TIME I EVER ASKED FOR FISH. I DONT ASK FOR IT
MUCH AT A CAFE. I AM A KIND OF A MEAT HOUND MYSELF, BUT
WE HAVE SPENT ALL WE HAD IN CLAREMORE TO BUILD A KIND OF
RODEO GROUND FOR FISH, AND NOW WE HAVENT GOT ENOUGH LEFT
TO GET THE FISH WITH, BUT WE HEARD THAT YOU ALL HAD FISH THAT
YOU DISTRIBUTED AROUND TO THE VOTERS• COURSE RIGHT AFTER AN
ELECTION IS A TERRIBLE TIME TO ASK A REPUBLICAN ADMINISTRATIC
FOR A HAND OUT, EVEN IF ITS JUST FISH, COURSE THE CHAMBER
OF COMMERCE WITH THEIR USUAL BAD JUDGEMENT OUGHT TO HAVE
GOT THE FISH BEFORE THE ELECTION. CAUSE I AM LIKE GEAORGE
WASHINGTONX, I CANT TELL A LIE WE VOTED AGAINST YOU,
XXXXXXXXTXXXXTXXQMXIXXTXERXXXXXXXXXXXXXXX BUT WE DID WAN T XXX
YOUR FISH. IF YOU FILL THE BOYS UP ON FISH FOR THE NEXT
FOUR YEARS IN GOOD SHAPE, I BELIEVE I CAN MAKE EM SEE THE
LIGHT, AND SPRINKLE IN A FEW REPUBLICAN VOTES.
WE GOT A LAKE THAT A FISH WOULD BE PROUD TO CALL HOME,
EVERY FISH GETS A ROOM AND BATH. WE WILL TAKE GOOD CARE OF
EM, WE WONT CATCH MANY OF EM, MOST OF OUR FOLKS ARE TOO LAZY
TO FISH.
         WHAT WE WANT TO DO IS MAKE ANOTHER RAPIDAN OUT OF
CLAREMORE. AND WE WANT MR HOOVER TO COME AND CATCH SOME OF
HIS OWN FISH. WE ARE A BROADMINDED PEOPLE AND OUTSIDE OF
ELECTION TIME WE TREAT A REPUBLICAN THE SAME AS ANY OTHER
HUMAN. WE WANT TO GET COOLIDGE DOWN THERE TOO•
         SO PLEASE SEND US SOME FISH, FOR PAT HURLEY WILL BE
BACK THERE, AND HE WILL WANT TO FISH• SO YOU WOULDENT
KEEP PAT FROM FISHING WOULD YOU. •
LET US KNOW WHEN THEY ARE COMING AND WE WILL HAVE THE
CHAMBER OF COMMERCE AND THE BAND DOWN TO MEET EM, WE WILL
GIVE THESEFISH XXXX A RECEPTION LIKE THEY NEVER HAD BEFORE
         SEND EM BEFORE ROOSEVELT GETS IN THERE FORH HE IS
A DEEP SEA FISHERMAN, AND MAY SEND THE WRONG KIND.

WESTERN UNION

Received at SANTA MONICA BLVD., BEVERLY HILLS, CALIF. PHONE Oxford 4700
BV18 141 DL CNT PCTNS=WILL ROGERS=BEVERLY HILLS CALIF 18 933A
WALTER HARRISON= 1931
    EDITOR DAILY OKLAHOMAN OKLAHOMACITY OKLA=

WHATS ALL THIS MESS OVER SOME DEGREE. BILL ESTES AND HIS
OKLAHOMA CHAMBER OF COMMERCE BEEN WIRING ME ABOUT IT. THEY
ARE AS BAD AS I AM. A DEGREE WOULD READ AS FOREIGN TO ANY OF
THEM AS A PRESCRIPTION. WHAT ARE YOU TRYING TO DO MAKE A
JOKE OUT OF COLLEGE DEGREES? THEY ARE IN BAD ENOUGH REPUTE
AS IT IS, WITH OUT HANDING EM AROUND TO COMEDIANS. THE WHOLE
HONORARY DEGREE THING IS THE "HOOEY". I SAW SOME COLLEGE
GIVING MELLON ONE, AND HE IS A BILLION BUCKS SHORT. I GOT
TOO MUCH RESPECT FOR PEOPLE THAT WORK AND EARN EM, TO SEE
EM HANDED AROUND TO EVERY NOTORIUS CHARACTER. I WILL LET
OOLAGAH KINDERGARDEN GIVE ME ONE D A (DOCTOR OF APPLESAUCE).
YOURS=
    WILL.

[Below:]
Left to right:
Betty (Mrs. Will Rogers),
Collier (Mrs. Will Rogers, Jr.),
Astrea (Mrs. Jim Rogers),
Will, Jr., and Jim.

5.The Last Days

People ask me, they say, "Will, why do you run around? You got a nice home and why don't you stay home?"

I've got to travel. I've got to go places in order to see things to talk about. I don't want to fly all night on a plane just for the pleasure — just to be there. It's to get around and see something and find out something, so when you do talk a little about it, you know. I don't ever plan ahead for anything. I don't even like to have dates ahead, if I can help it. I like to do anything right now. So I am off on a little sightseeing trip. I got to go and see that Alaska.

You see, I have been working pretty hard on some movies. I been making a lot of faces lately. I have used up all my expressions two or three times. You know, us actors just got certain little grimaces that we make for hate, fear, merriment, exhaltation (well that and merriment are pretty near the same). Scorn is one of our good ones. We can just wipe you out with a look, that we label "scorn." About the same situations come up in every picture, so it's really just like a politician's speech. If he's asked any questions from the audience, they are generally the same ones in every town, and he has the same answers — and that's the way we are. An actor is a fellow that just has a little more monkey in him than the fellow that can't act.

Anyway, it just happened that I almost had three movies right in a row. Now that don't mean that they will be released as fast as we made them. They only come out about every four months, but we got a couple ahead, already made, and that means that I will have a little time off to do a few things I been planning on. You see, after I finish a long siege, I sorter begin to looking up in the air and see what is flying over, and Mrs. Rogers, in her wise way, will say, "Well, I think you better get on one, you are getting sorter nervous." So when my wife knew it was with Wiley, it dident matter where it was we was going, and she was mighty fine about it. Well, she is about everything. You can't live with a comedian long without being mighty forgiving.

So I went out to the flying field at midnight in Los Angeles to catch the plane for Seattle. You see, day or night means nothing to 'em now. With the courses all lighted they run schedules in the nighttime the same as in the daytime. Bill, that's the first born, and his mother were with me, and I was off on this little sightseeing trip with Wiley Post. By the way, Mrs. Rogers is no mean aviation enthusiast herself. She will make all the short trips with you. In fact, she was flying the next night after I left on this trip, clear back to New York, and to Maine, to see our Mary.

I dropped off in Frisco to tend to some business early the next morning and caught a plane out of there at eleven the next morning, and then to Seattle at five in the afternoon. The pilot in the big Boeing just scraped Mount Shasta. There's snow all over the old anthill. We looked down and saw a big forest fire in the mountains. Pilot said it had been burning for

days. Lots of great timber going to waste. Into Portland, Oregon, a beautiful airfield on an island, and a beautifully located city. Girl stewardess come along with a fine lunch. It had more dainty little sandwiches and knickknacks than I had ever seen in any lunch in my life; it was arranged lovely. They say it was made up at the St. Francis Hotel in San Francisco.

Into the Puget Sound country, beautiful bays and islands. Tacoma, who had the first slogan that I can ever remember. It was when I played there in vaudeville, about 1908. "Watch Tacoma Grow." It did.

Seattle! The gateway to Alaska. Yes sir, a plane is a great place to see anything, only the wings are right under where you want to look, and you can't see anything.

It's a beautiful morning in Seattle, Washington. Wiley and Mrs. Post have been here for a few days, getting the ship from wheels to pontoons. Mrs. Post and Wiley and I drive out to the field. It's a combination land and water airport, right on beautiful Lake Washington. Our plane looks mighty pretty. It's a bright red with a few trimmings of white stripes. It's a Lockheed body, Sirius wings, three-bladed pitch propeller, big Wasp engine. Wiley calls it "Aurora Borealis," I call it "Post Toasty." The pontoons are awful big looking things, but Wiley says, "None too big." Wiley is kinder of a Calvin Coolidge on answers; none of 'em are going to bother you with being too long.

Mrs. Post decides at the last minute to go up to Alaska a few days later by boat, so it's only Wiley and I that are taking off. Mrs. Post asks me to take good care of Wiley. I said, "Of course you mean in the air. After we get on the ground he is able to look after himself."

There was an extra single seat ahead of a double seat. Wiley took it out, and there is left a world of space, as there is this comfortable double seat. It could be possible to be a six-passenger job. Wiley has got a rubber boat and a canoe paddle, some life vests, or protectors. Oh, yes, and his gun case. I don't know what kind it is. I don't hunt or shoot; it's a long looking thing. I expect there is a Springfield rifle in there. Oh, yes, and his fishing rod and 80 reels. Oh, yes! And two or three coils of rope — and they are not mine. They are to tie the ship up and pull it up to the banks. That will be my job, to get out first and tie the rope and then vault ashore and haul it in. I will have to have a card from the Longshoreman's Union.

What, no camera? No! That's what we are going on this trip for, to get away from cameras. Then, too, I don't know nothing about 'em and can't work 'em. We may see some fine sights, but you can always lie about a thing better than you can prove it. Besides, you always have to explain that "This picture don't near do the scene justice."

Oh, yes, and some sleeping bags. Wiley got them; said they was great to sleep in. I never was in one of 'em. You zip 'em up around you after you get in 'em

THE COMPANY WILL APPRECIATE SUGGESTIONS FROM ITS PATRONS CONCERNING ITS SERVICE 1201-S

CLASS OF SERVICE

This is a full-rate Telegram or Cablegram unless its deferred character is indicated by a suitable symbol above or preceding the address.

WESTERN UNION (04)

R. B. WHITE PRESIDENT — NEWCOMB CARLTON CHAIRMAN OF THE BOARD — J. C. WILLEVER FIRST VICE-PRESIDENT

SYMBOLS
DL = Day Letter
SER = Serial
NM = Night Message
NL = Night Letter
CDE = Code Cable
LC = Deferred Cable
NLT = Cable Night Letter
Ship Radiogram

The filing time shown in the date line on telegrams and day letters is Standard Time at point of origin. Time of receipt is Standard Time at point of destination.

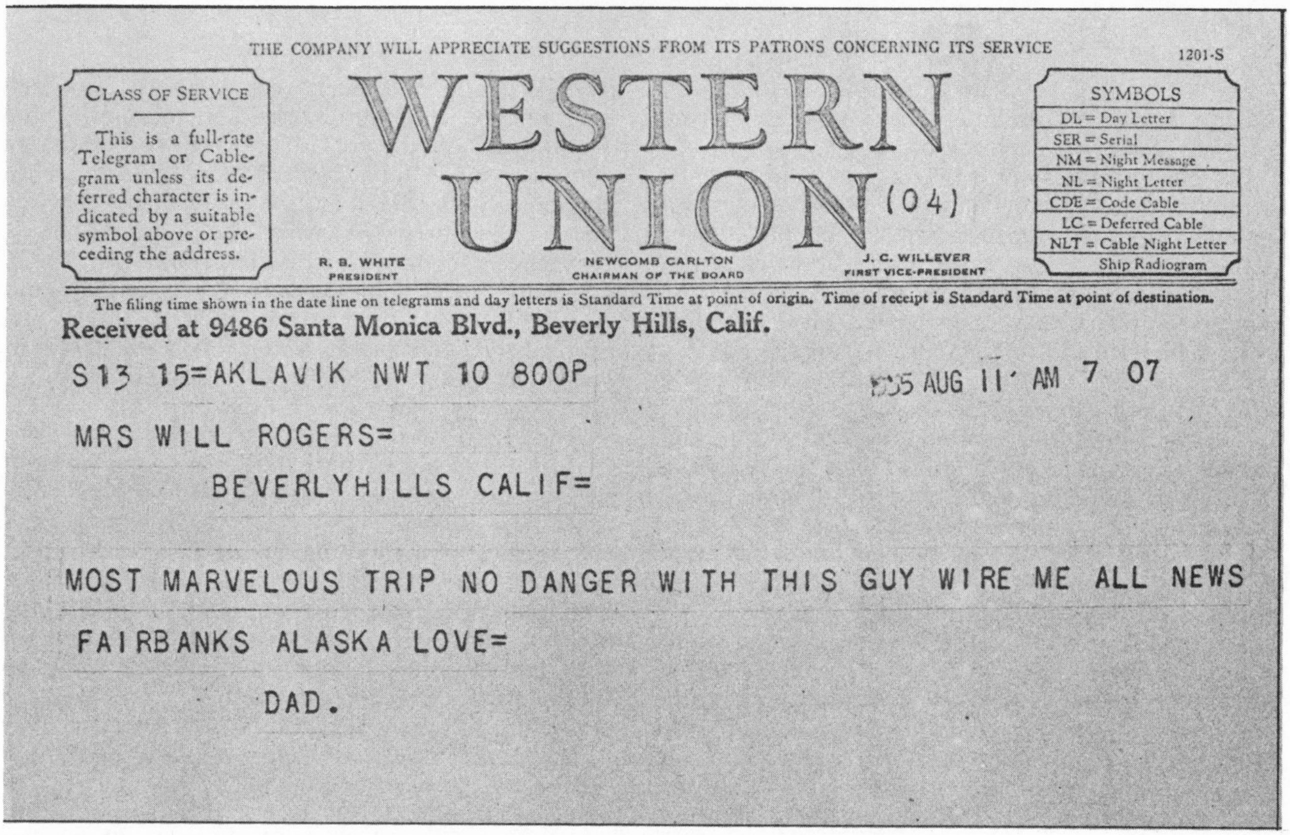

Received at 9486 Santa Monica Blvd., Beverly Hills, Calif.

S13 15=AKLAVIK NWT 10 800P 1935 AUG 11 AM 7 07

MRS WILL ROGERS=

BEVERLYHILLS CALIF=

MOST MARVELOUS TRIP NO DANGER WITH THIS GUY WIRE ME ALL NEWS

FAIRBANKS ALASKA LOVE=

DAD.

A reassuring telegram sent four days before crash.

some way. I always have trouble with those zippers, so I can see myself walking around in one of those things all day.

There ain't any unemployed in Alaska. What the so-called idle are doing is getting autographs, and say they are working 24 hours a day. Fellow comes up and says, "I see all your pictures," and I ask him which ones, and he can't name a one. Woman brings a little five-year-old girl up and says, "Tillie wants to meet you. She reads all your little articles in the papers and enjoys 'em." Tillie says, "Who is he, Ma?"

Girl newspaper photographer, very efficient and pleasant. They seem to know we don't know where we are going ourselves and they don't insist on us telling 'em. Well, they about got the gas in; Wiley is getting nervous. I am anxious to get going, too. I think we are going to have a great trip, see lots of country that not too many have seen. But you can't tell. You could go to the northernmost part of Hudson Bay and expect there would be a pack of folks having a picnic, or maybe some holding company stockholders, sending telegrams to the President.

I was telling you, I think, about taking off in Seattle. Well, she took off like a bird, with an awful short run and with about 260 gallons of gas. Seattle is awful pretty from the air — well, from anywhere. Then you start above those channels and islands and lakes, and then up and up the coast. If there is a prettier trip in the world than from Seattle to Alaska by what they call the Inland Passage, I never saw it.

Victoria over on the left. That place is the most English of any place outside of England, and even more English than 90 percent of England. Beautiful gardens, beautiful flowers, a lovely, dignified city. It's England. Then up the coast. Big timber coming right down to the water edge. I don't know where they would ever get any shortage of timber.

We had pretty weather for about the first 300 miles, then it began to kinder close in. We had expected to stop at Ketchikan, our first Alaska city, but Wiley, I guess, figured that if he stopped there, we would get closed in and wouldent get any further up the coast. So he flew low over the very pretty little city right along the water edge, with the high mountains to the back of it. It's a great fishing center.

It's a great country, is Alaska, where you have to live off the country, hunt, trap, kill and live. There is a queer streak in me, I'm no hunting man, or fishing either. I wish I was, for there must be a lot of pleasure in it, but I just don't want to be shooting at any animal, and even a fish, I havent got the heart to pull the hook out of him.

Fairbanks. We was trying to get off, and the river was sorter narrow and had many bends, and Wiley was afraid that with a full load of gas, that we might have difficulty in taking off. So we had some gas sent out to a lake, about 50 miles out. And then we flew there and loaded up.

Now we will be headed for Point Barrow, the furthest north of any piece of land on the North American continent.

Well, Wiley's got her warmed up. Let's go.

Wiley Post's plane being tested after the pontoon had been added in Seattle, Washington. Will then sent this picture back to the family with appropriate comment.

—S38—148—GOVT RUSH RC—5 EXTRA. PUR—FORTMACARTHUR—SANPEDRO CALIF

MRS WILL ROGERS=   Skowhegan   16 1037A

LOSANGELES—CALIF—OR—FORWARD=   Maine   935 AUG 19   53

FOLLOWING FROM POINTBARROW DATE QUOTE TEN PM NATIVE RUNNER

REPORTED PLANE CRASHED FIFTEEN MILES SOUTH BARROW STOP

IMMEDIATELY HIRED FAST LAUNCH PROCEEDED TO SCENE FOUND PLANE

COMPLETE WRECK PARTLY SUBMERGED TWO FEET WATER STOP RECOVERED

BODY ROGERS THEN NECESSARY TEAR PLANE APART EXTRACT BODY POST

FROM WATER STOP BROUGHT BODIES BARROW TURNED OVER DOCTOR GREIST

ALSO SALVAGED PERSONAL EFFECTS WHICH AM HOLDING ADVISE

RELATIVES AND INSTRUCT THIS STATION FULLY AS TO PROCEEDURE STOP

NATIVES CAMPING SMALL RIVER FIFTEEN MILES SOUTH HERE CLAIM

POST ROGERS LANDED ASKED WAY BARROW STOP TAKING OFF ENGINE

MISFIRED ON RIGHT BANK WHILE ONLY FIFTY FEET OFF WATER STOP

PLANE OUT OF CONTROL CRASHED NOSE ON TEARING RIGHT WING OFF

AND NOSING OVER FORCING ENGINE BACK THROUGH BODY OF PLANE STOP

BOTH APPARENTLY KILLED INSTANTLY STOP BODIES BADLY BRUISED

STOP POST WRIST WATCH BROKEN STOPPED EIGHT EIGHTEEN PM UNQUOTE=

KUMPE SEATTLE WASHINGTON.

50

[Above:]
The overturned wreck, broken and twisted,
resting in the lagoon's shallow waters.

[Right:]
Solitary memorial marks the
crash site through the
Arctic night.

WILL ROGERS
AND
WILEY POST
"AMERICA'S AMBASSADORS
OF GOOD WILL"
-
ENDED LIFE'S FLIGHT HERE
AUGUST 15, 1935

THIS STONE WAS TAKEN FROM
THE SAME QUARRY AS THAT
USED IN BUILDING OKLAHOMA'S
MEMORIAL TO WILL ROGERS
AT CLAREMORE, OKLAHOMA, U.S.A.

[Left:]
Close-up of the original
tablet on the crash site marker.
Damaged by the elements, it
was replaced in 1973.

[Below:]
The Will Rogers Memorial at Claremore, Oklahoma.
Dedicated in 1938, it is visited annually by
well over half a million people.

WILL ROGERS

QUARTER-BLOOD
CHEROKEE

ROLL NUMBER
11384

"LIVE YOUR LIFE, SO
THAT WHENEVER YOU
LOSE YOU ARE AHEAD."
WILL ROGERS

WE HONOR THE MEMORY OF OKLAHOMA'S
BELOVED NATIVE SON. A MODEST, UNSPOILED
CHILD OF THE PLAINS, COWBOY, ACTOR,
HUMORIST AND WORLD TRAVELER WHOSE
HOMELY PHILOSOPHY AND SUPERIOR
GIFTS BROUGHT LAUGHTER AND TEARS
TO PRINCE AND COMMONER ALIKE. HIS
AVERSION TO SHAM AND DECEIT, HIS
LOVE OF CANDOR AND SINCERITY, COUPLED
WITH ABOUNDING WIT AND AFFABLE
REPARTEE, WON FOR HIM UNIVERSAL
HOMAGE AND AN APPROPRIATE TITLE,
"AMBASSADOR OF GOOD WILL."

PRESENTED BY
THE CHEROKEE NATION
NOVEMBER 4TH, 1946, THE 67TH
ANNIVERSARY OF HIS BIRTH

Tablet at the Memorial.

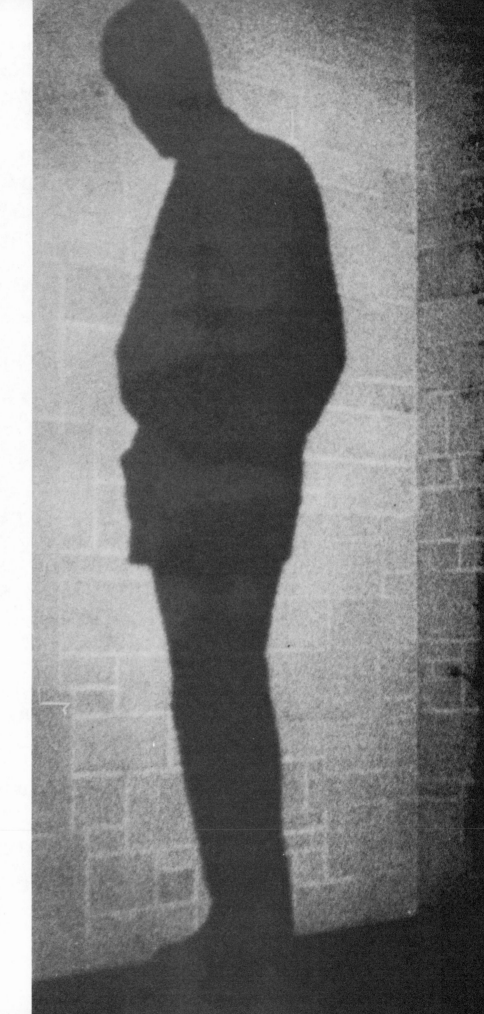

Jo Davidson's larger-than-life bronze statue greets all visitors to the Memorial's foyer. An identical copy is in Statuary Hall in the nation's Capitol.

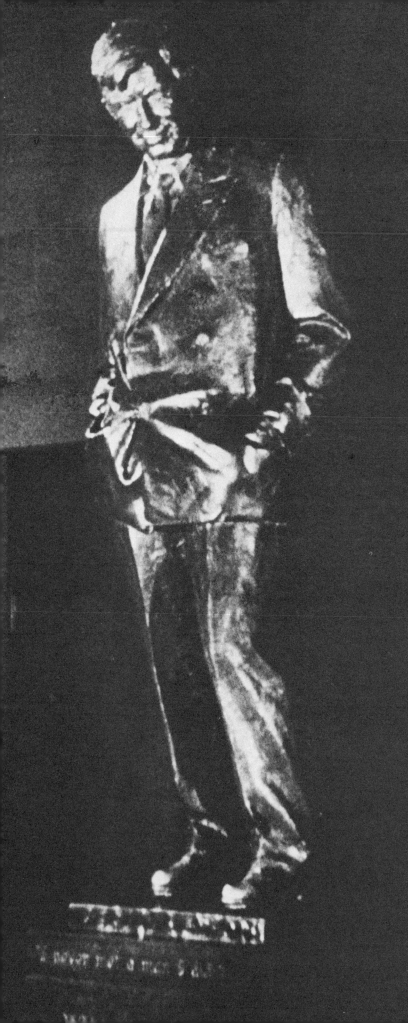

Postscript

His humor and his comments were always kind. His was no biting sarcasm that hurt the highest or the lowest of his fellow citizens. When he wanted people to laugh out loud, he used the methods of pure fun. And when he wanted to make a point for the good of mankind, he used the kind of gentle irony that left no scars behind it.

He loved and was loved by the American people. His memory will ever be in benediction with the hosts of his countrymen who felt the spell of that kindly humor which, while seeing facts, could always laugh at fantasy. That was why his message went straight to the hearts of his fellow men. From him we can learn anew the homely lesson that the way to make progress is to build on what we have, to take from the lessons of yesterday a little more wisdom and courage to help us with the task of today.

—Franklin Delano Roosevelt

All I Know
Is What I Read
in the Papers

6. Recession
and
Inflation

There is quite a few problems that is agitating the country, that I am not really 100 percent decided on myself. I would never make a good economist. You know, an economist is a man that can tell you anything about — well, he will tell you what can happen under any given condition — and his guess is liable to be as good as anybody else's, too. You know, if there is one man in this country that hasent had a pamphlet printed, giving his view on "How to Solve the Current Situation," it's because there is no more paper to print 'em on. You keep reading about things getting better, but most of the articles are written by folks that are doing well themselves.

I just read where this fellow got back a couple of weeks ago from the Fiji Islands, or some outlandish place he had been. He said that down there you could live on 90 cents a week. Why, that's about 10 cents more than what some have to live on here!

I have read where certain folks have appealed to the President. It's a tough time for any group to start making demands. The farmer deserves his profit, but the guy that's not eating deserves a meal more. The stockholder deserves his dividend, but the unemployed deserves his job more. But I still believe that there is not a man in this country that can't make a living for himself and his family. But he can't make a living for them *and* his government, too. Not the way this government is living. What the government has got to do is live as cheap as the people.

Here we are, worrying and reading in the papers about a hundred different problems that they got us all excited about, and making us believe they amount to something. This country has got just one problem. It's not the balancing of the budget; it's not the League of Nations; it's not the silver question. None of those things mean a thing in the world to us, as long as we have seven million of our own out of work. You see, there's not an unemployed man in the country that hasent contributed to the wealth of every millionaire in America. Everyone of us, that have anything, got it by the aid of these very people.

And yet, we just ain't doing something right, we are on the wrong track somewhere. We shouldent be giving people money, and them not do anything for it. No matter what you had to hand out for necessities, the receiver should give some kind of work in return. So what I suggest is that every city, and every state, should give work of some kind at a livable wage, so that no one would be in actual want. You wouldent be accepting charity, but you would be doing honest work for it, until you could get employment in some line that wasent public work, and at a regular wage. It wouldent cheapen labor. It would only cheapen public works, the thing that belongs to all the people, and the thing we would like to have cheapened. So that's our only problem: to so arrange it so that a man, or a woman, that want work can get work, and give 'em a more equal division of the wealth the country produces.

Now if our big men can't fix that — well, they just ain't big men, that's all! So what we got now is substantial unemployment, and this is the thing that needs fixing. It sure taught us an important fact, that we havent got as many "Big Men" as we thought we had. We used to think every head of a big organization was a "Big Man," and he was, as long as everything was running in spite of him. But when old man "get-back-to-earth" hit us in the jaw, why, we dident have an industry that shrunk like the "Big Man" industry. Now "Big Men" are just like livestock; they are selling at just what they are worth, no more.

We sure had enjoyed special blessings over other nations, and we couldent see why they shouldent be permanent. We was a mighty cocky nation. Why, the thought never entered our head that we wasent the brightest, wisest, and most accomplished people that ever was on this earth. We had begun to believe that the height of civilization was a good road, bathtub, radio and an automobile. And hadent we figured out Mass Production? We been honoring and celebrating the inventor who could save a dollar by knocking somebody out of work, and now we are paying for it. Machines are great things, but if one replaces a hundred men, it don't buy anything, it don't eat anything, while a hundred men would spend their pay back for food, shelter and hundred of various commodities for themselves and their families. So they can have all the theories and plans, but till you put people back to work, you ain't going to be able to fix it. Folks got to have work.

But did the thought ever enter our boneheads that the time might come when nobody would want all these things we were making? Honest, as we look back on it now, somebody ought to have taken each one of us and soaked our fat heads. We bought everything under the sun, but where was our payments going to come from, if we lost our jobs? Why, that had never entered our heads. Why should we lose our jobs? Wasent all our big men telling us things was even going to get better? Was our prominent men warning us? If we had had a "prominent" man, he would have; but we just dident have any.

The President said the other day that "During the last twelve months we have suffered with other nations from economic depression." Yes, and we have suffered a lot alone, too. In fact, I would go even further than the President and say that we suffered substantially, or even gross substantially. You see, that's how a lot of people try to make us feel good, is to tell us how bad somebody else is off. I don't believe that I could get much nourishment to be starving in a room, and have the keeper come and say, "The other fellow has been starving two days longer than you have!" I still believe that I would be just as hungry as I was before. But, I guess, there are some people that could just get fat on nothing but such news.

But I think the trouble with us is that everybody is just sitting, waiting to see what the government is going to do for 'em. You know, what can we get the government to build for us; how much relief will the government give us? Then you have the fellow with money. He's afraid to invest, cause he is so scared the dollar will change. What difference does it make, it will still be a dollar. So everybody tries to kinder explain the cause of this depression. That's where they all fall down. They offer every kind of different excuse. Why don't some of 'em just say, "Boys, I don't know where this thing come from." But no, they go on explaining their theories, and by the time they get through, they have forgot how to settle it. With this thing riding the headlines, I have read till I'm bleary eyed, and I can't get head from tails of the whole thing. We are living in an age of explanations, and plenty of 'em, but no two things that's been done to us have been explained twice the same way — not even by the same man.

In the first place, there is no reason to know where all this come from. If a snake bites you, you ain't going to stop and study out where he come from, and why he was there at the time. You want to start figuring on what to do with yourself right then.

I really don't know any more about it than a prominent man knows about relieving depression. But it looks like the financial giants of the world have bungled as much as the diplomats and the politicians. This sure would be a great time in the world for some man to come along that knew something. But still every day brings new schemes in the papers. The Russians got a five-year plan. Maybe it's terrible, but they got one. I guess we will just have to save ourselves accidentally — that's the way we stumbled on prosperity.

I've been accused of being worried over this inflation. I wasent worried, I was just confused. Now there is quite a difference. When you are worried, you know what you are worried about, but when you are confused, you don't know enough about a thing to be worried. But even my confusion is all over now. Everybody I meet has explained this whole thing so clearly that now I am going around explaining it myself. You see, medical science has two ways of actually tracing insanity. One is if the patient cuts out paper dolls; and the other is if the patient says, "Hey, listen, I will tell you what this economic business really means!"

I got a wire from an old boy in Parsons, Kansas, and he wanted me to enter in a hog calling contest. You know, I used to be an awful good hog caller when hogs were cheaper, but the way hogs have gone up in price, it's changed the whole system of calling 'em. I hollered all morning just for three slices of bacon and it dident come, so there ain't much use of me hollering my head off to try and get a whole hog to come.

You know, there was a time when we couldent spell a "billion" dollars, much less realize it, count it, or anything. But now, as a nation, we learn pretty fast, till it won't be long now, and we'll be working on the word "trillion." You know, trillion, that follows billion. You'll read in the papers, "Congress has just been asked to appropriate two trillion dollars to relieve the descendants of a race of people called 'Wall Streeters.' " The paper will go further on to say, "This is a worthy cause, and no doubt this small appropriation will be made, as they are the wards of the government."

Then there's another thing. The papers tell every day in big headlines what gold sells for. They just as well tell us what radium sells for. Who has any of either? So we read that gold is going up and it's driving us almost nuts because we ain't got any to sell. I let three gold fillings go on the first day of the sale, and now that gold has gone up, I'm not only sick at heart, but I've got a toothache from the loss of the fillings. A female movie staress in Hollywood, for whom things havent been breaking any too good lately, she's just getting along great. She's turning in an old gold wedding ring every day. And she told me, she's set for several weeks yet.

Now the House of Representatives is going to limit debate on inflation to five hours tomorrow. I wish to goodness there was a way to limit individuals that try to explain it to you, to five hours. We thought technocracy was a tough bird to get the lowdown on, but it's only a first reader compared to a guy explaining inflation. So I am going to Washington tomorrow and hear Congressmen bite into it. You see, there's one thing about it. It's made every man's intelligence equal. All you can hear about it is, "Money will have to be cheaper." Cheaper than what? Even if a dollar is worth only ten cents, how are you going to get your clutches on it any easier than now? Unless they give it away, I can't see where it's going to be any big help to anybody. You see, our problem is not what is the dollar worth in London, Rome, or Paris, or what even it is worth at home. It's how to get hold of it, whatever it's worth.

Then I see a committee down in Washington, who were investigating the high cost of living, turned in their report. "We find the cost of living very high, and we recommend more funds to carry on the investigation."

You know, no matter what we pay, high, low, or medium, the yell is always the same. I bet you when the Pilgrims first landed at Plymouth Rock, and they had the whole of the American continent, and all they had to do to get an extra hundred and sixty acres was to shoot another Indian, well, I bet you anything, they kicked on the price of ammunition. I bet you they said, just like we're doing now, "What's this country coming to, that we have to spend a nickel for our powder?" Of course we know our government is costing us more than it's worth. But do you know of any other, cheaper government that's running around? If you do, they'll sell you a ticket there anytime. You can try Russia, I was over there, there's no income tax in Russia — but there is no income.

Oh, I don't know what it's all about. I don't know any more about this than an economist, and God knows, he don't know anything.

7. The History of the Automobile — Part I

The automobile show has just been held here in New York. They hold it every year. They have the same cars every year, only painted different. You can go in a showroom in your hometown any day and see the same thing with no admission. Every year they try and concentrate on something new. This year they are featuring a square doorknob to their closed cars, instead of the old-fashioned oblong ones, and the cigar lighter lay flat in a little compartment, instead of being placed up and down. They don't work any better than any cigar lighter does, but they lay different. And the funny thing is that thousands of people will come there, pay admission, and walk up and down the aisles for hours, seeing the very things they have had in their own cars for years. Why don't they, if they have a mania to look at cars, just walk along the streets of any town, where there are more different kinds of cars parked than was ever in any automobile show in the world? You would feel then that the ones you were looking at would run. Because the cars in a show are hauled there by trucks.

In the old days, when they had new inventions coming out, there was some excuse for holding a show. If somebody wants to do something for the automobile public, let him invent a car that will sell secondhanded, one week after you bought it, for at least one-fourth of what you gave for it. It just seems to totally ruin a car to have an owner drive it for a few weeks. They instruct buyers to not go over 25 miles an hour for the first 1,000 miles. You might just as well run it 70 miles an hour, because at the end of 1,000 miles, it will only be worth an old secondhand kimono and a box of candy, anyway.

The rise of the automobile industry sounds like a William Fox movie scenario. Once upon a time, 1893 to be exact, the World's Fair in Chicago opened. If it hadent been for the streets of Cairo, Illinois, it just as well might not have opened, for that is all that was ever remembered. Well, a man named Charles E. Duryea, and another named Elwood G. Haynes, saw the girls there on the streets of Cairo do their stuff, and also sitting in the front row at every performance was a kid named Ford. Henry was his christening handle. Well, these three boys, Haynes, Duryea and Ford, all got the idea, "Women like these can't be messing their time away buggy riding behind an old horse. We got to do something to get ladies like these somewhere right now." So, as their excursion tickets were about to run out, they all went back to their respective homes, and each started in to eliminate the horse as a national commodity.

Ford was working for Edison at the time, in Edison's Detroit electrical factory. His salary was one hundred and twenty dollars a month, with no profit sharing allowed. Mr. Ford built him an automobile. Used most of Edison's time to do it on. The timing gear he took out of Edison's factory clock (replacing it with a shorter hour one). The fly wheel he took from Edison's machinery. The one cylinder which was used was an inch-and-a-quarter pipe that he borrowed from a burglar who was not using it that night. The steering apparatus was the handle of a spade, also appropriated from Edison.

He sewed all this stuff onto an old buggy, all on Edison's time, mind you, and the funny part about it is that the thing run. But it took him over a year to tell where it was going to run. That started Ford in the automobile business, but it like to put Edison out of the electricity business. It took Edison three years to replace everything that Ford had copped out of his factory to put into this mechanical groundhog. That is why Ford has always tried to remain friendly with Mr. Edison. He is afraid he will sue him for royalty on all his cars, because Edison put more into them than Ford did. If a man worked in Ford's factory and carried out as much junk as Ford did in those days, it would put Ford's factory out of business for weeks. Why, just the dropping carelessly of one bolt will stop ten thousand men for minutes.

Now in the meantime, Mr. Duryea and Mr. Haynes had also made them a horseless carriage. Of course they didn't have the equipment and pay while making it that Mr. Ford did, but they turned one out. No one knew for years which was the best car of the three, as they were made in different parts of the country, and none of them could go far enough so they could get them together.

Mr. Ford tried his car out in the room at his boarding house, and it made so much noise that Mrs. Ford said it kept Edsel awake. They moved it into the street, and since then it has kept everybody awake.

Along in 1895, they had a road race in Chicago — from there to Evanston, and return — 52 miles. They would have had a longer race, but it dident stay light only 12 hours. In '96, they dident make much headway. That was the first year William Jennings Bryan ran for President. Everybody's mind was on Bryan; as a consequence, the auto and Bryan were both forgotten. In '98, cars arrived back home which had taken part in the Chicago road race of '95.

Spanish-American War broke out April 22. Broke up August 12. If wars were that short nowadays, neither side could get their armies there until after it was over. May 1, 1898, Ford found some more old piping and added another cylinder. Another minor event on the same day, May 1, 1898, Dewey made the first second-hand navy out of Spain's flotilla at Manila.

'99 was a quiet year; no one could get their engines started. The Czar called a peace conference at the Hague, and like all peace conferences, it was followed by a war, which broke out the following week between England and South Africa. The Philippine-American War also started as soon as our delegates could return from the peace conference.

1900 was a very eventful year in the social life of America. The first automobile show was held in Madison Square Garden, and the drainage canal was opened in Chicago. In opposition to the canal, Paris opened their World Exposition. The Paris Exposition lasted a year. The Chicago drainage canal was such a success, it was made a permanent attraction.

1901 saw the first horse that was not afraid of an automobile. He was used for towing them back home. Buffalo put on a Pan-American Exposition, and most everybody going to Niagara that year stopped to see it.

1902, Barney Oldfield races auto against tandem at Salt Lake City. Time of race: four six-inch cigars. Steering wheel replaces stick-handle drive. You couldent kill as many pedestrians with the stick drive.

1903, limousine with a rear entrance makes its appearance. That was so the driver couldent tell the class of people he was hauling. Panama had a revolution that year, and the minute it was over, America recognized them. The Wright Brothers also flew that year, the same thing the Spaniards had done back in '98.

1904 brought out the first windshield, also the Alaskan Boundary question, and the opening of the New York subway. St. Louis, jealous of Chicago's drainage canal, opened the World's Fair (where I was an attraction with a Wild West Show on the Pike, until we all starved to death and had to ride our ponies back home to Oklahoma). The automobile made no progress with me personally that year.

1905, Olds put the first garage in his house, and Russia and Japan had a war. (I don't think it was over the garage, but it was something about as trivial.)

1906, Olds introduced the first house in a garage; Wall Street had a panic — found an honest man, I suppose.

1907, in Chicago they built bumps in the road to keep autoists from speeding. This custom has been followed out faithfully in most cities ever since. Jamestown heard about the drainage canal in Chicago, and they put on an exposition for the few people who were looking for excursion rates to nowhere in particular. Judge Landis fined the Standard Oil Company $29 million for speeding, but on account of them controlling the government, they got it back.

1909, Indianapolis built a speedway for advertising and Peary discovered the North Pole for the same reason. New York wanted to offset Indianapolis and Peary, so they put on the Hudson and Fulton Celebration. Sailors rode in a subway for the first time.

1910, whipsockets were removed from auto equipment, and that started a war in the Balkans.

1911, the first self-starter appeared, and President Diaz of Mexico resigned intact. Those were both unprecedented events. Turkey and Italy couldent put on an exposition, so they put on a war during the tourist season. The South Pole was also discovered that year, for no apparent reason whatever, and the minute it was, why, China declared a Republic; and they held the first motor truck show in Madison Square Garden; and Ray Harroun felt so elated over China and the Pole that he made 74 miles an hour on the Indianapolis Speedway, without killing a mechanician.

1912, linen dusters, goggles, and gauntlet gloves were introduced as standard equipment on all moderate priced cars. A second edition of the Balkan War was put on for late comers. The Lincoln Highway was suggested, probably by some road contractor.

That brings us up to 1913, the year I bought an Overland, the sinking of the Titanic, the flood in Ohio and Indiana, the christening of the Peace Palace at the Hague, just prior to the World War.

Now events have been so plentiful in these intervening years that it would be foolhardy for me to deal with the life of the automobile industry in the short space I have left. So I will take it up later at 1914 and show what car caused the war. Besides, from '13 on, I had a car, so I can speak with so much better authority than I have up to now.

8.The History of the Automobile– Part II

1923 Buick

This is really a continuation of the last novel by the same author. But I better explain what was in the last installment, as I never get the same reader twice. I took up the history of the automobile from its first stalling, explained who made the earliest one, and brought the industry up to the year 1914. Now we have to pick it up there and see what we can do with it on up to the present.

1914 saw several changes in this great vehicular movement. The Ford Company passed its first one thousand a day production. People thought then, "My Lord! Will they ever stop turning those things out?" They were multiplying something terrible. So America woke up and said, "We got to have somewhere to put these things!" And somebody thought of the idea of building roads to store them on. So they commenced to make roads. And as fast as they would make roads, why, Uncle Henry would clutter them up with these things. It got so it was the entire nation organized against one lone man. Every state said to themselves, "We will build some vacant roads!" But the minute they got 'em built, why, they found there were thousands of people there waiting to twist a mechanical thing's tail and away it would go and fill up their road, just as much as it had been with rocks and trees before they had it built. He has filled every road that was ever built. I don't care where you try to hide a road, one of Mr. Ford's road-fillers will find it.

The *Manufacturers' Review* tells us that in 1914 builders of cars commenced to study where to put baggage in a car on a trip. Then the thought struck some of them to put it on the feet of the people in the rear seat, a custom which must have had more merit, because it has been used ever since. Also in 1914, the Chicago Automobile Trade Association decided that 85 cents an hour was the correct pay for a mechanic doing repair work. They were right; it was the correct pay, but the mechanic still received $1.25 an hour. Nineteen hundred and fourteen also saw the first filling station painted white with a red roof. The World War in Europe also started, but the history of the automobile makes no mention of that fact; perhaps they don't know it. But I want to tell you that my history of the auto will embrace everything worthwhile, including prohibition.

In 1914, in addition to Archduke Francis of Austria being assassinated, and causing a war for the least reason that any war had ever been started, why, chauffeurs demanded a room and bath over the garage for the first time in automobile history. Germany had some land over in China, so Japan declared war on Germany, not on account of the shooting of the Archduke, but they thought it would be a good time to get this land, Germany's army being busy somewhere else. So on August 20th, Japan declared war on a nation they had never seen. On August 21st, 1914, rubber horns on automobiles were replaced by sirens. They found that pedestrians were used to the rubber honk-honk ones, and could get out of the way, but with the siren ones, they would scare you so bad, you would be very little trouble to hit.

1914, United States Marines landed at Vera Cruz, Mexico, to protect Standard Oil's interests. Next week, Standard Oil, in repayment for the Marines' courtesy, raised price of gas three cents. 1914 also saw the only woman driver who looked back before turning off the road. Another novelty that year, in addition to this lone woman, was the opening of the Panama Canal, to allow ships which couldent make it all the way around to come through and see this side. Congressmen, at government expense and pay, also went down, and all that were sober enough saw the Canal. Massachusetts, through good manipulation of their senators and congressmen, got in on the government pork barrel under the guise of the Rivers and Harbor Bill. They opened up the Cape Cod Canal, to allow Cod fish who couldent make it around the Cape to cut through and exchange courtesies with the Cod on the other side. It's been a big social success for the Cod fish, but financially it hasent paid the lighthouse keeper.

1914 also saw the first, and only, tire blowout that ever happened in front of a garage. So, all in all, it was, as I say, a very eventful year.

In 1915, Twin-Sixes come on the market. The name was better than the design. British had a naval victory of Dogger Bank also, and the jitneys overrun every town and city in America. It was worse than the Germans invading Belgium. Panama-Pacific Exposition opened so Frisco would have something on Los Angeles. They did, till they counted up. Chicago Drainage Canal reopened. John D. Rockefeller misses golf ball, and gasoline goes up two cents.

In 1916, Clover Leaf Body was invented. Germans attacked Verdun, which caused a slanting windshield to be feature of the 1916 automobile show, and also Pancho Villa attacked Columbus, New Mexico. We had a man on guard that night, but Villa, the villain that he was, wouldent come up on the side this fellow was guarding. Our soldiers chased him over the line, till they run into some red tape and had to come back. Safety First Federation was formed by what few pedestrians were left; the first president, and the executive consul were run over that year. Pershing enters Mexico and gas goes up three cents that fall.

1917. A man in Claremore, Oklahoma, put up the first "One-Man-Top" single-handed. America declared war on Germany. These were the two outstanding features of that eventful year.

1918. Motorless Sundays were invented, not to save gas, but life. Undertakers make strenuous objections. First tractor is used for plowing, instead of just for an advertisement. First mirror invented to see what the people in the back seat were doing.

1919. Automobile makers (outside of Ford) worried over the price of steel. The price of steel is the last thing to worry him. Peace Conference opens in Paris.

Peace is harder to decide on than war. There were then 15,500 cars in manufacturers' hands, and they dident know what to do with them. Then they thought of the idea of painting them different colors and striping the wheels, and they sold them. Everybody tried that year to fly the Atlantic. Some of them made it. Wire wheels look pretty on cars. Boston police strike for the benefit of Calvin Coolidge. Four-door Ford Sedan invented.

In 1920, automobile agents started playing golf. Self-starters started to work, and national Prohibition started everybody to drinking. In 1921, New York puts in traffic towers to keep their policemen from getting run over. Latter part of 1921, cross-town traffic allowed to cross Fifth Avenue. Disarmament Conference called at Washington to devise treaties to have America disarm. Women's cigarette holder and mirror first introduced in closed car, biggest sales feature in years. First woman found who didn't sit in back seat and tell husband how to drive.

1922. Every street crossing had four-corner lots. This is the year that an oil filling station was put on one corner, a real estate office on one, and a drugstore on each of the other two. Irish Free State was established on account of lack of ammunition. Hole in gasoline tank (to fill it) put under tire rack, so you can't get at it.

1923. Insurance policies charged on automobiles to cover real value, instead of cost. Insurance companies believe many cars deliberately destroyed. (Insurance companies' belief well founded.) Ford puts in self-starter and saves 40 thousand broken arms. The World's Friendship aeroplane leaves Rio de Janeiro. (Nobody ever heard how it ever got back.) Overlands cut their price, and there was an earthquake in Japan. Buick tried to make their car look like Packard; costs them 25 dollars fine per each for doing it. Balloon tire had its reign during the last two weeks of this year.

1924, we had 17 million cars in this country, 20 percent of them paid for. Four-wheel brakes come in 1924, and Senator Johnston of Minnesota was beat in a milking contest by Secretary Wallace of Agriculture. First taxicab driver gave another one the right of way.

9. Have You Seen Your Doctor Lately?

Well, all I know is just what I read in the papers, and what I hear over the radio during the various toothpaste hours. I tell you, it's a lucky thing for us that people's teeth are in such bad shape, or we never would get any amusement at all. In the old days, when we did nothing with our teeth till we died off, why, we had no amusement at all. We couldent turn a dial and get our favorite "Amos and Andy." Toothpaste has been responsible for more good laughs than Barnum's Circus has. And you can use the wrong kind, too. According to the announcers, there is various kinds that cause decay, while their kind brings on added growth, so you got to be mighty careful.

Course, the best thing in the world in the old days was to chew on a tough piece of steak, or kinder gnaw on and around a bone. But nowadays, on account of having to buy so much toothpaste, why, it don't leave enough to get the steak to whiten and toughen the teeth. A good old rump steak would give your teeth more exercise and build up a stronger foundation than a steel toothbrush would.

But these lettuce sandwiches just don't offer much resistance to the old molars, and they don't get much exercise on them. Malted milk over a soda fountain just might as well be inhaled, as far as the teeth is concerned. This caviar assisted by cocktails is another national dish that don't offer much physical resistance to the eyeteeth. In fact, as far as the old tusks are concerned, there is really no reason for owning them.

An old toothless man or woman is not inconvenienced in the least with our modern type of food. There is nothing that comes in cans that they can't bulldog with ease and comfort. Our more rough type of food nowadays is a ham sandwich, and the boys that slice it, fix it so that the teeth have no function to perform in its digestion.

Most of our up-to-date food is by absorption. It melts in your mouth, so when the old toothbrush gets a crack at the teeth, it's about the only thing they have encountered since babyhood. You have to brush 'em for they have had nothing rub up against them lately.

A wolf has the best looking teeth in the world. They are always white. Even the announcer won't tell you that a film forms over them. A wolf has nothing to console his lonely hours, only chewing on some competitor. He has the whitest teeth, but he is not informed on how many times a day the little baby wolves should grab a tube of "Never-Tarnish" and scrape the wisdom teeth.

On account of no particular demand for teeth, it will only be a short time till we will be hearing over the radio ways and means to maintain 'em at all, for we will quit growing 'em. You quit walking, and you will soon have no legs. You stop arguments, and you will soon have no Senators. You stop anything, and nature provides that it will be discontinued. And you stop using the teeth or use 'em only for artificial purposes, and you will soon see there will be none. So

then we will have to find something else to occupy our time and ads.

If this country had no ads for a solid month, there is no telling what would become of people's teeth. But everything is drifting to the sanitary, anyhow. In the old days, when we wasent sanitary, why, we were strong enough to withstand the germs. But nowadays, we have to be careful of the microbes, for if they get a hold on us, we are goners. We are not physically able to withstand 'em. In the old days, as many as wanted to could drink out of one cup, and the last one would just shake his head and swallow down microbes just as fast as they would accumulate. But now, the old individual cup won't go for over one sitting, or it will knock the second individual right into the infested class. The old-fashioned gourd that the whole family drank out of, from birth till death, would kill more of the modern population than a war. We just ain't built to stand the assaults and batteries of an unwrapped-in-paper container. New handkerchiefs, everything is bundled up separately. Nothing comes by the gross anymore.

But while we have lost in strength and endurance, we have gained in amusement and instruction. For there is not an hour of any day that some one on the air don't keep us warned of what lies in wait for us in case we don't use their remedy. There is just more different things that can happen to us than there used to be.

But the two biggest medical problems that confront this country nowadays is face remodeling and teeth removing. Both of these adornments in the old days were thought to have been put there permanently. Your face, if it took on queer contours and shapes as it grew into manhood and disrepute, you never minded it much. You just figured it's getting pretty tough looking, but when I look at others, mine is holding its own. And your teeth, why the person that would have one taken out until it almost killed him you would think was crazy. You might go and have vacancies filled that might occur in it, but you dident ever in your life have over one removed at a time, or in a single year. But you see, that is because we dident know anything. We were just living, but we were not living according to doctor's orders. Nowadays what happens? You go to a dentist to get him to fill an old molar that has been rarin' and pitchin' because you have had your mouth open, talking too much, and cold has got in there and she has found this dugout.

The dentist will just glance at it for a minute and then commence to browse around with his little side-view mirror off an old car, and he won't say a word. He will just start shaking his head. You have your mouth propped open so wide, you can't even ask him what he is so disturbed about. But he don't pay any attention to you, anyhow. He just goes right on down the line, first on the south-bound traffic, and then he starts working back on the uptown side of your row of mileage posts. Finally, when you have slobbered all over your chin and necktie, he will stop picking and exploring and come out of there, still shaking his head, and acting as though he is going to tell you, "The jury is about to find you guilty of murder and you are to be hung Tuesday!"

Finally you say, "What's the matter, doctor. Does she need filling pretty bad?"

"Filling? Oh that one is nothing! It just needs a couple of fillings and a hanging bridge and a little interior riveting. It's nothing at all. It's those others. You got some bad babies in there. I think, though, by proper work and by getting them in time like this, I can save — oh, about 60 percent of them. My, but you are lucky coming here to me when you did."

"Why, Doc, there is nothing the matter with any of the others. That is the only one has hurt me in years.

"Well, I wouldent advise you wrong. I'll just take out a couple of these big ones, and that will give me more room to work around that little one. There is some little gold filling in there that will have to be taken out. They are not wearing that any more. Then the work is beginning to show bad anyway!"

"I know, Doc, but they never have caused me any trouble. They was put in there years ago by a little small-town dentist, and I thought they were fine."

"Why, you won't go a week. They are just liable to start bothering you tonight. It's getting teeth in time that is the big thing today. Now I can get these all fixed up, and you come in here, say, about every other Thursday, and you will see that you will have very little trouble with your teeth."

"But I havent had any up to this one. But if you think it's best, why, go ahead."

And he starts in. That is the start, not only of him digging into you, but you digging into the little monthly saving account that you had been trying to lay by for a larger tub set. But this is just the start of it. Now they have the regular doctors working with them. Maybe you have had rheumatism, or a bowed tendon, or the black leg, or something, and your doctor has been working on you for perhaps years. Why, he will say, "Let me have a look at those teeth. Yes, I have thought so a long time, but I wanted to wait to be sure. They have got to come out of there!"

"What's got to come out, Doc?"

"Why, those teeth. They are what is causing you to have dandruff. But I am going to do it slowly. At first I am only going to have you take out the first row in the balcony. I will give you a card to the man who will do it. Then you come back to me and I will be able to start curing you of that asthma that has been bothering you so long. I am going to have those x-rayed first and see just what ones are the worst.

Well, you go then to an x-ray guy. The doctor sends over a blue print of the ones he wants stills made of. He has a thing that shoots right through you and shows any bad spots. It should be compulsory before marriage, and not before teeth pulling. Then you could tell if either of you had a kind of a faulty heart, and it was maybe going to give out caring for the other. Well, they get the scenics of the bicuspids,

and if it shows a dark spot away at the back, it may be the brass collar button on the back of your shirt, or it may be a fly speck on the film. But, at any rate, it's too late to call for a change of venue. These teeth that were unfortunate enough not to photograph well, are coming out of there. Just think, we have had, and have, presidents that don't photograph well. But they don't pull 'em out of office for it. But a tooth, if it just happens to have some corn likker lodged down in there, and happens to photograph like bran mash, why, out the tooth comes. He explains to you, "See that small speck? Well, that is on a nerve that goes directly to the Madull Oblong Gotto, and it has a sideline that runs right through the Appendix!" So the x-ray bird gets his cut out of the savings. The man that's sent you there gets his. No dentist pulls your teeth anymore. That's a separate branch altogether. All he requires is a strong arm, two nurses, no conscience, some gas, or a hammer. Then the Appendix guy gets his. That is also a sideline, or accessory, to the medical highwaymen's profession. In other words, they are making four fees grow, where only one grew before. There is four industries flourishing of that one dark spot!

A broken leg is generally traceable to a cloudy molar. Gunshot wounds from an unreasonable husband is traceable to a faulty wisdom tooth. Water on the knee? They take out a tooth and drain that off. They remove the eyeteeth to prevent blindness, and if you are blind, they remove them to restore sight. Another great gag with them now is, "I don't know that it is your teeth that is causing you trouble, but we will just take them out, and if that don't cure it, why of course you will be out nothing but your teeth. It's worth the try. That might just accidentally be what is the matter with you."

The best joke I know of that you could play on a modern doctor would be to go to a dentist first and have every tooth pulled out, and then go to the doctor and say, "Doctor, those fallen arches of mine are killing me. What can I do?"

He would say, "Let me see those teeth of yours, that is just about what is causing the trouble." Then, when he looked, there wouldent be any teeth. You would have a big laugh on him.

It's funny. Babies without teeth at all, are sick, and old people that havent got any at all, die. So I don't know how these doctors get away with this laying everything onto the teeth.

There are two things that seem like they got started wrong in life. One was the Constitution of the United States. The men that layed that out dident seem to know what we needed, and so these modern, smarter men have been all these years trying to improve it and get it fixed up properly. And the other thing, was teeth.

It seems the Lord, when he layed out our original teeth, dident know much about teeth, so He just put those we have in temporarily, till the doctors amounted to something.

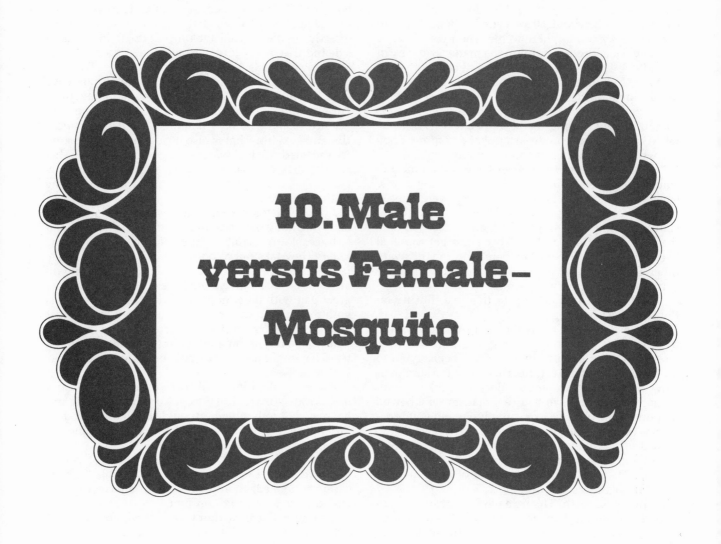

10. Male versus Female-Mosquito

We are always reading statistics and figures. Half of America do nothing but prepare propaganda for the other half to read. Insurance companies have guys figure out the very day you will die. In fact, they won't insure you till they have it investigated and find out — then you, like a sucker, go bet them you will live longer than that.

But just the other day, a fellow in Atlantic City, New Jersey, come through with some statistics that really ought to set us thinking! It wasent one of those, "The average working girl makes $33 a week, spends $10 for board, $12 for silk stockings, and the rest for lipsticks."

This guy is a professor and chief "entomologist." That word will stop you ignorant ones. But you got a fifty-fifty break, I don't know what it means either. Well, this professor delivered this address at a convention of the New Jersey Exterminators Association, duly assembled in the very heart of the mosquito belt. So I gather from that, that an entomologist is a man that has devoted his life to a study that must include this New Jersey product. He has either given his life's work for, or against, the mosquito. It's a surprise that New Jersey had such an organization called "The New Jersey Mosquito Exterminators, Inc." Anyone who has ever visited that state, could not possibly understand how there could be an organization devoted to the annihilation of those comical little rascals. Or if they have got such a society, where have they been exterminating, and when?

But you see, what they been doing is holding dinners. All you do in America nowadays, is get a name for some kind of an organization, then you start holding dinners. An organization without a dinner is just impossible. Now the only mosquitoes exterminated was at the dinner. Well, during the scratching and slapping and singing of the mosquitoes, this guy read off the following authoritative statistics.

"The normal productivity of one lone female house mosquito in one year is 159,875,000,000 offsprings."

Now you statistics hounds, get that. There is four sets of those three figures. So according to my remembrance of Ray's elementary arithmetic, that runs us up into the billions. So that first 159 you see there ain't nothing but *billions!* Now just wait and let that soak in a while, 159 billions of offsprings. You mothers that think you have done something for your race when you have brought into the world two to eight or ten young hyenas, you certainly can't boast after reading what the female mosquito has done to leave her imprint on the ankles of humanity. Now I don't know what was done at the dinner about it. Perhaps they all signed a pledge to go out and, during the coming year, to exterminate as early in the season as possible one female mosquito, thereby lessening the yearly yield by 159 billion.

Now wait a minute. You ain't heard nothing yet. Only half of these, or 79,937,500,000 should be counted as pests, for they are the active, buzzing, biting and egg-laying females. The others are mere males, which do not bite and are harmless. These figures, which are based on the known rate of mosquito reproduction, and which disregard infant mortality, indicate the urgent need for control measures that begin early in the season.

Now women, what have you got to say for yourselves? Get that, the males are harmless. They don't bite, buzz or lay eggs! That's great. It makes me proud I am a male. That fellow Kipling had it right when he wrote (or maybe it was Shakespeare, or Lady Astor, or somebody over there), "The female of the species is more deadly than the male." Women denied it then and there was a great mess raised about it. But this New Jersey entomologist has finally got the dope on 'em.

Now we are getting down to the main part, and like all speakers, he dident explain that. It is this. He told you to go out and exterminate a female as early in life as possible. You are liable to go out with the best intentions in the world and kill one, and what might it turn out to be but an innocent male. A poor male mosquito that had never done a soul a wrong in its life. It had never sung to you, it had never bit you, it had never laid eggs on you. In fact, it had gone through life acting in a gentlemanly way, and here it is killed. Why? Because you havent been taught to distinguish the sex! He has given up his life, this poor mosquito has, just as a martyr to the ignorance of the human race. What we need is literature of two kinds. One to teach us to readily realize the sex, and the other is a pamphlet for the female mosquito on birth control. Show them that they are not only doing their part, but they are going over their quota! Teach them that the days of the big families in mosquitoes are past, that what we want is fewer and better mosquitoes. Try to get them to move out of New Jersey, and to Fifth and Park Avenues, New York, and let 'em see there that being prolific in offsprings is only for the lower classes.

Don't try and kill off the females. Educate 'em up to modern ways. They are not so crazy about laying eggs, it's just because they think it's their duty to do it. Course the whole thing is kinder mysterious to me. I don't see how the female can be the one that lays all the eggs, raises all the young, does all the biting, and still has time to sing.

Now when do they find time to raise all these children? There must be times when they can't be singing or biting. Now the way this entomologist has left us now, about the only way we have left open to do, is to watch a mosquito till he bites you, and then destroy him — I mean her. In other words, if he bites you, he is a her, and if he sings, he is a her. Watch him and if he lays an egg, then it's a her. But if he just sits there all day and don't do anything, why, about the only conclusion we can come to is that it is a *he.* Don't kill him, he does no harm, he just sits and revels in the accomplishments of his wife. So when you find a male, the best thing to do is just to sit there and wait till his wife comes between bites.

How does the male live? That's what they are going to take up at the next dinner.

11. Hollywood: The Galloping Pictures

All I know is just what I read in the moving picture ads, and say, boy, what an education it is! I thought the underwear ads in the magazines were about the limit in presenting an eyeful, but these movie ads give you the same thing without the underwear. Even I, myself, appeared in a nightgown in *The Connecticut Yankee*, so on the billboards it would add a touch of romantic glamour, to say nothing of a smattering of sex appeal.

Mind you, you mustent let the ad have anything to do with what you see on the insides. You are liable to see the wildest stuff facing you on the billboards, and then go inside and everybody is dressed as Eskimos all through the picture. In other words, the big trouble is getting pictures that will live up to the pictures on the ads. And, too, the off-colored, or risqué, pictures havent been going so good as they used to. It isn't that tastes are improving, it is that there is nothing new they could shock folks with.

Now about this movie business, and how I got my start. To be honest about it, I havent got a real good start. The way I figure things, a fellow has to be a success before he goes lecturing and crowing about himself. Out here in Hollywood, they say you're not a success unless you owe $50 thousand to somebody, have five cars, can develop temperament without notice or reason at all, and have been mixed up in four divorce cases and two breach-of-promise cases. Well, as a success in Hollywood, I'm a rank failure, and I guess I am too old to be taught new tricks. Besides I'm pretty well off domestically speaking, and ain't yearning for a change. I hold only two distinctions in the movie business, ugliest fellow in 'em, and I still have the same wife I started out with.

Now about how I actually got started. Mrs. Rex Beach was really the one who helped me get started, by selling the idea to Sam Goldwyn that he ought to star me in the movies. Anyway, Sam signed me up, and I starred in a series of six-reel comedies for him during 1921 and 1922.

Now, I had been on the stage a few years, but I never yet had any of that junk on my face. I was told I would photograph black if I dident make up. I asked to make it a black-face part, then I could play it straight.

Well, they had to put a hitch on my upper lip to get me to smear paint all over my contour. Even that could not disguise this old, homely pan of mine. They said the day of the pretty actor is gone. You are so ugly, you are a novelty.

We then went up into what they call the studio. It's a big, glassed-in place like those up in the Bronx Park, where they stable those big South American palm trees. It reminded me of Amarillo, Texas; in the old days, with about six herds waiting to ship at once.

It was a bad day outside, and it had hazed all those companies under cover. You couldent move around without stepping on a five- or six-thousand-dollar-a-week star. And moving cameras were thicker around there than Army Commission hunters in Washington.

I got lost from my director and started to take a near cut across, when some guy bawled me out. It sounded like a Roosevelt speech. I was only between Mabel Norman and three cameras, and them all cranking on her most particular scene in a picture called *A Perfect 36*.

So I had really gone in movies quicker than I had figured on. Imagine me, a principal in a perfect 36. When they all got through cussing me, a fellow said, "What company are you working for?" I told him, "Goldwyn." He said, "It's all Goldwyn! I mean, who is your director?"

Miss Norman was looking at me, and I couldent think of that guy's name to save my life. This bird says, "He must be in Madge Cannedy's company. They are taking a Bowery lodging house scene!" I got pretty sore at that and walked away.

Now you wouldent think a fellow could pull the same bonehead twice, but leave it to an old country boy, to horn in wrong. I was feeling my way around among scenery and sets, trying to locate my man, when a big, burly guy nabbed me by the coattail and yanked me back and said, "You poor boob! I saved your life. That's Miss Geraldine Farrar taking close-ups for *The Hell Cat*. I heard what she did to Caruso one time, and I thanked him. I watched her a while, in hopes she would sing, but I tell you what she did have, she had an orchestra playing appropriate music in all her scenes.

This man said he would show me where I belonged, so we passed through an Irish farm house of Tom Moore's, stopped to see May Marshe's propaganda picture of choking the Kaiser, passed through the Metropolitan Opera House and Cheyenne Joe's saloon, on the way to my gang. By the time I got there, they thought I had given up the picture and gone home. It was now ten-thirty, and I thought I was late. We took the first scene at exactly three forty-five in the afternoon.

The director says, "Now, Will, we are going to take the scene where your old pal dies. You have broken out of jail and he gets hurt, and you are bringing him into the doctor's office at night to get him treated, and he dies. It's the dramatic scene of the whole opera."

I says, "But I haven't got out of jail yet!"

He says, "No, you won't for a couple of weeks yet. Besides, the jail is not built yet."

That's the first time I learned that they just hop around any old way. Once we took a scene that was the start of a fellow and I fighting outdoors, and then a lot of rainy weather come, and a week later he knocked me down in the same fight.

The director says, "I am not going to tell you how to act." I said to him, "Why, these correspondence schools do that." He instructed me as follows: "Now, thought photographs. If you are thinking a thing, the camera will show it!" So I told him I would try and keep my thoughts as clean as possible. He said, "Now we will rehearse the scene, and then take it. Now carry your old pal in. Ha! Wait a minute, you

12 SHORT FEATURES

—That Will Be **The** Feature Attraction in **Thousands** of Lucky Theatres Throughout America!

C. S. CLANCY   presents

Will Rogers

OUR UNOFFICIAL AMBASSADOR ABROAD

Pathepicture

[Left:]
Filming Laughing Bill Hyde, *Will appears in a flowing beard.*

[Below:]
With director Hobart Henley on set of Laughing Bill Hyde, *Will's first film.*

With Peggy Wood in 1919 silent film Almost a Husband.

wouldn't carry him in that way, would you? You will hurt him worse than he is even supposed to be in the story!''

I told him to change the story around and let me be hurt and him do the carrying, that the other fellow was the biggest.

But those guys are set in their way and won't change anything.

Then we took it, him ballyhooing at me through a megaphone just what to do. He says, ''That's fine, very good.'' Then I heard him say to the cameraman, ''Mark that N.G.''

The next take I was really getting along fine on it. I was drama-ing all over the place, holding this pal, a-pleading with the doctor to do something for him. My mind was more on my art than on the load I had, and I dropped him.

Well, I want to tell you folks, somebody could have bought my moving picture future pretty cheap right then.

The director kept impressing on me that my only pal was dying. Well, he didn't have anything on me. I was almost dying. He looked and he saw I had tears in my eyes, and he says, ''That's great!'' He thought I was crying about my pal, and I was crying about getting into the darn thing.

Anyhow, the outstanding picture of this group was *Jubilo*, based on the theme of the song of that name.

Ben Ames Williams wrote *Jubilo*, where I played a tramp. Everybody that sees me in street clothes says that I excel on tramp parts. I like to play tramps. There is something about an old tramp that kinder hits me, especially a kind of a good natured one that don't take things too seriously. Anyway, *Jubilo* was the only story ever made out here where there was no scenario made. We just shot the scenes from the various paragraphs in the story in the *Saturday Evening Post*. When we took a scene, we just marked it off, and went on to the next. I think that it was the only story ever made that was absolutely filmed as it was written. And here is the big novelty to it, we didn't change the main title either. They will film the Lord's Supper, and when it is made, figure that that is not a good release title and not catchy enough.

Why, I passed a theater down by the ranch the other night, and we wanted to go in but what stared us in the face was something like *Fast Company*, or some such idiotic title, and we just drove on. A few days later, the children got to talking about a good and funny picture they had seen, a baseball picture. I got to asking them about it. It was the one by Ring Lardner, *Elmer, The Great*, based on his famous stories of the rookie in baseball. Well, here this thing called *Fast Company*, and featuring some girl, was nothing but *Elmer, The Great*. Now I know that title they had drove out more people than it ever brought in.

So no matter what famous book you have read and want to see in the pictures, why you better start going into every theater you come to. Don't look up at the title, for *Passionate Pal* may be just what you was looking for as *Romeo and Juliet*. Sometimes you just think there ain't enough crazy titles to go round, and that when they end, that will be the finish of pictures.

But I must get back to how I got started. I also made *Doubling For Romeo* for Sam Goldwyn. It was the story of a cowhand who went to sleep and dreamed he played Romeo in Shakespeare's immortal drama. I liked my work in this one a lot, but they had a sales convention at the studio and showed the film to the gang. Although I thought the picture was very funny, the boys seemed to think different and refused to laugh. At the time I was nearly heartbroken. I felt that I was a flop and was about to quit pictures. Gosh it was awful!

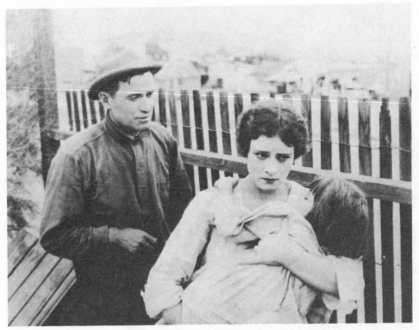

Will and Irene Rich in 1919 Water, Water Everywhere.

I wasent writing much in those days, although since then the papers seem to like my stuff and pay me for making wisecracks, which doesn't make me a bit sore. For recreation I used to keep some horses and goats on the lot, back of the studio, and I spent most of my time enjoying the companionship of dumb, but honest, animals. They couldent laugh at me, which was encouraging.

From Goldwyn's I went to work for Hal Roach and made a series of two-reel comedies there. It's a serious business — this making people laugh. But wisecracks and picture work pays better than the old rope throwin' act, and that salves by bruised feelings.

Say, did you ever see a picture company on location? Well, now that we have to carry all that sound equipment and men with it, why, it looks like Barnum's Circus coming — I bet there is about 50 of us. It takes lots of folks to make these things, even when you see 'em sometimes you think they ain't so hot. And the funny part about it is that a bad one takes just as much work as a good one, for we have never found anyone that can tell when it's going to be bad. You see, bad pictures are not made with a premeditated design. It looks to you sometimes like we must have purposely made 'em that way, but honest, we don't. A bad picture is an accident, and a good one is a miracle. We do our best all the time, and all the crew, the cameramen, the carpenters, property men, sound technicians, and dozens of other expert men in their lines, they all do good work on all of 'em, but it's us actors, and writers and directors that just don't click in some of 'em. This is the only business in the world that nobody knows anything about. Being in them don't give any more of an inkling about them than being out of them.

The exhibitor says he wants better pictures for less money.

The producer (that's the fellow that spends a lot of somebody else's money making pictures somebody else wrote, somebody else directed and a lot of others acted in) says he wants better stories and better directors and better actors for less money.

The actor says, "You are not giving me a fair share of what I draw at the box office!"

Will Hays said, "They got to be cleaner!"

The exhibitor says, "If you get 'em too clean nobody is interested in them!"

The novelist says, "What's the use of selling them a story, they don't make the story they buy!"

The scenario staff says, "It reads good, but it won't photograph."

The exchange salesmen say, "The exhibitors are a dumb lot, they don't know what their audiences want!"

The exhibitors say, "We may be dumb, but we know how to count up. Give us pictures where there is something to count up!"

The so-called intellectual keeps saying, "Why don't they give us something worthwhile in the movies that we can think about!"

The regular movie fan says, "Give us something to see, never mind think about. If we wanted to think we wouldn't come here!"

The old married folks say, "Give us something besides all this love-sick junk and the fade-out behind the willow tree!"

The young folks that pay the rent on these temples of uplift say, "Give us some love and romance. What do we care about these pictures with a lot of old folks trying to show what they do in life. We will get old soon enough without having to see it now!"

Wall Street says, "We want more interest on our money!"

The producers say, "Look at the fun you are having

[Left:]
*Will Rogers and son
Jimmy in* The Strange
Boarder, *1920.*

[Below:]
With Guinn "Big Boy" Williams in
Cupid, the Cowpuncher.

by being in the business. Dident we give you a pass through the studio; what do you want for your money?"

The actors that aren't working say, "They don't want actors any more, they only want types!"

The actors that are working say, "Thank God, they are beginning to realize it's us actors they want, and not just somebody that looks like the part."

Now speaking of looking like the part, I must tell you that since I have been out here working in pictures, I have had a chance to see quite a lot of movies, and observe the looks and style of dress on the screen.

Now the thing I want to speak about was really prompted by my being asked to speak before a doctors' convention. I had not been sick for a long time and did not really know what a doctor looked like, only of course, the ones I had seen on the screen, who all wore Van Dyke beards, trimmed very neat, and a cutaway coat. So I went to the hotel where I was to speak on the subject "Odd and Ends Left Inside after Operations," or "Mistakes Doctors Have Made and Covered Up." I saw a room full of men but not a one had a Van Dyke beard, so I thought I was in the wrong room. Finally I spied one lone guy with a Van Dyke, so I immediately rushed up to him and said, "You are Dr. Alibi, aren't you?" He said, "Why, no, I am only a clerk."

Now I wouldent believe these men were doctors at all, as not a one had the earmarks of a doctor, and to make it still more doubtful, there wasn't a cutaway coat in the room. So you see, by not knowing how to look or dress, I just realized what fools moving picture actors were making out of these doctors. Now it wouldent be so bad if it was only the doctors in real life that were making themselves ridiculous by not knowing how to dress and look, but the same thing has percolated into almost every other line of business you can think of.

Another bunch of men are the bankers. Anyone with a grain of movie sense knows that all bankers are big and fat. Still, in New York, just before I came out to Hollywood, I spoke at their banquet where the richest were gathered from all over the U.S. I spoke on the subject, "Widows You Have Foreclosed On." Well, when I got into the room, the first fellow I saw looked like the ideal screen banker. He had on a dress suit and was big and fat, so I said, "You are one of the bankers. Can you give me some information?" He said, "Why, I'm one of the waiters here. I am no banker." So I asked him where the bankers were. He said, "Why, they are all around here." I said, "What! These little weasely undernourished men?" Well, I tell you how bad they looked. I got so scared I went to the manager and told him to, "Feed 'em before I talk to them, because some of them look like they ain't going to live anyway."

Another case that I had forcibly brought to mind lately was a fellow who sold me a lot and took part of the money down. I found later he had sold the same lot to three other people. He was a little, fat, blond, jolly fellow. Now anybody in the world that's ever seen just one picture knows that a crook, or villain, that would do a thing like that is tall with black hair and eyes, has a mustache and smokes cigarettes all the time. That little fellow will never get any credit at all for being a crook. His whole life's work is wasted, simply because he don't look right.

Even women, who as a rule are much smarter than men, make the same mistakes. Now I have seen young women with babies who they said were theirs, and some really young ones that claimed they had a whole bunch, maybe five or six. Now you know, and anybody that has ever been to movies knows, that that ain't right. A woman doesent have any children unless she is at least gray-headed. As for being the mother of five or six, why her hair must be snow-white and she must be on the way to the poor house. No, I don't see how these young women in real life ever make anybody believe these children are theirs.

Sheriffs in real life are a source of great merriment to all movie fans. A lot of them will persist in appearing without being tall and lanky and having a mustache. What a joke they are to regular movie fans! Can you imagine a sheriff on the screen that is not tall and has a mustache?

Another thing I saw the other day when visiting a big ranch out West. Here was a cowboy chasing an animal, and he was running it part of the time uphill. Well, that struck me, who had been looking at pictures for years, as being a strange thing to do. I had always seen everything chased downhill, and never up. So I just thought how foolish of this cowboy, doing this, when on the screen it had been proved absolutely unnecessary. But then, this cowboy was away out there on that ranch and didn't know much. Why, he was even chasing where there was no road! That was a novelty to me. I had always seen a fellow chasing like mad *down* a road. So I asked him why he dident run down a road when he was after something, and his excuse was that he had to follow what he was after. Silly remark, wasent it? Why, out here in the movies, we train everything to run down the roads. That's all they would have to do on a ranch. But then in lots of places they havent got as good roads as California, so I guess that's why they don't chase their stock and outlaws up and down roads like they do in the movies. Of course, everything can't reach the perfection we reached in our industry.

Another practice that they tell me is still in vogue in certain parts of the West is to shoot a gun so much that you have to reload it. Now what a silly practice, when producers and actors have been working and striving to educate people for years to know that, no matter how many times a man may shoot a six-shooter in a battle, he don't have to reload it. Of course, sometimes it gets so hot you have to dip it in water to cool it off, but I never saw one shot so many times it had to be reloaded. But, as I say, it will take some people years to learn what we are trying to teach them. But I am proud to be connected, even in a small way, with an industry that is trying in every way possible to set real people right, and make them see where they are wrong. They have either got to change, or be the butt of every movie fan's ridicule.

It's kind of a cuckoo business, but trains have been

Waiting on set of Doubling for Romeo.

full for twenty years of so-called smart people that were coming out here to fix the movies, and they have all gone back. There are things that look like they ought to be changed, but the wise ones can't seem to be able to think of anything to improve 'em. It's sorter like our government. It's the cockeyedest run thing, we sometimes think, but darn it, we keep living under it and nobody can scare up anything any different.

Like the other day, at the studio, they was talking about a story. They said it had to be changed a lot, that the old idea of a mortgage on the old farm was all out-of-date, that the villain robbing the train and hiding the money was all the hooey! They claimed that all stories had to be made modern and up-to-date. So I told 'em, "Say, listen! There never was a time in our lives where the foreclosing of a mortgage was as timely as it is today. It almost comes as standard equipment with most homes and farms. And as for villains being out of date, why, villains are getting as thick as college degrees, and sometimes on the same fellow!"

No sir, there is no new situation. Wives are leaving husbands, husbands are leaving wives. Robberies, where they used to take your horse, and if they was caught they got hung for it, now they take your car, and if they are caught, it's a miracle, and they will perhaps have the inconvenience of having to go to court and explain. The old horse, if the horse thief ever let him loose, or give him half a chance, he would come home. Our automobiles don't stay at home long enough to know where home is, even if they could get back. So our movies won't be changed much more than your morals, or your taxes, or any other of the things that you think should be remodeled.

But this old town is just a-humming, don't we have the Academy of Motion Picture Arts and Sciences? I was always a little leery of this organization. The name "Arts and Sciences" has bluffed out more people than it has attracted. If I didn't know so many of the people who belong to it personally, I would have taken that name serious. Call them "Arts and Sciences," but do so with your tongue in your cheek. Everything that makes money and gives pleasure is not *art*. If it was, bootlegging would have been the highest form of artistic endeavor.

And those little statues they hand out! They are lovely things. They were originally designed for prizes at a nudist colony, but they didn't take 'em. It must be terribly artistic, for nobody has any idea what it is. It represents the triumph of nothingness over the stupendousness of zero. When they hand out those awards, there is greater acting in the room than you will see on the screen. We all cheer when somebody gets a prize that everyone of us knows should be ours. Yet we smile and take it. Boy, that's acting.

Or take adapters, commonly known among authors as book murderers. They are the people that show you how the book should have been written in the first place. If given the Bible to adapt, they would claim that it started too slow, that the love interest should start in Genesis, and not in Leviticus, and that the real kick of the story was Noah trying to have each animal find its mate. They would play that for suspense. There has always been the suspicion that an adapter is one who wants to bet you you won't recognize your own story. Now, original writers are men who have had good enough lawyers to protect them from plagiarism suits. Or take photography! That's an art, where, if you shoot enough weird shots that get the audience's mind off the actors, you will get a medal — not only from the Academy, but from the audience.

So you see, I am the one that started American pictures. I was in them before they were referred to by the press agents as an "art." I was in pictures in Hollywood away back, when some of these big stars

80

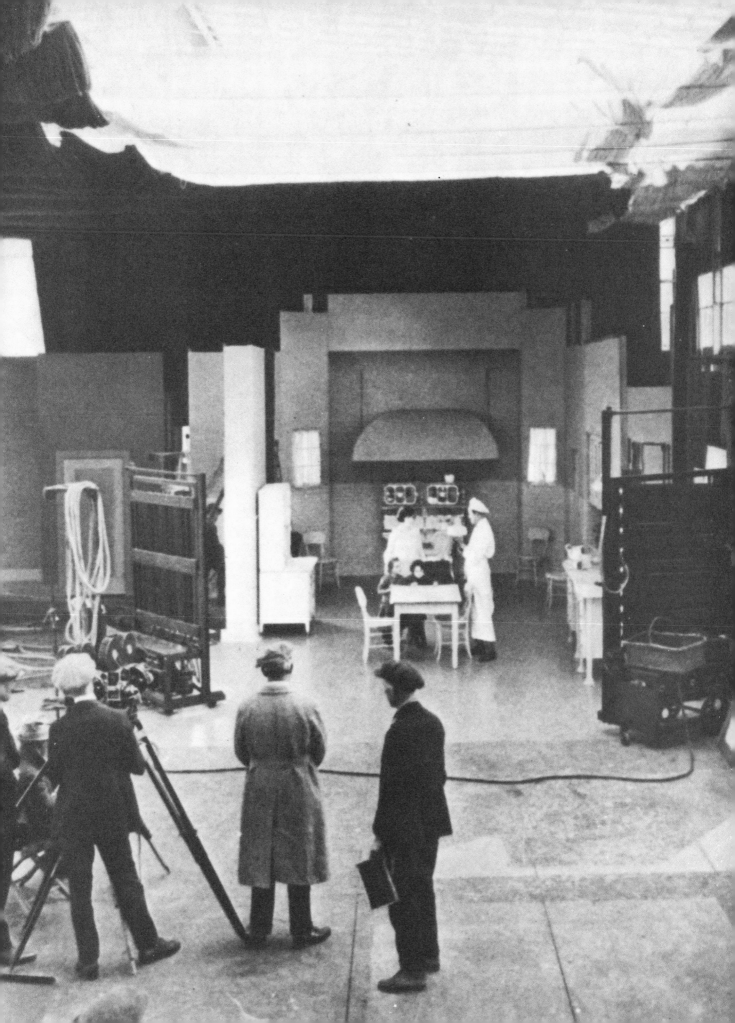

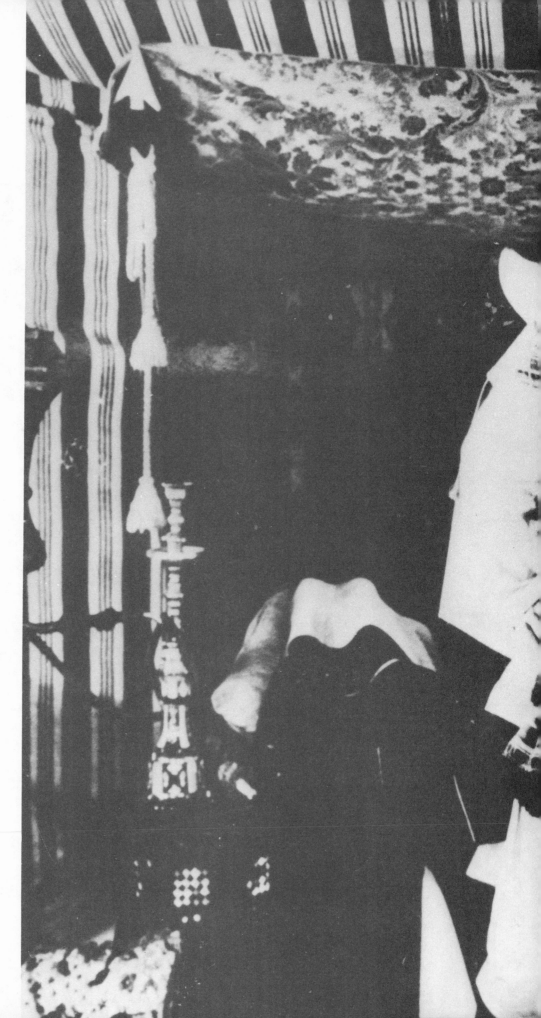

Imitating Rudolph Valentino in Uncensored Movies, *a spoof of great stars.*

[Above:]
Will, far right, as a Keystone Kop.

[Below:]
On a rearing horse à la Tom Mix.

were just learning to get married. You see, pictures have to undergo a poor, or what Will Hays would call a "mediocre," stage before they can get to be big. Well, there is the stage that I assisted the great film industry through. The minute they commenced getting better, why, my mission had been fulfilled. In other words, I am what you might call a pioneer. I am all right in anything while it is in its crude state, but the minute it gets to having class, why, I am sunk. After anything begins to take itself seriously, I have to gradually drop out, some times suddenly.

But really, the whole motion picture business is flourishing and weddings were never more at a premium. Divorces permeate the air. High-powered roadsters are skitting here and yon. So let's everybody connected with this business, and everybody that loves to go see movies, as we go to our beds at night pray to our Supreme Being, that He don't allow it to be found out what is the matter with the movies; for if He ever does, we will all be out of a job.

[Will Rogers starred in almost 70 motion pictures from 1918–1935 — 21 of them "talkies." In the last three years of his life, 1933, 1934, 1935, Will Rogers was America's top male box-office favorite. ED.]

[Left:]
Here Will Rogers
assumes a typical
Tom Mix pose.

[Below:]
Next to Stan Laurel, Will
mimics strong, silent
look of William S. Hart.

Bull-fighting for the camera.

Reading a newspaper between takes.

With indisposed Blue Boy in State Fair, 1933.

Shot from travelog about Ireland, 1927.

Poster for Will Rogers' first sound film.

Quick peek at book before the next scene.

Left to right: Brandon Hurst, William Farnum, and Rogers as Sir Boss.

Russian poster for A Connecticut Yankee,
starring "Vyll Rodshers and Myrna Loy."

Russian poster for A Connecticut Yankee,
starring "Vyll Rodshers and Myrna Loy."

[Right:]
Rogers, as Dr. Bull,
exchanges banter
with Andy Devine.

[Below:]
Will practicing on
the way to a set.

[Left:]
Rogers, as David Harum,
with Kent Taylor.

[Below:]
Whittling away
with Charles B. Middleton.

[Above:]
In serious discussion with Mickey
Rooney in The County Chairman.

[Right:]
Stepin Fetchit, Evelyn Venable,
and Will Rogers.

[Above:]
*Catching up on the
news on* David Harum
set.

[Left:]
*Douglas Fairbanks,
Sr., and Tom
Mix greet Will
as Mayor of
Beverly Hills.*

[Right:]
In Old Kentucky,
*Will gets dancing
lesson from
Bill "Bojangles"
Robinson.*

[Below:]
Frank Borzage, Ethel
Barrymore visiting a modest
Will Rogers on a movie set.

[Left:]
Two interested spectators
at a polo game, Spencer Tracy
and Will Rogers.

12. Our National Follies

It's going to be awful hard to keep politics from creeping into the news from now on. We have various pestilences every once in a while, and we have floods, but the only advertised and known calamity is our elections. We got one coming on, and there is no use denying it. We just as well harden ourselves to it. It's just like an operation. The anesthetic (or whatever you call the gas they give you), why, that is the worst part of it. An election without all the gases wouldent be so bad, but it's these weeks of slowly putting you under the influence that is the trying part of an election. So we just might as well start steeling our systems to it.

You dare not turn on your radio now for fear some presidential candidate will be spouting "What this country needs!" When as a matter of fact, what this country needs is more working men and fewer politicians. But everything will be fixed this fall, if you just listen to what the candidates say. In fact, that's about all we are doing, just listening to what the candidates say — so you see, even our minds are not working.

All the politicians are trying to stir up some excitement in their line of work. But I can't find much interest around the country in their graft, outside the ones that are in it. The outside people have just about come to the conclusion that there ain't a worry's worth of difference in any of 'em, and they just try to forget it and live it down if they ever did take any interest. By the way, the way they are raiding the Treasury now, there don't look like it will do anybody any good to get elected. What's the use running your head off to get to a table where the food has just been all eaten up? If I was an office seeker, I would kinder be doubtful whether there was enough in there left to pay my regular salary, much less what I wanted to run for office for in the first place.

You see, I did quite a bit of prowling around down in Washington, to see what our hired help was doing. This is the time of year when Congress really works, but it's for themselves and you can't blame 'em. They have had a taste of it, and they like it. There is something about holding office that must just get right next to 'em. And they are seldom ever any good anymore for anything else. But they are likable cusses. You can't help but like 'em, and they are always smarter than the people that elected 'em. So our elections are just what we need. We don't know what we need it for, but it's for something, if it's only to get one half of our folks sore at the other half.

Anyhow, in Washington, everything was politics there. All you could hear was "Who is going to run?" The Democrats have got more candidates than they got voters. Every place wants to run a different man. The Republicans are just as bad. They want to run everybody, too, but they can't run anybody but the President. If they run anybody else, they would be repudiating their own administration, so they are up against it. If things pick up, the President has a good chance, but if they don't, he is kinder snowed under.

But I know things are going to get better, in spite of both sides. Then, when things do get better, you'll hear the yell that will go up. Now watch this! The Democrats will swear that recovery was due to them. And the Republicans, they'll say it was due to them. Nobody wants to claim the credit for the country blowing up, but wait until it starts picking up, and they'll both be on it then. I don't think either one of these parties knows what it's all about, to be honest with you. Both sides are doing nothing but just looking at the next election. You don't hear anybody talking any more about when these unemployed folks are going back to work. All you hear now is "Do you think the President is going to be elected?" And, "Who will the other side run?" Their minds are on political business, that's all it's on.

Everybody is always asking, "Has women voting made any real change in our political system?" It has. It has just doubled the amount of candidates. The only way we can possibly have more people seeking public pensions is to give the children the vote. We have done it for the wife; let's do it for the kiddies. Don't children have the same qualifications for office that the grownups have?

A while back the Democrats were having a lot of fun exposing the Republican campaign corruptions, but they would have had a lot more fun if they knew where they could lay their hands on just a little of it for next November. The difference in corruption in the two parties was 7 million last election. So the Democrats have got to investigate and find out how to improve their corruption. You see, politics has got so expensive that it takes lots of money to even get beat with, nowadays.

So now you hear a lot of talk about the campaign this year being awful cheap, and maybe on the level. But I want to tell you that I would hate to offer $150 thousand to either side. I'll bet they would grab at a promissory note, or even an anonymous check. So don't be afraid to contribute! Both sides are doing business at the old stand.

Well, anyhow, as I said, every four years we have politics. Every seven years some people have an itch; in a malaria country, every other day people are scheduled to have a chill; every 40 years France and Germany fight; and there is just hundreds of these calamities that hit us every once in a while. But of all of them, I think politics is really the most disastrous. It hits a country like a pestilence. There is no telling where it will hit. People that you would think was smart, and would know better, are sometimes struck by it, and when they are, they are as dumb as the dumb ones. Why, we got people that are really taking the whole thing serious. They think a President has got something to do with running the country.

Well, let's take a look at a campaign right from the jump. You might wonder, "Just when does a campaign really start?" Well, they really start about 15 minutes after the official returns are in from the last election, on about the fifth drink after the counting is over, or the radio has announced that "So-and-so concedes the election to his honorable opponent." That is the first hooey of the following campaign. Right there is when the boys start laying their traps for the open office-holding season, which is four years away, but they start cutting their bait that very night. "Well, Jim, I'll tell you where we made our mistake this year and how we can beat that 'ham' next time!" So they start soaping the tracks right away.

Course, the President, he is usually conceded the nomination of the next election, unless he has been notoriously incompetent. But all things being as they usually are, why, he, of course, can have the nomination if he wants it. And history has never recorded the one that dident. Coolidge dident, but he had had already practically two terms. But it wasent a third term bugaboo that kept Calvin out; it was horse sense. He knew just to an inch how much American wind the financial balloon would hold, and he got out just two days before it busted.

We have about 100 senators in there, all of whom think they are only in there till the next election, when they will move to the other end of Pennsylvania Avenue. But there is some great moves go on in politics.

These politicians would make that old horse trader David Harum go and burn up his barn. He never saw the day he could pull off swaps like these babies can. Two-thirds of the men in politics are not "free-born Americans of lawful age and a fair break in intelligence," as the Constitution calls for. They were born, but not free; they are of age, but it wasent lawful; and the break they got in intelligence was not fair.

What I mean is that they are just a lot of pawns. They belong to their party, and mess around and do odd chores, and do all the dog-robbing that is handed out to them to do. Then a bunch of men meet in a room and start moving these blocks around. The poor nut don't know if he is to be advanced from an alderman to senator, or sent back to garbage inspector. These babies at the head move him and he goes and likes it, or gets out. There is a hundred things to single you out for promotion in a party politics, besides ability.

All of this is in the "organization." And what is it for, outside of just keeping the jobs in your own hands? Where does your justice and "free born" come in on that, when one gang organizes to keep the other from working? That's really a violation of the restraint of trade law, and those guys just work their heads off, scheming to kill off the other side. What difference does it make who is in, they are all about alike. The whole business is taken too seriously. We never had a man so crooked that he would like to ruin the country. We may run into one or two every once in a while that want to grab off part of our possessions. But they feel there is plenty left where they got that. So the old country just rambles along, not because of the politician, but in spite of him. Anyway, politics is a business where most of the men in it are looking for glory and personal gratification more than they are for money. It's one of the easiest ways of

horning in on something publicly. You can talk all the modesty you want, but it's just not one of our major industry. The old boys like to get their names in the pot. They like to pose as advisers and leaders.

Why, these old birds that are on all these national committees, and are always delegates to conventions, why, you could no more pry one of these jobs loose from them, even if they had to pay their way and the convention was held in Moscow, Russia. But they are a harmless sort, and really at heart mean well. And I think most of them are really wise to themselves, but it's gone so far they can't admit it.

A newspaperman spoiled my last convention by asking me if I was an alternate! Now, a delegate is bad enough, but an alternate is a spare tire for a delegate. An alternate is the lowest form of political life there is. He is the parachute in a plane that never leaves the ground.

Now, our National Conventions are nothing but glorified Mickey Mouse cartoons, and are solely for amusement purposes. Conventions are like locusts, they come every few years. It takes a great country to stand a thing like that hitting it every four years.

I was drafted to cover all these conventions. Of course, no one would have gone of his own free will and accord. I was asked to write something funny. All you have to do to write something funny about a convention is just tell what happened. And there is always excitement at a Democratic anything. It don't make any difference, there is always something that will stir up an argument, even if they all agree. Especially those platforms. You take any one of our party platforms and they promise anything before election. The same fellows that make 'em out, make out these insurance policies. That is, what they say on one page, they can deny on the other.

As for drafting a platform, that's a lot of apple sauce! Why, I bet you, there is not a Republican or Democratic office holder today that can tell you one plank in the last election platform without looking over the minutes. Those poor delegates will be allowed to sit and sweat and finally vote on something that he thinks is a platform, but when he gets home it will be found to be a trick floor! One of those things that you can raise, or lower, without the audience even seeing you do it. It will have a false bottom, and when you think you are standing on it, you won't be at all — you are over it but not on it.

And then those speeches, those terrible nominating speeches. Every man would talk for half the time about what his state had done. For instance, a Wisconsin man gabbed for an hour telling what Wisconsin had accomplished, including the milk and butterfat per cow. Another guy, from Tennessee, was nominating somebody from perhaps Vermont, or Arizona, I forgot which, and he went on for an age about what Andrew Jackson had done for the Commonwealth, and the records and traditions of his state. As a matter of fact, about all old Andrew was responsible for, was the system that made us all have to sit there and listen to such junk. Andrew was the one that said, "If you don't get out and work for the party, you don't get in on the gravy after election!"

Some man from Illinois got up to nominate somebody, and we knew we would hear something about Lincoln being from Illinois, and sure enough we did. He kept quoting Lincoln's famous remark about, "God must have loved the common people because he made so many of them." Well, this bird kept talking about his man being for the common people, and he flopped terribly. You are not going to get people's votes nowadays by calling them common. Lincoln might have said it, but I bet you it wasent until after he was elected.

One delegate started his speech out with, "As I look into this sea of faces!" So that shows you about how far speech making has advanced. It was Noah that first pulled that when he looked over the bunch just before pulling in the gangplank! I have watched and heard men burlesquing political speeches. It kinder made you wonder, "Are we doing all this progressing that we talk about all the time?"

They say practice makes perfect at anything. But I tell you, 'tain't so! No nation that was ever invented under the sun does as much practicing "talking" as we do, and if you think we are perfect at it, you just listen over the radio, or worse still, in person, to the speeches at these political conventions.

If oratory was devoted to some legitimate cause and reason, it might be the means of revolutionizing the world. But it's just gab, gab, gab, with not a laugh, or a new idea in it. There should be something that before a speaker gets up, they go over his stuff that he is about to perpetrate on the public, and take it apart before he delivers it, and see if there is a new thought or idea in it. Then, if there is not, he is told that the best place to dispose of that is at some radio station. They have to fill in all those hours every day, 365 days a year, and naturally they run pretty short of stuff. So, no matter how few ideas it may have, it won't be noticed there.

Then, if it does have an idea, why, take it out and let him go before the convention and just deliver that idea that it has, provided that all the other speakers havent delivered the same idea all week. Now, with this board operating, it would shorten the time of conventions to almost nothing. Because I don't believe there is over three or four new ideas at any given convention.

And further, if you will just eliminate the names of Lincoln, Washington, Roosevelt, Jefferson, Jackson and Wilson, why, both conventions will get out three days earlier. Every nut that gets up to spout off always has to refer to one or more of these past favorites. In fact, I think a lot of our past great men would be a lot bigger in public estimation if it was made prohibitory for them to be referred to by some of our politicians. For instance, people will say, "My Lord, if Roosevelt kept company with that fellow, and was as near him as this fellow seems to imply, I don't think as much of Roosevelt!"

Those speeches are straight applesauce! "These are momentous times! The eyes of the world are on us! Let us act with foresight and deliberation!" You hear

that from every speaker. Now just take that apart and see why they fall over if you try and let 'em stand alone. "These are momentous times!" Now what is momentous about 'em? Time is time, momentous things happen to individuals, not to everybody at once! What might be momentous to one, would be just wasting time to another. They are only momentous times with the speakers. For if justice gets its due, it's the last time he will ever get to address a National Convention! The only guy a convention is momentous with is the bird that gets the nomination.

Then the prize bromo of all: "The eyes of the world are upon us!" Now if that is not insulting your intelligence. The eyes of the world are not paying any attention to us. The world is shortsighted as far as we are concerned. Why, the eyes of our own country are not even on us. They know this thing is just an ordinary routine. Somebody is going to be President. It don't make any difference who it is. None of them, from any party, are going to purposely ruin the country. They will all do the best they can. If weather and crops, and no wars, and a fair share of prosperity is with them, they will all go out of office having had a good administration.

Or take the topic of "past records"! That's another thing that should come under strict censorship. They always tell you "What my party has accomplished." Now, as a matter of fact, any time a man says that, he is insulting the intelligence of his audience, for no party can put over one sprig of legislation without the aid of some members of the other party. Everything that is put through during a Republican administration is always referred to as "Our Legislation," and all that come off during the Democrats, is "Our Policies." Now neither can even pass a motion to adjourn without the other side. All legislation is put through by the aid of swaps and trades. They are just a lot of horse traders. "You help me put over my new Post Office, and I will help you get your creek widened!"

So make 'em leave all the so-called Party Accomplishments out of the speeches. Make 'em leave out all that "It's an honor for me to have been chosen" stuff! Our public men take themselves so seriously. It just looks like they are stoop-shouldered from carrying our country on their back. It takes weeks after one of these conventions is over to really start appreciating the finer comedy points. The reason a thing don't look ludicrous to us, is that a man at the last convention did and said exactly the same thing. But it's when we get home and see what was really inside it, why, then is when our sense of humor asserts itself. But it's too late to do anything about it then. So we just smile, and wait four years and they are all back again. The ones that failed to save the country the last time, they are all back again for another trial. The same issues are dragged out again, lower taxes, all the old gags are dusted off, and away they go again. The same old leaders are there again, just raring for something to lead with the same old speeches.

You see, here is what has made bad speeches stand

out so over what they used to be. Maybe in the old days speeches were just as idealess. But they were only listened to by the delegates. And the man making the speech was a delegate, so he only had to appeal to the intelligence as high as his own. But nowadays, this radio thing changed all that. They are not just talking to a lot of politicians; they are talking to the world. And people are getting wise to the type of man that is supposed to be saving the country. Right away we compare the intelligence of their talk with the talk that we hear in other lines of business, and it just don't stand up. So the old radio thing has given us a true line on our public servants. And speech making was never at a lower ebb in the history of the world than it is today, here in America.

So let's get a censorship board for public speakers at National Conventions and it will just about eliminate public speakers. And that will leave nothing but the flags and the band, and that will mean a perfect convention.

And the women, poor souls, they havent been able to harrow much of a row as far as cleaning up our national pastime is concerned. I think they take it too seriously. I believe they would get further if they kinder ridiculed and kidded the men. They can do that in everything else, so why can't they do it in politics?

And the ones that do the nominating, where do they dig them up? And do the men that are being nominated know of it in advance? I don't believe they do, or they would never allow 'em to go on. These nominators can't be friends of the man they nominated, or they would never go on and handicap them as they do. Talk about presidential timber! Why, man, they have whole lumber yards of it. There are so many nominated that some of the men making the nominating speeches have never even met the men they are nominating. I know they never had, from the way they talked about them.

But it's always great to meet all the old newspaper boys who will all be there, grinding out dope to the home papers, trying to make "copy," where none exists. They are the ones that keep it interesting. It's not the actors themselves. Political conventions would die standing up if it wasent for the inventive genius of the boys that make the actors look colorful. They will write back to your paper and make you, at home, think that it is the most exciting place you ever saw, while as a matter-of-fact, there won't be a thing in the world doing but some old, long-winded bird talking about "getting back to the early Lincoln diplomacy!" There won't be an original saying, or a new passage uttered during the entire fiesta. But the old newspaper boys will smoke it up and tell it to you over the radio, so that you will imagine that Henry Clay, Daniel Webster and Calhoun are there in droves. Personally, I think the camera has done more harm for politics than any other one faction. Everybody would rather get their picture, than their ideas, in the papers. What does the platform of a political party amount to, compared to the photography? There is ten cameras to every plank in the platform.

There is more film wasted on the two conventions than was used making the *King of Kings*. Speakers get up early in the morning, not to find out how their speech was received by the press, but how the pictures turned out.

It's just as I say, one of our follies that we built up, that no other country in the world would understand, or know for what reason it was being held. But we like it, and it's distinctly ours. It's the one place where our public men can do foolish things, and due to the surroundings, they kinder look plausible at the time. It's a great game, this convention game is. I don't suppose there is a show in the world with as much sameness in it as it has got. You know exactly what each speaker is going to say before he says it. You know what the women seconders will wear. You know before you go who will be nominated. You know the platform will always be the same, promising everything, delivering nothing. You cuss yourself for sitting day in and day out and looking at such nonsense. But the next four years find you back there again.

But it's a show that no American should miss. It's entertainment, and it's enlightening. Most men that emerge from it with any spoils were more lucky than competent. A good campaign manager can do more than an able candidate. "Trades" makes presidents more than ability. But as bad as we are, and as funny as we do things, we are better off than the other countries, so bring on more conventions — the bigger, the noisier, the crazier, the better! No nation likes "hooey" like we do. We are all cuckoo, but we are happy.

Well, finally, the nominations are over and now the campaign is going. The Democrats must attack. He is the "Out," as usual. He has to tell what he would have done. Then the "In" must come out and must tell "why he didn't do it." Then it's up to the voters to believe one man's promise, or another man's alibi. But this has been going on since George Washington started it.

But everything is changing. People are taking their comedians seriously and the politicians as a joke, when it used to be vice versa. So will you do me a favor? If you see or hear of anybody proposing my name, humorously or semi-seriously, for any political office, will you maim said party and send me the bill? I hereby and hereon want to go on record as being the first presidential, vice-presidential, senator, or justice-of-the-peace candidate to withdraw. I not only "don't choose to run," I will say "won't run." No matter how bad the country will need a comedian by that time!

I couldent run anyhow, I can't make up my mind which side to run on. I don't know which side of some of these issues the most votes is on, and I can't straddle them, for that's where all the rest of the candidates are now.

I hope that in doing this I have started something that will have far-reaching effect. Who will be the next to do the public a favor and withdraw?

13. The Roman Senate

Our President delivered his message to Congress. You know, that's one of the things his contract calls for. It's one of the few stipulated duties of the President, and that is, that every once in a while he deliver a message to Congress to tell them the "Condition of the Country."

This message, as I say, is to Congress. The rest of the country knows the condition of the country, for they live in it, and are part of it. But the senators and congressmen, being in Washington all the time have no idea what is going on in America. So the President has to tell 'em. The country must have been in pretty bad shape, for it took 12 thousand words to tell how bad it was. You see, when a thing is in fine shape, it don't need much explaining — you can then just write, "Country OK."

Now we will just see what he says about this land of "A dollar down, and a dollar a week." In the first paragraph he says, "In complying with the Constitution that I from time to time give to Congress information on the state of the Union. I wish to emphasize that during the last year this country has grown in strength, advanced in comfort, and gained in knowledge." Well, that don't look so bad for us. We have "gained in strength." In plainer words, we have got stouter, that proves that our reducing has been a failure. If a country can get stouter while they are on a diet, what could we gain if we wasent? This observation of the President will be of no knowledge to lots of middle-aged women of the country. They have realized their strength, ever since they had procured a bathroom scale. "Advanced in comfort." Now why have we advanced in comfort? Maybe it's because we have gained in strength, or have we got more comfortable in spite of our fat. At any rate, we are fat and comfortable. Now in both of these I think his observations are absolutely correct. I have never seen a President more right than he is there. We are "fat and comfortable."

Now I wish he had gone into it a little further there and kinder discussed the fact as to just how good it is for a country to be fat and comfortable. A pig being fattened for slaughter is fat and comfortable, but that's just about all he is. He ain't worth much to get out and do some rustling around for himself. So I wonder if the President dident just about sum up the condition of this country in those two observations. Wasent it Rome that was in that very shape one time? I never did read much about Roman history, outside of the life of Mussolini, by Zurfatti. But I have gathered from Hollywood photographic annoyances that Rome gained her exalted position at a time when they were anything but "fat and comfortable." They were, as a matter of fact, "skinny and ill at ease." In other words, little pangs of hunger drove them to deeds far beyond their natural capacities. They went out and cleaned up on the rest of the world, not for glory, but for calories. Just look at pictures of them in their great bales of tin armor. They wasent comfortable by any means. I know, because I wore one of

those things in a picture once. That's what made them fight — to get out of that thing. And Caesar wouldent unlock it and let 'em out till they had practically whipped the world.

Caesar was kinder the "head man" down there then. He knew that senators were a useless lot, and that especially the ones from the backward states should talk "darn small." Brutus was a senator from Sicily, kinder the Alabama of the Roman Empire. The other senators wanted to have Caesar investigated. You see, Caesar had really no official capacity. He maintained a suite of offices in Rome, and every time there was a convention, or an election, he would bob up. There was two political factions in Rome then, the Republicans and the Christians. Caesar was, of course a Republican, and contributed generously to their campaign funds, and would kindly furnish Christians for the Sunday afternoon affairs in the arenas. In that ingenious way they kept the Christians the minority party. But the Christians said, "If we can't rule, we will investigate."

But Brutus, being a learned man, far beyond the knowledge of other senators, was the first person to have no confidence in investigations. He knew they were good for recreational purposes, and for a pastime, till the next session was called, but not as a means of arriving at anything. So instead of investigating Caesar, he procured a bowie knife and stabbed the gentleman, practically ruining him. It was a rather crude way of arriving at the facts, but you must remember that Brutus was an honorable man. That called for a trial, to see if it was a penal offense to stab a senator. The jury was to decide whether Brutus was to get a medal, or be reprimanded. Nero was called in to judge, while he was rosining the bow. Mark Anthony was the first district attorney to have ambitions of becoming governor. When he started speaking, they couldent tell if he was for Caesar, or against him, for it was the first time that satire had ever been used publicly. When he kept saying, "Brutus was an honorable man," why, Brutus was taking it on the level, and Mark Anthony had to repeat it over twenty times to drive home his brand of humor. The Roman Senate at that time was a kinder modern House of Lords, and, after Anthony for the 19th time said, "Brutus was an honorable man," why, they got looking at each other and saying, "This guy is either kidding us, or Brutus." And they got to paying closer attention and they found it was both of them. Anthony made a wonderful speech, but it practically ruined all senates to follow. For they figured that all legislation must be based on oratory, make up in gestures what they lack in ideas. So all these intervening years, senators have tried to emulate Anthony, and the only thing they have ever approached him in is endurance. Anthony had one quality that the boys following have never been able to grasp. Anthony dident take himself seriously, that's how he got Brutus off with a tune by Nero and a small bail.

But all this is just to show you that Rome's turning point was just at that time. She had reached her heights through the American magazine plan of hard work, perseverance and taking advantage of her opportunities. Now she was fat and comfortable. She started putting in baths. Up to then, when a nation got any dirt on 'em, they wore it off. But the Romans commenced to getting "high hat." They had up to then walked everywhere, or rode horseback. But an ingenious fellow named Chariot, first name Henry, got to getting out a contraption to ride in, a thing where you dident have to walk. You looked like you was walking, but you wasent — you was in fact riding. Well that just upset the whole life habits and customs of a nation. "Ride in a conveyance and take a bath!" Rome was sitting pretty. Then somebody decided with these conveyances, they must have some roads. Up to then they had had nothing but trails, for they dident need anything else to walk on. Then they appointed a Highway Commission, and that's where the first graft enters history. The Highway Commission wanted to build from Rome to Naples, as Naples was where a great many of the boys spent their weekends. They called it the Appian Way, for the same reason we call one the Lincoln Highway. Lincoln was never on it, and neither was Appian. Then there was a fellow on the Highway Commission who lived a-way over in Venice, so he built a road by his place, thereby starting a custom which has been faithfully handed down. A smart state nowadays will appoint all their highway commissioners from one place, then one road will do all of them.

Anyway, the lads commenced burning up the boulevards, more people crushed under wheels than met their death in fair competition with the lions. But what mattered the deaths, wasent progress on the rampage? "We are bathing and moving. What else do you want?"

With the riding came the flesh. Where they used to walk and keep theirselves in shape to meet and defeat any enemy on a moment's notice, now they were taking on beef. But they were happy; they were riding and bathing. To solve the industrial situation, why they decided to sell on credit, making the chariot within reach of all. Up to then, Romans had never been in debt. But now they were really becoming to amount to something. They could afford to look down on the Greeks, and the Medes and the Persians and the Pharisees. For those backward people dident not only not have a bath, or a chariot, but they dident even know enough to owe something. They were a backward lot! So the Romans just kept riding, bathing, for now they were selling tubs on credit. Well, that was great. They framed themselves up a stock market, where they could sell something they dident have. They started selling shares in Vesuvius Limited.

Well, these other nations got to watching 'em, and as their waistbands expanded, their endurance lessened. Instead of standing on guard to see if any enemy approached, they was weekending on the yacht in the Bay of Napoli.

14. Political Corruption

Well, all I know is just what I read in the papers, and what I get an eyeful of as I wander from tabernacle to tent, preaching a sermon on "Tolerance toward Politicians." It's rather a thankless job and sometimes gets mighty discouraging. When you start out to educate people "up to some cause," you are just about sunk before you start. I try to tell 'em that those men are doing the best they can, according to the dictates of no conscience. But it's hard to change the old established idea of what the politician is. People think I am a paid propagandist, sent out by the politicians just to foster goodwill toward them. But it's not that at all. It's just that I don't think the politicians are getting what's coming to them. They are lucky.

But with an election coming on, I want to draw your mind off of golf as much as I can and onto a few of the big issues of the day. But it's awful hard to get people interested in corruption, unless they can get some of it. You take a fellow that hasent received any corruption, and it's kinder like the fellow that has never drunk sauerkraut juice. He ain't much interested in whether it's good or bad. People just figure, "Well, there couldent be so much corruption, or some of it would have come my way." And the fellow that has received any of it, naturally he is in favor of a continuation of the policy.

Corruption is supposed to be a Republican measure, and they are supposed to have perfected it up to the high standard that it occupies today. It's really not new. It has been in existence for years, but mostly in a small way, and practiced by the minor politicians.

In fact, the Democrats were supposed to have started it in what was called Tammany Hall. But a good thing can't be restricted and is bound to spread. So the Republicans had their eyes open for all the new wrinkles that would help them stay on the U.S. pension list. So, like everything else, they took it and improved on it and brought corruption up to the high standard that it is today.

The Democrats always were a kind of a cheap lot. They never had much money to operate on. They were always kinder doing business on a shoestring basis. The type of man they had with them went in more for oratory than he did for stocks and bonds. They would rather make a speech, than a dollar. They cultivated their voice instead of their finances. You give a Democrat a high hat and a frock and put him on the speaker's list, and he would turn down the chairmanship of the board of a big corporation. Give him a horse in the parade every year and that was just about all the glory he wanted.

The Democratic graft was mostly confined to sorter rounding the saloon keepers into line with a campaign collection every year. They thought that was just about the height of "big business." They knew that as long as a saloon keeper was on a good corner, and no opposition allowed near him, that he was good for quite a touch in the latter part of October. Lord only knows why the Democrats thought that the saloon keeper was the only man that would pay for a good location. They never give any other business a tumble. I guess it was because they dident know there was any other business.

They dident know that a man that was owner of some mines, or lumber or coal, might also dig up something for the pot — if promised a little break in the tariff, or railroad rates, or suppressed opposition. But their mind was on a saloon, and that's as high as they could elevate it. So the Republicans just was wise enough to see that the same principle applied to one business, as to the other. If it was good for the saloons to stand in with the government, why, it was good for all other business.

The men who were thinking of running for office got to looking 'round the various states and seeing what some other men wanted, and they went to them and said, "If you will sorter help me out at the polls, I think I can help you out getting these big things." While the Democrat was still fooling his time away with the "jitney" fellow, the Republican said, "There is only one way to be in politics, and that's to be in a big way! What's the use of being a piker?" So, instead of getting a hundred dollars from some poor little guy, they grabbed off a couple of thousand from the big fellow that was looking for something worthwhile. And they just kept working and building their business right up, till, look what it is today.

They had vision; they had foresight. They really deserve to prosper. There is two types of larceny, petty and grand, and the courts will really give you a longer sentence for "petty," than they do for "grand." They are supposed to be the same in the eyes of the law, but the judges always put a little extra on you for "petty," which is a kind of a fine for stupidness. "If that's all you got, you ought to go to jail longer!"

But the parties will never be changed as long as we live, for you can't change human nature. You can't broaden a man's vision if he wasent born with one. And another thing. It's hard to get people to believe a thing as corruption, when it's something that has always been going on. These deals gradually come under the heading of legitimate campaign business. You promise something in return for something, whether it is a post office, or an oil well. It's what the lawyers call "sharp practice." So it's going to be awful hard to make an issue of corruption. It's like the poor. It's always been with us.

If you promise a man that if you are made senator, that he will be made a judge, why, you have sold him something. His votes have helped you to get your salary. You might promise him a river to have a dam built on, but you have always promised something, either directly or indirectly, and you can't get voters to distinguish the difference — if there is any. The Republicans have always been the party of big business, and the Democrats of small business, so you just take your pick. The Democrats had their eye on a dime, and the Republicans on a dollar.

15.The Congress

You know, every year it gets harder and harder to tell the difference between a Republican and a Democrat — course, outside of looks. Their platforms and policies become more and more alike. But I believe I have found out the sure way to tell one from another this year. It's just the way they talk. The Republicans say, "Well, things could have been worse!" And the Democrats say, "How?" But I don't want to lay the blame on the Republicans for all the things that have happened to us lately. They're not smart enough to have thought 'em up.

Anyhow, now there are the early-bird variety of candidates for president. You see we have all these senators in there, all of whom think they are only there till the next election, when they will move to the other end of Pennsylvania Avenue. There will be dozens and dozens come in, mostly through starvation, and partly through thinking that the Democrats can win with practically nothing. And there will be some enter the race that will qualify for nothing. And all the speeches you hear are just preludes to the next presidential election. Of course, this early in the game you don't have to offer any constructive remedy. Just to shout what is wrong is enough, and it's all in the game. In fact, the Democrats can call a man more things than the Republicans. Cause there has been so much more that they had practice at. Denouncing is not only an art with the Democrats, but it's a profession. But for what little practice the Republicans have had, why, they are not doing bad at all. They, for amateur denouncers, are doing fine and may soon be as good as the Democratic denouncers.

I went down to Washington a couple of times to see what our hired help was doing. They was just appropriating right and left. The U.S. Treasury to them is just a rainbow, there is no end to it. You see, appropriations for the boys back home is what gets you the votes. Putting on taxes to get the money to appropriate is a sure way to lose votes. So everybody is handing it out, and nobody has the nerve to replenish what they are taking out. Those birds, naturally, have an eye for their own employment. Every little, old one-cylinder senator and punctured-tired congressman from all over the country is trying to put over his little local scheme. You know, that's the sad part about politics. These are the men that will get elected every time, the ones that are able to hornswoggle the government out of something for some kind of a scheme, just for his own district's special benefit. Any man that looked after the interests of the majority in politics, why, he wouldent even be nominated the second time. He has got to come in with some loot from somewhere. And the more he drags in, the more solid he is at the next election. I tell you, if it was in private life, and he put over some of the polite banditry that he does in official life, he would be caught and sent to jail, instead of back to Congress. And then they wonder why our real big men never go into politics.

You see that's why I have to go to Washington every so often, to see what the senators are doing. I can't just leave 'em, they wouldent do a thing, or if they did, it would be the wrong thing. I got to go there and kinder prod 'em up every once in a while. You know, the same as our President has to bring 'em in and pat 'em on the back every so often. You see, that's the way he works 'em. He never scolds 'em, he knows that they are just children at heart. So when he wants something done, he just coaxes 'em, brags on 'em, and first thing you know, they have voted *yes*. Well, I can't do that. In fact, there's few that can. I am not that even tempered. Our President is almost a freak in that respect. He seems to know just where their back itches, and there is where he scratches. But I can't do that. I have to cuss 'em a little sometimes. I like 'em maybe at heart as much as the President, maybe more, but they do vex the very devil out of me, and all of us, at times.

Now these fellows in Washington wouldent be so serious and particular if they only had to vote on what they thought good for the majority of the people of the U.S. That would be a cinch. But what makes it hard for them is, every time a bill comes up they have things to decide that have nothing to do with the merit of the bill. The principal thing is, of course, "What will this do for me personally back home?" Politics and self-preservation must come first, never mind the majority of the people. A politician's thoughts are naturally on his next term more than on his country.

Now I see where they introduced a bill to raise senators' and congressmen's salaries. Most of the congressmen run away and wouldent vote on their salary raise. Imagine, they run on a "fearless ticket, not afraid to come out in the open on anything," and then they run from this. It sure looks like, with Congress charging more, the people are getting harder to displease than they used to be. But the bad part about the whole structure of paying our congressmen is that we name a sum and give 'em all the same, regardless of ability. No other business in the world has a fixed sum to pay all their employees the same salary. If some efficiency expert would work out a scheme where each congressman would be paid according to his ability, I think we would save a lot of money.

Now I read where they are having what is called a filibuster in the Senate. Boy, we pay for wisdom and we get wind. You know what a filibuster is, it means that a man can get up and talk for hours at a time, just to keep some bill from coming to a vote. The whole foundation of our government is based on the majority rule, so they have done their duty when they merely vote against it, or for it, whichever they like. Why, if a distinguished foreigner was to be taken into the Senate and not told what the institution was, and he heard a man rambling on, talking for hours, he would probably say, "You have lovely quarters here for your insane, but have you no warden to look after their health — to see that they don't talk themselves to death?" Imagine a ball player standing at bat and not letting the other side play. Or an actor talking all night, to keep the rest from going on. You know how long he would last. Anyway, one senator even threatened to read the Bible into the record as part of his speech — and I guess he would have done it, too, if somebody in the Capitol had had a Bible.

Now I see where they are finally going to limit debate in the Senate. It used to be that a man could talk all day, but now, as soon as he tells all he knows, he has to sit down. I guess most of these birds will just be getting up and nodding now; why, some of them won't even be able to answer roll call.

Say, did you know that Congress has over 1,000 bills introduced in there? They got 'em in there for everything from birth control to mass production. One fellow from Indiana contributed a bill to do away with "slugs" in beating vending machines. Another fellow from New York introduced a bill to stop war. Now that's an original idea. Another representative wants a bill to stabilize money. Bills to build over 300 bridges are in there. Nothing beats a bunch of bridges as a national graft. And then they ask me, "Will, where do you get your jokes from?" I just tell 'em, "Well, I watch the government and report the facts. That is all I do, and I don't find it necessary to exaggerate."

I must tell you, I am to go into Ziegfeld's new Follies, and I have no act. So I run down to Washington and get some material. Most people and actors appearing on the stage have some writer to write their material. I don't do that; Congress is good enough for me. They have been writing my material for years, and I am not ashamed of the material I have had. I am going to stick to them. Why should I go and pay some famous author, or even myself, to sit down all day trying to dope out something funny to say on the stage! No sir, I have found that there is nothing as funny as things that have happened. So I just have them mail me every day the *Congressional Record*. It is to me what the *Police Gazette* used to be to the fellow who was waiting for a haircut.

I tell you, this country runs in spite of parties. In fact, parties are the biggest handicap we have to contend with. If we dident have to stop to play politics, any administration could almost make a Garden of Eden out of us. You could transfer the Congress over to run Standard Oil, or General Motors, and they'd have both things bankrupt in two years. No other business in the world could afford to carry such deadwood. But I know these guys personally, and they know in their own hearts that it's all a lot of baloney. So, if they are smart enough to make us feed 'em, why, then we are the yaps, not them.

It must be something in the office that makes 'em so ornery. Outside the Congress hall, when I meet all my old friends, representatives from Oklahoma, Los Angeles, Texas, Kansas, Arizona, and from all over, I want to tell you, they are as fine a bunch of men as anyone ever met in his life. They are all full of humor, and regular fellows. That is, as I say, when you catch 'em when they havent got politics on their minds. But

the minute they get in that immense hall, they begin to get serious, and it's then that they do such amusing things. If we could just send the same bunch of men to Washington for the good of the nation, and not for political reasons, we could have the most perfect government in the world.

But we sure are a good-natured bunch of saps in this country. When the President is wrong, we charge it to inexperience. When Congress is wrong, we charge it to habit. When the Senate is right, we declare a national holiday. When the stock market drops fifty points, we are supposed not to know that it's through manipulation. When a bank fails, we let the guy go start another one. When a judge convicts a murderer, that's cruelty. Boy, we sure are going on the assumption that nothing in public life — or out of it, for that matter — is any good. Now what we have set out to do is to find the worst. Now it's no trouble to pick out the bad, but I tell you, when you sit down to pick out the worst, boy, you sure have set some task for yourself. You see, it takes years in this country to tell whether anybody is right or wrong. It's kinder of a case of just how far ahead you can see. The fellow that can only see a week ahead, he is always the popular fellow, for he's looking with the crowd. But the one that can see years ahead, he has a telescope, but he can't make anybody believe he has it. There is no country in the world where a person changes from a hero to a goat, and a goat to a hero, or vice versa, as they do with us. We are the only fleas weighing over 100 pounds. We don't know what we want, but we are ready to bite somebody to get it. So quit listening to the politicians. The country is not in as bad a shape as the rumors have it. If we did pass out as a great nation, our epitaph should read, "America died from fright!"

You know, I generally give the party in power, whether Republican or Democrat, the more digs, because they are generally doing the country the most damage. And besides, the party in power is drawing a salary to be knocked. Now Congress adjourned for only a week, so they been back at it again for about ten days. Back at what? Why, back at what they was back at before! What was they back at before? I don't know, but they still is back at it, whatever it was. So you see, Congress went to work. What are you laughing at? Honest, they went to work. Anyway, they come in and sat down!

We have never had a Congress where the politicians were so eager to get going. But if you think politics are based on patriotism and not on business, you just watch the press. Five hundred men in Congress, and about another hundred in the Senate, will argue on what to do with the taxpayer's money. This will be a mighty noisy session of Congress, for every man will have a scheme to relieve the unemployed, and it's going to take months just to read all the bills that will be introduced. Of course they have to go to committees first, but it will take the entire Congress and Senate members to make enough committees, just to read all of 'em.

Say, this sure is a funny thing about being a U.S.

Senator. The only thing the law says you have to be is 30 years old. Not another single requirement necessary. They just figure that any man that old got nobody to blame but himself if he gets caught in there. You know, I kid about these fellows, but I believe it's not really intention on the government's part that they don't do better, it's ignorance.

Now take the budget. Early in the year the President sends what they call the "budget" to Congress. It takes the head of every department in Washington six months to think up that many figures. You see, you have a budget like you have a limit in a poker game. You are not supposed to go beyond it till at least an hour after the game has been started. So we won't run over the budget limit till about next month. When we do, it makes work for another department in Washington. You see, here is what Congress does. It votes mythical beans into a bag, then tries to reach in and pull real beans out. Anyhow, here in front of me is a whole financial statement of how we stand. Now a lot of us don't pay much attention to our government finances, because it's all so complicated. Oh, we read 'em, and we look like we are doing fine, and then there is another bunch of figures way over on the other side that deny what the ones on this side say. There is a thing in there that you had no idea existed. Take, for example, the "Commission of Fine Arts" — I guess it don't include politics — they grabbed us for only $9 million. Then there's the Department of Agriculture, they got us for $154 million, and that's just for giving the farmer advice. Or take the Department of Labor, that only runs over $11 million. You see, if they only had to keep track of the ones that work, they could do it on a few hundred bucks. It's keeping track of the idle ones that runs into dough. You see, an idle fellow is much harder to watch than one that's working. Then I see where the Department of Justice costs us $28 million. Well, that ain't bad for justice. In fact, justice is one of the cheapest things we got on our list. Maybe that's why we don't get anymore of it. I'm in favor of paying more and naming some people that ought to have what's coming to 'em. But Lord, the money we do spend on government, and it's not a bit better than the government we got for one third the money twenty years ago.

Now, only today I received a wire from a congressman friend of mine, who wants a copy of something I said to read into the *Congressional Record*. Now I feel pretty good about that. That's the highest praise that a humorist can have, to get your stuff into the *Congressional Record*. Just think, my name will be right there, alongside all those other big humorists. I'm not bragging, but I feel pretty big about it. Say, did I ever tell you — I don't know whether I ever did — did I ever tell you about the first time I ever had any of my stuff in that daily? Well, I had written some fool thing that pertained to the bill that they were kidding about in there in the Senate, and some senator read my little article. Now, everything that a senator reads goes into the *Record*. So another senator rose and said, as they always do, if you have ever seen them, "Does the gentleman yield?" They always say that. They call each other gentlemen in there. But the tone that they put on the words, it would be more appropriate and it would sound better, if he come right out and said, "Does the coyote from Maine yield?"

Then the man says, "I yield." For if he don't, the other guy will keep on talking anyhow. So the coyote from Maine says, "I yield to the polecat from Oregon!" He don't say polecat, but I mean he says "gentleman" in such a way that is almost like polecat.

Well, anyhow, that's the way they do it. They are very polite in there, but I must get back to my story. When this senator read my offering, the other senator said, after all the yielding was over, "I object to the remarks of a professional jokemaker being put into the *Congressional Record*." You know, meaning me. He was taking a dig at me. They dident want any outside fellow contributing.

Well, he had me wrong. Compared to them, I'm an amateur. And the thing about my jokes is they don't hurt anybody. You can take them or leave them. You know what I mean. You can say they are not funny, or they are terrible, or they are good, but they don't do any harm. But with Congress, every time they make a joke, it's a law! And every time they make a law, it's a joke.

16. Investigations, Hearings and Cover-ups

Say, did you read what this writer just dug up in George Washington's diary? I was so ashamed, I sat up all night reading it. This should be a lesson to presidents to either behave themselves, or not to keep a diary. Can you imagine, 100 years hence, some future writer pouncing on Calvin Coolidge's diary? What would that generation think of us? Calvin, burn them papers!

I bet you, many a public man wishes there was a law to burn old records. Because there is still many an investigation going on in Washington. I never saw such an eager Congress. You see, there is something about a Democrat that makes 'em awful inquisitive, especially if it's on a Republican, and there is an awful lot to find out about most Republicans.

Now the Democrats are investigating slush funds. If they can find out where it comes from, they want theirs. Imagine a Congress that squanders billions, trying to find out where some candidate spent a few thousand! But these boys in Washington have had a lot of fun investigating. You see, a senator is never as happy as when he is asking somebody a question, without that party being able to ask him one back. But the only trouble about suggesting that somebody, or something, ought to be investigated is that they are liable to suggest that *you* ought to be investigated. And from the record of all previous investigations, it just looks like nobody can emerge with their noses entirely clean. I don't care who you are, you just can't reach middle life without having done and said a whole lot of foolish things. So I tell you, if I saw an investigating committee headed my way, I would just plead guilty and throw myself on the mercy of the court.

Once I was called to Washington before an investigation committee, to explain about a dime I gave to Rockefeller. Did you know that in Washington, even the porters are afraid now to take tips? Why, there are politicians acting honest now that never acted that way before. But I tell you, you can't believe a thing you read in regard to official statements. The minute anything happens connected with official life, why, it's just like a cold night back home — everybody is trying to cover up.

The queerest investigation that has sprung up in Washington — and it has to go some to be queerer than some of the others — is one that happened lately. One of the senators, a questioneer at one of the various investigations, was himself indicted in his home state, and he turned right around and caused an investigation to be made, and a committee formed, to investigate where they got the grounds to indict him. Now the people who had him indicted will appoint a committee to investigate where he found out that he was indicted.

So, all we have been able to read lately is about somebody testifying before somebody else's committee. Now I have a scheme that I think would add to the efficiency of these investigations. That is, have certain days for certain things. Say, for instance, Mon-

days. Everybody that wants to confess, come and confess Mondays. Tuesdays is for accusations. If you want to accuse anybody, come Tuesdays and accuse from 9 A.M. to 6 P.M. Then that leaves Wednesdays, Thursdays and Fridays for denials. You see, it takes longer to deny than anything else. All you'd hear is, "It's absolutely false. I dident receive the money, and if those 18 witnesses have testified that I did, they must have been mistaken!" Or here is a favorite line, "I don't remember!"

I tell you folks, if American men are as dumb as some of them have appeared on the witness stand, civilization is tottering.

But say, do any of you know what does the Senate do with all the knowledge they demand from other people? They never seem to use it.

Anyhow, I'm back in Washington to see this Senate investigation. Some think that these things will not do much good. But any time one half learns how the other half lives, why, it does us all good. You see, there is a lot of things these old boys in Washington have done that maybe are within the law. But it's so near the edge, that you couldent slip a safety razor blade between their acts and prosecution. It's too bad that they can't do something with these men that they are finding all this stuff on. The American people would trade ten investigations for just one conviction. If they would only hang somebody, no matter if they were guilty or not, just for an example, why, we would forgive them for all their investigations. Still, these senators may be doing this just to get out of the Senate during the day.

You see, the reason investigations drag along so long is that these people who are testifying have all testified before many times. But the first time you testify, they don't expect you to tell anything. It's just to kinder get you used to testifying. It takes sometimes about five or six trials with you, before you really tell much that you know. In other words, they have to find out what you know before you will testify to it. No witness yet has ever told what he knew, until the committee had known first what he knew, and then made him tell it. They let a witness go for a while till they find out some more on him, and then bring him back and make him testify to this last thing that they have found out.

Anyhow, I've been reading all this testimony. But the very day that all this latest testimony came out, in the same papers, there was a picture showing a Negro with one of those truth machines fastened on him. You know, they are supposed to tell when you are lying. And that very day in Washington, there were guys testifying with nothing on their wrists but silk shirts. God bless America for a sense of humor. I tell you, if they had ever taken one of those truth machines to the investigations in Washington, there would have been more Americans sailing for Europe than went during the war.

Now I have an idea that I want to lay before you. Everybody is offering suggestions as to how to improve education. We are learning them all kinds of courses. We have courses in Business Administration, Salesmanship, Public Speaking, Etiquette, Banking, Dairying, Fertilizing, everything that a person can think of, we have a course in it that you can take at some college. Now what I want to propose is a course in "Public Testifying."

Most of our public men spend over half their time testifying on the stand, especially the Republicans. Now what has brought forth this idea of mine is the testimony that has been delivered on the stand. Did you ever in your life see men get as flustrated and tangled up as these fellows do on the stand? It looks like the smarter the man, the bigger sucker he is when he's being questioned. You know, the greatest testimony in any case, and about the only convincing testimony we have, is some child's testimony, or some old farmer or laborer. They are the ones that always make the hit on the stand. They can answer every question without flinching.

But the moment a witness has had any education, or thinks he knows something, why, the less convincing he is on the stand. I think, of all the bunch on the witness stand, that lawyers are the worst. You never read a lawyer's testimony on the stand in any case in your life and could tell heads or tails of it. They think they are so smart that they have to hide something, and they are generally more scared than any other class of witnesses there is. The reason the child, or old lady, or ignorant workman make such good witnesses is, they only have one story, and the prosecuting lawyer knows they only have one story, so there is no chance of tying them up in cross examinations. But the smart fellow has so many different angles that he is trying to use a little of all of them, and winds up making everybody believe that he dident tell half he knew and dident know half he told.

So I am going to start a school of "Public Testimony." Instead of being layed out like a school, it will be layed out like a court. Instead of teachers, we will have 'em made up as sheriffs, and bailiffs and jurymen and judges. The minute a man is elected to office, like senator or congressman, why, we will have him come and spend a few weeks in the school, and then, when he goes on to his public office, he will be all set for the first investigation. We will teach 'em not to be nervous, not to let the other fellow get 'em

rattled, and have 'em all trained to tell where they got every dollar they used in their campaign, and how much they paid for each vote.

You see, if they would keep all that straight, it's just like the income tax; it's merely a matter of records. If you can show the committee where you received so much — and spent so much — and they both come out even, you need have no fear on the stand. So that's what my school will teach. In other words, it will persuade our big men to turn honest after election and trust to the mercy of the jury. And we will coach 'em to tell everything the first time. That will save having to spend your life on the stand. Even if it takes a little longer the first time you testify, why, it will save time in the long run. If it takes a whole day to tell the thing, why, my school will instruct you to go through with it. In other words, we are going to try and instill honesty into our pupils, and get them to get used to telling nothing but what happened, and all that did happen.

Of course, when some of my early pupils first start testifying, they won't be believed. It will be such a radical change from the usual testimony that the committee will think that it is a clear fake. But as they grow used to my pupils, they will begin to realize that they can depend on them.

I think I will open the school at Claremore, Oklahoma. That's about the hub of everything. In fact, I will do a little local state work there just to practice getting politicians to testify correctly. Remember, after you have gone through a course, why, you will never have to fear any other investigation that you may be called on to face. Remember, it opens next year, "Will Rogers' School of Public Testimony," at Claremore, Oklahoma. After one term in my school, you will welcome testifying, instead of fearing it.

It's really patriotic reasons that make me want to do this, for I am afraid that foreign nations will read some of our papers and find the testimony of some of our men who are in the Cabinet and high in public office. And they will judge them by that testimony. They will think they are no smarter than their testimony. Well, that will leave a bad impression, and if I can change that and get them to make their testimony as smart as the men really are, why, I will have performed a public service.

Interviews

Joel McCrea

Bryan B. Sterling: *Didn't you first meet Will Rogers on the California-Nevada border?*

Joel McCrea: It was on the California side, at Lake Tahoe. He was Fox's biggest star, and he was doing a picture called *Lightnin'*. I was cast as his son-in-law, the juvenile lead. I met Will sitting in a buggy. The director, Henry King, asked me whether I had met Mr. Rogers and, when I said "no," he introduced me. That was 1930, and it was the beginning of a friendship which you kind of felt the moment I got there. Our first scene was on that buggy. Will was supposed to talk quite a bit, then I had a line, and then he talked on quite a bit longer. He improved it as he went along, and everybody got to laughing, but when the time came for me to talk, there was no cue. So the director said, "What's the matter, McCrea, isn't it your turn?" I said, it was, but that I had not received my cue. So Will just said to me, "Joe," he always would call me "Joe." "Joe, you ain't like these other actors, you're kinder like me. You ain't very good looking and you ain't a very good actor. You're just a cowboy and I'm going to help you. You see what I do. I change the dialogue. I write a great deal of it myself — sometimes I improve it, sometimes I don't, but I go along with it. And when I think I've said enough, I'll stop, and then I'll poke you and then you talk. I'm not going to do it for the other actors, but I'll do it for you." That was the beginning and we went through that day. That evening he asked me how I was going to get back to the hotel where we were staying at Tahoe. I told him I guessed I'd ride in the bus. And he said, "No, you ain't an extra anymore." He knew that I had just come out of the extra ranks. He said, "You ride in the studio car, but why don't you ride back with me?" He had a LaSalle, a coupe, which he drove himself. So I drove back with him. That was the first day of a friendship that lasted until he passed. One evening he invited me to go with him to Calneva, on the line between California and Nevada and have dinner. There were a number of very important people, including Winfield Sheehan, the head of Fox Studio. Now, none of these men knew me. I was just starting and not at all important in the picture business, but during dinner Will said to Winnie Sheehan, "Winnie, I'd like this boy in all my pictures that he'll fit in." Well, you can imagine what that did for me at Fox. Then, when we finished that location and came back, he said, "If you don't get a better offer . . . ," he always used that phrase. "If you don't get a better offer, meet me Wednesday for lunch." I would meet him at the studio for lunch, and he wanted me to come to his Santa Monica ranch because I knew a lot of the cowboys he had there. I'd be out there Saturdays and days off and rope with him, and then, Sundays, I'd often go and watch him play polo at the Riviera Club. It's obvious why this friendship meant so much to me. Of the people I knew with Will, so many are gone. I am one of the few left that did pictures with him and saw quite as much of him. I look back over those years — the years when I would rope with him and hear the different things he would say to me, and I got to thinking about the whole period; and I got to thinking of his effect on me — because he had tremendous effect on me, both as a motion picture actor and as regards buying ranches, which has been the most remunerative thing that I have done. But he had an influence on everything that he touched. And the key word is "glory." He glorified everything. When he came to the studio, instead of the dull, drab kind of a studio with a lot of actors and actresses, life came into it. He brought glory to it. The behavior on the set was improved, the attitude toward America, the attitude toward foreigners, the attitude toward colored people, the attitude toward Jews, he could do all that without ever preaching, by his example. He glorified the roper, he glorified the cowboy, he glorified really the politician by kidding him when he was hypocritical — and he didn't care whether it was a Republican or a Democrat. He glorified radio, by coming on it, the newspapers, by writing something that was so popular. Everybody bought the *Los Angeles Times*, just to read that. And there never was anything but a very clean, uplifting kind of humorous crack. And then he took over the airplane, when it was new and people were afraid of it, and he glorified that. So the word came to me that he glorified everything he touched — and in the overall sense, he glorified God. I never heard of him going to church much; I never heard him talk about religion, but just by his example, he glorified God. So this man affected near everything that I have ever done, including making me behave sometimes when I might not have, just because I would want him to think well of me. Yes, he brought glory to everything, but Will might add "but not to education."

BBS: *Have you ever wondered how he became the voice of the people? Of course, the fact that he did come from the country gave him the essence of the people.*

JMC: I would judge that coming from the kind of background he had, being born in that little place, being part Indian and immediately seeing the injustice we had done to the Indians, gave him greater insight into human nature. But, you know, something interests me and I believe it had something to do with his greatness. Now I hope this won't affect school children, but he never adjusted to school, to education as such. He didn't conform to anything. That's why he went from school to school. He didn't finish, and, I am sure, it was quite a disappointment at times to his family. But it showed his individual approach to life; he took no one's, he copied no one. He became an original. You see, when he started — I remember him telling me — he went away to South America, then joined the circus — well, he didn't do it so much to escape reality. He did it to express himself. Of course, he was born with something important to say — a gift that comes along quite seldom. But this was a completely creative and original man. His motivation was that he loved people, and he used the medium of humor to carry the message.

BBS: *Did he ever speak to you about his mother, who died when he was ten years old?*

JMC: He spoke of his mother with great devotion and love, but he never talked too much about her. I knew, of course, his wife, Betty. She was wonderful, sweet, patient, and it was like he was another boy in the family, like he was the oldest. I remember going to a polo game at the Riviera Country Club once and sitting in a box with Mrs. Rogers and the three children, Bill, Mary and Jimmy, and Mrs. Rogers commenting, "You know, everything that Will wanted to do, he was pretty near able to do. If he wanted to make a speech somewhere, or if he wanted to make a picture, if he wanted to play polo, if he wanted to go roping, he seemed to be able to do those things without any effort at all." Well, this time he was playing polo, and she said, "Watch him now. Do you see he is whipping that horse? There is nothing wrong with that horse, but he wants to buy another one." When Will came back to the box, sure enough, he said, "You know, Betty, that horse ain't fast enough. I'm ashamed out there. I'm trying to keep up with them fellows, and they just run away from me." It was just exactly as she had said. He had found a horse he wanted to buy. And Betty, very much like a mother, was sympathetic. She helped him in everything. She facilitated his doing the different things he wanted to do. There was never any talk on her part about "Take me along." It was always his idea that, whenever he could, he would take her along.

BBS: *Do you think that Bill, Mary or Jim realized the importance of their father?*

JMC: Well, it was from 1930 to 1935 that I knew him, and I saw a great deal of him. I saw him every week probably. Sometimes, when he was working, or I was working, I would only see him Saturday or Sunday, but I saw him regularly. But Will was so busy, either roping, or practicing, or working in a picture, or doing benefits. He did so many benefits. Eddie Cantor used to get him to do benefits all the time. Will would say, "I always do benefits for Eddie, 'cause he's a good man. He's doing good things for people." Now with all these activities — and he loved his family almost better than any man I ever knew — but he just didn't have that much time. And the children, at that time, were still young. It must have been difficult for them. I remember Mary. I took her out when she was sixteen; it was to one of her first parties. And during the evening, she said, "You know, sometimes we resent you a little bit." And I said, "Oh, is that right?" And she said, "Yes, you take so much of our father's time." You know, I hadn't realized it. You see, the people, America, everybody, this was their man and they loved him and wanted to hear him, they wanted to see him — everybody wanted his time.

BBS: *Was working with Will Rogers much different than working with any other star?*

JMC: Every actor that ever worked with him — not just I — the late Rex Bell, who became Lieutenant Governor of Nevada and was married to Clara Bow, he was one Will helped start; Irene Rich, one of his favorite leading ladies; Louise Dresser; Rochelle Hudson; "Big Boy" Williams; everyone who ever worked with him, or had contact with him, would brag about it. Even though they were the biggest directors or cameramen, and they had worked with the Barrymores, or Valentino, it's always Will Rogers that they would brag about.

BBS: *Did you call him Will, or Bill?*

JMC: If you really knew him well, if you were close to him, you called him Bill, instead of Will. But you know, I called him Mr. Rogers for quite a while until he told me not to, and then I used to call him Bill. But when I speak of him, I always refer to him as "Will," because most people know him better as that. I'm not trying to impress anyone with how well I knew him — I know in my heart.

BBS: *Let me ask you some little personal things. Before a take, or a retake, was Mr. Rogers at any time nervous, or was he really as relaxed as he always appears in those old movies?*

JMC: He always knocked on wood, just before a take. We'd be standing outside a door, and he would have to enter and do something, and he'd knock on wood. It got so that I did it too. I don't know why I was doing it. He was never nervous to the extent that he was shaken, but he was keyed up. Every nerve of his body aimed toward whatever he was doing. He was absolutely intent.

BBS: *Strange, but this inner tension does not come across on the screen.*

JMC: As far as pictures were concerned, he was not really nervous, not basically. He would just knock on wood and go ahead and do the thing, and he helped you, because it seemed that you were just carrying on what you had been doing off the set. He was one of the easiest men to work with, one of the best. And he was so original and creative himself. Even the top directors of his films, and he had the top directors, didn't tell him too much — he already had it. I remember one director, Dave Butler. He had been an actor; he had been in *Seventh Heaven*. He had been a good actor in the days when they overacted a bit, so he would say, "Will, when you come in, you do this, and you do that, and you go over and you see the man, and you say "Ah!" And Will nudged me and said, "Joe, watch Dave, he's acting." And I'd ask him, "Are you going to do it that way?" And Will said, "I can't. I can't remember what he done." And he went ahead and did it his own way and nobody could improve on that. He was just a natural.

BBS: *You mentioned that he affected everyone he came in contact with. Just how did he influence your life?*

JMC: He told me, "What are you going to do, Joe, if you make a success and make a lot of money? How much do you make now?" And I said, "A hundred a week, and I'm going to buy a ranch. I want to buy a

Rogers and McCrea in Lightnin'. *A friendship begins.*

cattle ranch. That is what I wanted to do, but I went into pictures to make enough money to do it." "Well," he said. "You say you will, but you won't do it. You will get in a convertible and drive down Hollywood Boulevard and wink at the girls." So, you see, he challenged me. And I became even more determined to prove myself to him.

BBS: *Did you ever see him just relax?*

JMC: This was a man that would never have time to drink, or smoke, or anything because that would take time. It would take time to go and buy cigarettes, or to clean the pipe. He had no time for that. He was always going. He must have had a premonition that he would be here only so long, and he wanted to get it all done. He was always going fast; his mind was clear and fast; he talked fast; he rode a horse fast; he was on fire the whole time.

BBS: *It's no wonder that he was so interested in flying.*

JMC: He was interested in flying and in flyers. He was very interested in Amelia Earhart and Charles

Lindbergh and Billy Mitchell. I remember talking to him one time about flying, and I wasn't enthusiastic. I was "chicken," and I said, "The horse is high enough for me, and I might fall off him!" I asked him, "Would you get up in one of those planes, like Lindbergh flew across the ocean?" And he said, "Sure, I would do that. People tell me I ought to be careful with my life, but every man's life is just as important as any other's." You see, he didn't take on that importance that he must save himself, even for others. He felt that life must be lived, not just as an existence.

BBS: *Obviously he did not consider himself important, nor did he take himself too seriously.*

JMC: I remember one time I was a guest at the Hearst ranch at San Simeon. There were about 90 people at a sit-down dinner, and most of them were big shots from the big studios. Louis B. Mayer, Irving Thalberg, big directors, and many of the MGM directors, because Cosmopolitan was then releasing through MGM, when the butler came and told Mr. Hearst that Will Rogers was down at the stables. Now the stables

were down from the castle. It was about three or four miles before you got to them. Will had been driving through, going somewhere, and he had stopped to say hello to the cowboys, and they had asked him to come and eat with them. So when Mr. Hearst sent his invitation down to Will, he sent word back to thank Mr. Hearst very much and to tell him, "I've got a little manure on my feet and I don't want to come up there right now." And he stayed with the cowboys. Later I asked him about it, and he said, "Oh, you were up there with them rich folks, weren't you? But I've been up there. I've seen that castle once. There's a lot of statues up there, naked."

BBS: *You knew ''Big Boy'' Williams, didn't you?*

JMC: I knew Big Boy, he was a close friend of Will's. Big Boy was a football player and a cowboy from Texas. He came out here and Will gave him that name. His name was really Guinn Williams, but Big Boy fit him perfectly, and it became his name on the screen. I remember one time we were standing out by a corral at the Santa Monica ranch, and Will and Big clowned around together. It was some kidding argument — oh, about strength, or something. Now Will was about twenty years older than Big, and he wasn't supposed to be a Charles Atlas, or anything. But Big Boy was terrific. He played a heavy in a couple of pictures with me, and I had to wrestle him and I said, "Don't forget to read the script — I'm supposed to win!" Because if he fell on you, it would hurt you. He weighed about 235 pounds. But on that occasion, Will just picked him up and threw him over the corral fence. I never saw such strength. You see he had this tremendous mental strength behind it. Whatever he set out to do, he could do. The last time I saw Big Boy, I was coming from my ranch in Nevada and I stopped at Bishop. The fellow that stood in for me for 25 years, and his wife, who was my secretary, they were retired, and they run a little pioneer hardware store in Bishop. They also arrange for location for films and television. So whenever I'm in the area, I stop in to say hello. Well this time, it was just a few years ago, they said I'd better go to the motel and see Big Boy because he was there and wanted to see me. I hadn't seen Big Boy for two years, so I went over to the motel, and he was sitting there with his wife, and he said, "Joel, I want to talk to you. The last three nights I have been dreaming about Bill Rogers, and he is riding Soapsuds, and he says 'Come on Big, get on your horse and go with me! Let's go!' I don't feel good, Joel. It's like he was calling me." Do you know, it wasn't a week before Big Boy died.

BBS: *That is quite a story. But I have come across several other premonitions connected with Will Rogers. Tell me this, did you ever see Mr. Rogers angry?*

JMC: I saw him mad once. We were on location, and we didn't have any fancy facilities. We had outhouses. Well, I went in there and Will came in, and he never said a word, and I never said a word. I started out first and waited outside for him, when just as he came out, there was a fellow coming in the door and he said, "Oh, Will Rogers! I want your autograph!" He reached for a piece of toilet paper to get that autograph, and you should have seen that look that came into Will's eye. He said, "No! I'll give you one later!" Then he turned and walked away. Will used to say to me, "Joe, the time to worry about this autograph business is when they quit asking you for 'em." But this time I saw a flash of anger — it scared me. He was no humorist then, and this fellow, this tourist, knew he had done the wrong thing, and he never came back. It was the one time I saw Will mad, and he stayed angry for about ten minutes, then he came over to me and mumbled, "Autographs, autographs! What a place to come to get one!" I never saw him angry any other time. Not ever on the polo field, where he got knocked off his horse when somebody cut right into him. His horse fell on him — it could have been disastrous. Will lay there for at least a minute, then he got up and said to those trying to help, "Now don't make an epic out of it! Where is my horse?" He wouldn't accept any sympathy, or be carried, or anything. Oh boy, he was tough.

BBS: *Which of Will Rogers' other friends do you remember meeting?*

JMC: I remember one time Will asking me, "Joe, do you know Tom Mix?" I said, "No, I used to deliver papers to him, when I was a newsboy." So Will said, "We'll go and see Old Tom." So Will took Irvin S. Cobb and me out to three empty lots in Santa Monica, where Tom Mix appeared in a three-ring circus. The three of us sat in a box and watched Mix come riding in like Buffalo Bill. I was watching the circus and everything, and as soon as Tom's act was over, and the other acts were coming on, Mix came up to the box. He stood straight as an Indian, and boy, those fancy clothes, and very serious faced; there was no humor in Tom Mix, but colorful, anyway. There were only three seats in that box, so I got up to give my seat to Mix, but Will said, "No, sit down," and Mix sat on the step down to the next box, and he looked at Will Rogers as though he were God, and he asked him, "How do you think it is going? Do you think it's all right?" And Will wanted to know, "How is the box office — how much money are they taking in?" "Well," Mix said, "it was fine last night, and the night before." So Will said, "Well, there is your answer." Tom Mix never glanced at Cobb or me. His eyes were only on Will. Here was this man that was supposed to be quite egotistical, Tom Mix, you know; but boy, he wasn't egotistical with Will Rogers. He just worshipped him, you could just tell.

BBS: *Here is a question I ask everybody. Did you ever see Will Rogers take a drink?*

JMC: The first drink I ever had in my life, was the first day I rode home with him in his LaSalle from location. The lights were on, it was about 5:30. You know, you quit location when the lights are going. We passed a little bar with a sign in the window. "Beer." I didn't say anything as we were going by, but Will said, "Do you want anything? Do you want a drink? There's a bar." So I told him that I didn't drink, or smoke, and I thought he'd like that. But Will asked me, "You don't? Why not?" And I said, "Well, my mother told me when I was young, that her father had quite a problem with drinking, and she was always afraid that it would make quite a family problem. When I was raised there was never any alcohol in the house, we never had it. And my mother didn't want me to drink. Anyway, I was an athlete, and I ride waves, and I just don't drink." "Well," Will said, "that's fine, but do you think that shows a strong character?" And I said, "I suppose so." And Will said, "Well, it don't. You never tasted alcohol, you don't know. If you tasted it, if you drink it, and then say you don't want to drink, that would show character. But you're just going on your mother's say-so. You haven't built any character yourself, because you're just doing what you're told to do. But if you try it and then say you don't care for it, then there's no argument, you're not a drinker. Then you got character!" I said, "OK." We went into this little bar. No one would hardly believe this, because of all people, you'd never think of Will Rogers connected with drinking. Well, we went in the bar. I didn't even know what to ask for. I had tasted beer once, my brother had it, or somebody. It was terrible; I didn't like it. Well, Will sat up at the bar, and I sit next to him. The bartender comes and wipes the counter and doesn't even look who it is, and just says, "What'll it be?" And Will said, "Sherry Flip." And I said, "The same!" I didn't know what it was, or what else to order. I didn't know what a "Flip" was; I figured it had to have some sherry, but I don't know what it was, and I've never had one since. Well, I had that Sherry Flip, and it tasted good. You know, sherry, I've had that a lot since, and it tastes good. Then Will said, "Do you want another?" And I said, "No, thank you." Will said, "I'll have another one," and he did. Then we both got up and went out, and never, from that day on did he ever mention drinking again, or did I ever see him take a drink — not even a sherry, not a beer, nothing. Anyway, I had my one first drink with him, and it was a Sherry Flip. But it just shows you! Here first of all I thought it would impress him that I didn't drink, but it didn't. Second of all, I had the drink with him and thought, well, after this, occasionally he will want me to have a drink with him, like anybody would, but no! He never mentioned it again. We'd be out together, and the waiter would come over and ask whether we would want a cocktail, and he would say, "No, thanks." And I would say, "No, thanks." He never tested me again. He had decided that my character would be stronger if I had had one drink, and then said "no," rather than taking my mother's word for it.

BBS: *He must have thought highly of you to bother testing you.*

JMC: He tested me right along; he took an interest in me, almost as if I were his son. He challenged me then, and I can feel it today. When I do something, I know whether he would approve of it. It was just fate that we were thrown together, but it was the greatest thing that ever happened to me. From the day I met him, everything changed for me. He picked me from a test I had made. Henry King ran it for Will, and Will picked me. And from that point on, even Mr. Sheehan said "Good morning" to me. He knew Will liked me, and he wanted Will to be happy. As I have always said, without Will Rogers I wouldn't be where I am today.

BBS: *Did you have a chance to observe Sheehan and Will Rogers often?*

JMC: No, but that reminds me of a story. Will went to see Winfield Sheehan one time and said, "Winnie, I think I ought to pick the parts I want to do myself. I have done all right so far. I'd like to choose some of my own roles. Irvin Cobb has written lots of things, and some of my friends have written stories." And Winnie said, "But Mr. Rogers, in running a studio we have tremendous investments in properties, we have bought scripts, we have stories submitted to us, and we have to build a program. That's sort of our department, and we would like to control it." Well, Will said, "I would like to pick a couple of things I would like to do. I know the kind of part I can play. I won't pick anything I can't do." There was nothing for Winfield Sheehan to say. Now this is what actually happened. Winfield Sheehan apparently spent a great deal of time thinking about it, not wanting to offend Will, not wanting to shake up his biggest star, and he finally got an idea. He got a five-ton truck with every script, every property, every book, every synopsis that Fox ever had, and he sent it to Will's ranch, with an inter-office communication, saying, "Dear Mr. Rogers, these are a few of Fox's properties. Will you read these and tell us which ones you want to do." Will just turned the memo over, and wrote on the back, "You win, Winnie!" and sent the whole truck back.

BBS: *Did Mr. Rogers talk at any time about his retirement?*

JMC: No! He never wanted to retire. He never had in mind cutting down on what he was doing; really, if he had had his way, he would have gone the way he did, rather than to ever get to the point where he would have to cut down. He was a man of such enormous energy, and he wanted to do everything to the fullest — always.

May 24, 1970

Peggy Wood

Bryan B. Sterling: *I was amazed to read that you are from Brooklyn.*

Peggy Wood: Why should you be amazed?

BBS: *I thought of you as having a British background.*

PW: Oh, no! My people have been here since 1630.

BBS: *Why were they ten years late?*

PW: I suppose they waited for the press agents to come back to tell them what they would find.

BBS: *You know Will Rogers had a line . . .*

PW: Yes, I know. "My people didn't come over on the Mayflower, they met the boat." Well, it was my folks that his folks met.

BBS: *But then your ancestors did come from England.*

PW: No. You know the Puritans? They tossed them out of England. They went to Holland, then Holland got sick of them, so they sent them off to America. But they weren't all "Woods." Some were "Woods," some "McFarlands," some Dutch. Some came through Maryland to Ohio; others came through the Hudson and Mohawk valleys.

BBS: *Let me try it again; your career started on the stage?*

PW: Yes. And after a couple of years, I met Will

Rogers. I was in a show, *The Lady of the Slipper*, with Fred Stone. You know, Montgomery and Stone, and Elsie Janis.

BBS: *And that was the first time you met Will Rogers.*

PW: He came backstage to see Fred Stone. Fred had a place on Long Island, what you might call a ranch, where he had horses and the great outdoors that he liked so much. And of course, that was a great place for Will Rogers to stretch his legs and stretch his rope, too.

BBS: *From what I have heard, the two met when Fred Stone wanted to learn roping.*

PW: That's true. Will Rogers had made his success in vaudeville as a roper.

BBS: *Then when you met him, he was already well known?*

PW: Oh, yes.

BBS: *Was he easy to talk to?*

PW: Certainly. He was there, around the theater, and he had plenty of conversation, he never lacked for that.

BBS: *Was it more in the form of a monologue, or was it conversation?*

124

PW: Conversation. Later, years later, when I saw him in London, when I was playing there, he came by. And he and I had supper at the Savoy one night, and I had the feeling that he was now doing a monologue. And he didn't have to do that with me; we had chatted, many times. He was a very alert man, and he was always waiting to pick up something that somebody else said, which would stir up some kind of response from him. So he really wasn't drowning out anybody else's talk, ever.

BBS: *Will Rogers appeared in London, in a Charles Cochran show.*

PW: So was I, but not at the same time. He and Cochran were good friends.

BBS: *The story goes that, when Cochran offered him a signed, blank check, Mr. Rogers tore it up.*

PW: That's quite like him! When Will Rogers and I appeared in the movie *Handy Andy*, we finished ahead of time, ahead of schedule, and that last day he stalled and stalled and stalled. In one scene he had to lie in bed, and he wouldn't get up. All because he wanted the crew to get their full accrued pay, if I may make a pun. Only when he was assured that the crew would get their full pay, did he get off that bed. He was going to get them their full money — and he did.

BBS: *Let's go back to* Almost A Husband, *which was Will Rogers' second film for Goldwyn. Was it your first?*

PW: Yes. He was so easy to work with. He was a pro.

BBS: *I have always wondered what actors said to each other in those silent films, when they were supposed to have a conversation. Obviously there wasn't any written dialogue.*

PW: We just talked about anything that had to do with the situation.

BBS: *Were you ever concerned about anybody lip reading?*

PW: I wasn't about to use some nasty·swear words, or obscenities that they could lip read. But do you remember in that famous war film *What Price Glory*, that was a silent film, do you remember what a soldier said? It was very carefully photographed so that it could be lip read. Do you remember what he said? The captain had given him an order and the soldier said, "That lousy son-of-a-bitch!" And everybody in the audience roared. That was so clearly shot, the camera was aimed at this doughboy, who had just been taken down a peg or two. He didn't say it out loud, even if it had been a sound film; it was his fury of saying it under his breath.

BBS: *In your work with Will Rogers, did you find him*

sometimes taking over the director's job, by wanting to do scenes his way?

PW: He had a great sense of taste, and if things weren't right, he would do them over. He, being a sensible man, didn't have to be told. He knew.

BBS: *Do you know that there is no copy available of Almost A Husband? Almost all of Mr. Rogers' early silent films were allowed to hypo [decompose] in the cans, and had to be thrown away.*

PW: I'm not surprised. The motion picture people at that time were just out after what was quick money, and they had no idea that they could save these films, that it was possibly an art form.

BBS: *Do you recall any idiosyncrasies Mr. Rogers might have had?*

PW: No, because he was a typical Oklahoman, and to a person from New York, that was idiosyncrasy enough. The language was different, the choice of phrases was different, there are lovely locutions they use — sure, he was full of idiosyncrasies! He was a puncturer of self-made balloons. If it was the truth, he said it! The most devastating thing that can happen to pomposity is comedy! The comedian can destroy so much better than the invector, the one who rages. George Bernard Shaw was the same. By way of comedy he punctured things that were the shibboleths of the Victorian era. And so Will Rogers punctured the poses and pomposity, or even slyness, or even lies — all he had to do was say what it really was in simple words. As my father used to say, "I can only understand words of one syllable and one letter." Also, the similes he used were things of the earth, that are eternal. What he meant was that people who lived by the earth, on the earth, have to do with living things. Therefore, his similes — I suppose the cliché is — homilies, were so true. And further, he put a little twist on the end of them, and that is where the corkscrew was that pulled out the cork! The funny part was that he was his own straightman, or the newspapers were his straightman, but he never used a dirty word, and he never was sly. He didn't have to be.

BBS: *Let's go back to the sound film you made with Mr. Rogers. Do you remember any other anecdotes about Handy Andy?*

PW: Neither Rogers nor I liked the film very much I thought what I had to do was just plain silly, and he thought so too. We all went to the Mardi Gras in New Orleans and we dressed up in silly clothes.

BBS: *Did Mr. Rogers ad-lib his lines, or did he stick closely to the written dialogue?*

PW: I am sure he ad-libbed, but the written dialogue was no great shakes — no great Shakespeare. Maybe that's where that phrase comes from. He knew what he was doing. He knew when he had to give cues. He wasn't being naughty.

BBS: *It has been said that he was a very restless man, always wanting to do something.*

PW: Oh, yes. That's true. When he wasn't doing his own shows, he was doing something for somebody else, in the way of a benefit, or going off to camps, performing for soldiers, or organizing something, or going off somewhere. He didn't advertise his philanthropic acts at all, because he didn't think it was good taste.

BBS: *Did you ever see Mr. Rogers affectionate?*

PW: He was a compassionate man; he was always pleasant, he was always kindly. That is the key word — kindly! But I never saw him affectionate. He was always talking to everybody. He'd come into the commissary and stop at every table. But with all this "Hail-fellow-well-met," I would say he was a loner.

BBS: *Did you ever see him angry?*

PW: Yes, I saw him angry — at injustices!

September 10, 1970

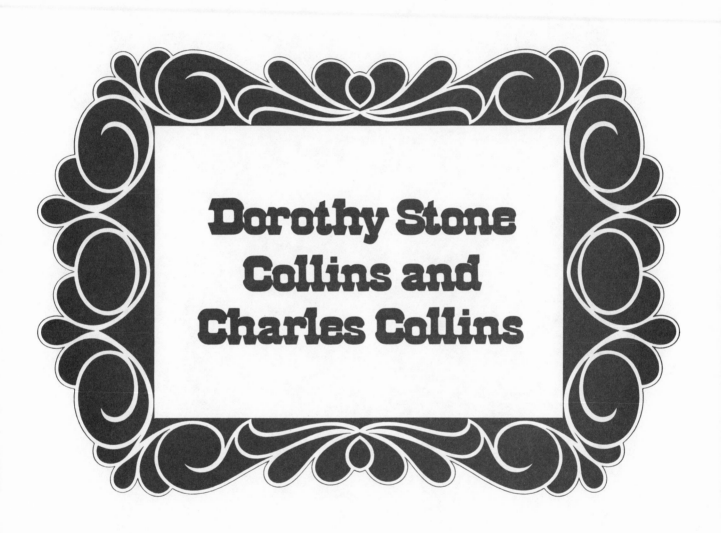

Dorothy Stone
Collins and
Charles Collins

Dorothy Stone Collins: This is going to be great fun, I love talking about Will.

Bryan B. Sterling: *Let's start with the meeting between your father, the famous Fred Stone, and Will Rogers. How did that come about?*

DSC: Daddy decided that he wanted to dance inside a lariat, for the show *The Old Town*. Nobody had ever done this. So he hired an Indian boy, called Black Chambers, to go on the road with him during the last part of the *Red Mill* tour, to teach him roping. Well, the following season, when *The Old Town* opened, that particular dance was one of the highlights. But all the time Black Chambers was with Daddy, he kept talking about another Oklahoman, Will Rogers. He kept saying, "This is a wonderful guy, Fred, and I think you ought to meet, because if you and Will met, you'd get along real good." One day, Daddy was coming out the stage door, when a man came up to the doorman asking, "Is Fred Stone around?" Since Daddy was standing right there, it was obvious to the doorman that the man didn't know my father by sight and he asked, "Who wants to see him?" The stranger said, "Will Rogers." Daddy remembered what Black Chambers had told him and he walked over and identified himself. "Black Chambers told me about you. You know he taught me to rope." And Will said, "Shucks, I would have taught you all the roping you want, just for the fun of it. Shall we go and rope now?" And Daddy and Will went back into the theater, and there, on the darkened stage, they roped together. They roped all afternoon, without dinner, until it was time for the company to come in. From then on, these two were just like . . . brothers. Daddy brought Will home, and you know how little girls are. I was about six years old then, I fell madly in love with Will Rogers. This, you must understand, just after I had been told, to my desolation, that I couldn't marry Daddy, as he could not wait for me, and that he was already married to my mother. So I decided that the next best thing was to marry Will Rogers, if he would just wait for me. So my mother patiently explained to me that Will Rogers also couldn't wait for me, and that he, too, was already married. So I said, that just for that, I would marry another Indian! And to finish this story with a point, I did marry Charles Collins, who is one-sixteenth Cherokee, and from Oklahoma. In fact, when Daddy found out that I was dating Charles, he said, "Oh, he is the same tribe as Will Rogers!" And that made it all right. As I said, Daddy and Will became inseparable. Will was appearing in vaudeville at the time. Then someone started what was called "Sunday Night Concerts at the Winter Garden." What it really was, was big-time vaudeville. And one Sunday night Will was slated to go on. Since the theaters were dark on Sundays and Daddy didn't have a performance, he came to see Will. Well, they put Will on, just ahead of the finale. Well, Will started to talk and rope, and he went over so big, and Daddy was just delighted. When all of a sudden — I guess they were running out of time — they turned the lights out on Will.

Now you know, Will could go on and on, as was his wont, he was liable to do that, but he had the audience with him, and he just didn't keep track of the time. So Will just walked off and they started the finale. Well, my father, who was well known to theater audiences in New York, leaped to his feet and turned to the audience and said, "Don't let 'em do that to Will Rogers! He's got a great act. We want Rogers!" And going up and down the aisle, he got the audience into a frenzy, and they all shouted, "We want Rogers! We want Rogers!" Will didn't know about any of this. He had gone to his little dressing room, way upstairs, thinking he had been a flop — that they had turned the lights out on him because he had been flopping. Well, the audience drove the finale right off the stage, and they had to go and bring Will back on stage. Then the audience gave him an ovation. Will was stunned. He didn't know what had happened. He started to rope again, but was so nervous he spilled his loop. Will stood there for a moment, scratched the back of his head and said, "I shoulda quit when I was ahead." But he continued his performance and the audience that night loved him. He was now their friend.

Charles Collins: I heard that story of Mr. Stone and Will Rogers at the Winter Garden first from the Stones, when I met them. Years went by, then a few years ago, when I was in New York, I saw Johnny Schubert. We were talking and reminiscing, and Johnny told me the same story. So I realized that it just had to be true, just as I had first heard it.

DSC: Yes, there could have been some coloration, because I was afraid that when you are young you build something up in your mind, when your parents tell you something with emotions behind it. After all, I come from a long line of actors, and they dramatize things. Well, the day after this happened at the Winter Garden, Will came over and he asked, "Did you like my act?" And Daddy said, "Congratulations! It was great!" and of course, he never mentioned his own part in it. But when Daddy left the room Mother told Will the whole story. Later, when Daddy found out, he was a little bit miffed at Mother for telling Will. But she was telling us later, that she started to tell Will, thinking that it would make him laugh, and she told it in a funny way. "You should have seen Fred, he was in a frenzy. He ran up and down the aisle. I was so embarrassed, I wanted to get out of the theater and go home." Then she looked at Will, and he had his knee up, with his arms clasped around it, and tears were coming down his cheeks. He was so touched. Will was a very sentimental guy. I don't know whether he cried over other people, but he cried over my Dad. He had such a love for Daddy, that anything that Daddy did, like that, it would just get to him. Well, the next summer, Will rented a house in Amityville, Long Island, opposite our house, so Daddy and he used to be together all the time. Every morning, Will would come over with his little rope, whistling under Daddy's window. Now Daddy was to sleep till noon, because he was work-

ing so hard at night. Mother would stick her head out the window, and she would say softly, "Will Rogers, you go away and come back at 12 o'clock! Fred's asleep." Then Daddy would stick his head out and say, "I'll be right down!" And the two would ride and rope all day.

BBS: *I remember reading that Will Rogers had a serious accident while he lived in Amityville.*

DSC: Yes, and it was that accident that got him to do more talking than roping. Daddy had a little creek back of our house, and it had low tides and high tides. At low tide, you shouldn't dive off the diving board, as there was only little water there. Well, this one day, Will didn't look, and he dived and hit his head and almost broke his neck. His right arm and side were completely paralyzed. The poor man was stunned. He was still in vaudeville, that's how he earned his living. Now how could he do roping without the use of his right arm? But from that very day on, he started learning every trick he knew with his left hand. It did two good things. True, it was a frightening, horrible thing to happen; but, it got him to talking more, which made a star out of him, and it made him an even greater roper than he ever was before, because he learned to rope equally well with either hand.

CC: You know, Will used to do hospital and camp shows all the time. But after the war, some cavalry outfit was quartered at the Rogers ranch. Naturally they had a lot of horses, and colored soldiers were looking after them. One night, in the middle of the night, everybody had gone to bed, one of the officers — the one who told this story — got up and felt a little restless. So he decided to go and see whether everything was all right. As he came to the corral, Will Rogers had the lights on, and there he was, in the center, roping and telling gags. All the colored soldiers were sitting on the fence, laughing and nearly falling off. So the officer asked Will, "Mr. Rogers, what are you doing here in the middle of the night, taking time to come out here, entertaining the fellows?" Will Rogers looked at him in his shy way and said, "Oh, well, I felt sorry for these boys. That old Colonel was mean to 'em today."

BBS: *I can just see him doing it.*

CC: I heard this story at some hospital. An Army officer told us about Will entertaining the wounded, when he suddenly left the ward. He was gone a long time, so finally someone went to find him. And here was Will Rogers, in the men's room, leaning on the window sill, crying at the plight of those young patients.

DSC: I tell you, he was the most sensitive and compassionate man.

CC: And he was nervous to the extent that he couldn't sit still. He would always jingle coins in his pocket while he was talking. And he didn't look at you very much. I remember Will telling about the Lindbergh baby. He had been out there, in New Jer-

sey. It was just the week before the kidnapping. He came up directly to Rex Beach's in the afternoon, Sunday afternoon, I think it was, talking about this little baby. He talked so much about it; what a cute kid it was, and how smart. Oh, I remember now! He was upset because there had been stories that this baby was a deaf-mute, or something — that something was wrong with it. He was just so angry about that, because the baby was just wonderful, he said. Yet all the time he was talking, he was jingling those coins in his pocket. Sometimes he would take the coins out and shake them in his hands, like a gourd.

DSC: My Daddy was a great marksman and won many cups, but Will would never shoot a rifle, nor did he want to go hunting.

BBS: *Will Rogers loved animals. Did you ever read the eulogy he wrote to his horse, Dopey?*

DSC: No, but I remember Dopey. We kids all rode Dopey. It seemed to have a great rapport with people. We all loved that horse; it was such a kind horse.

CC: Did you ever hear the story of when Dorothy's father was recuperating from his illness? He was living out here at the Will Rogers ranch. Well, they had a nine hole little golf course where the polo field is now. Fred Stone was walking, and Will was caddying for him, riding one of the polo horses, carrying the clubs. Will was kidding Fred, saying something like, "This is a silly game, anybody can hit a little ball like that!" So Fred Stone challenged him, "Let's see you hit one! Get down off that horse and let's see whether you can hit one straight down the fairway!" So Will said, "Give me a club." Fred handed him a five-iron. Will, without getting off the horse, took a polo swipe at the ball. Wham! And it went straight down the fairway, right up to the green. Mr. Stone said, "That was a lucky shot; come on and do one more!" But Will wouldn't shoot another one. He had shot one, and that was it.

BBS: *Didn't Will Rogers' film career practically start in your home?*

DSC: Oh, yes. Daddy's brother-in-law, our uncle by marriage, Rex Beach wrote stories like Jack London. Now he was going to form a film production company with some other authors, like Rupert Hughes. There were about seven authors, and they were called the "eminent authors." They joined with Sam Goldwyn to make fine movies of their stories. And Rex's first story was called *Laughing Bill Hyde*. And one day, my aunt Greta, Rex's wife, said, "There is only one person to play *Laughing Bill Hyde*, and that's Will Rogers!" And I remember it, because it was in our home in Amityville, and Rex said, "That's the most marvelous idea!" So, later, when Daddy and Will came riding in, they told Will about it. But Will just pulled away, "I'm no actor. I'm just a roper. I can't do it!" But they finally talked him into it. And after that film, which was made in Fort Lee, New Jersey, he went to Hollywood.

131

BBS: *Did he ever come back to visit you on Long Island?*

DSC: Yes, I recall early one morning, there was a banging on our door. We were all in our dressing gowns, so it must have been early in the morning. It was Will. He came in and he was ashen. Dad asked him, "My God, Will, where have you been? We didn't even know you were in town." And Will said, "I've had a plane accident. My plane came down in a pasture out here." You know, Will was always riding the mail planes. There weren't any cross-country flights in those days. He would just hitch a ride, back and forth, on those mail planes. So Will came to our house first, to clean up, before going to his home. "Don't you tell Betty," he said, "or she won't let me fly anymore."

CC: Tell about the accident your Dad had.

DSC: Daddy was flying his own plane. That was just before we went into rehearsal for *Three Cheers*. By that time I was appearing in shows with him. Anyway, Daddy was soloing, accumulating time for his pilot license. It was just the day before we were going to return to New York. What I am telling you took place in Connecticut, where we had a farm. Daddy's plane spun into the ground and he crushed both legs, his ribs were caved in, he was scalped, he bit his tongue half in two, both shoulders were dislocated — well, they didn't think he would live. When they brought him into the hospital, the doctor said that had this been anyone but Fred Stone, that he would have amputated both legs immediately. They were so full of mud and fertilizer, that it was impossible to clean them. He lay in a hammock for two weeks, while they cleaned the tissues. But the doctor said that he had seen those legs in action, that he could not bring himself to take them off, at least until he was absolutely sure that it was inevitable. As time went by, the doctor refused to make any predictions, "I don't know what this man can do," he said. "Everything that I predict, he upsets." First the doctor had said that Daddy would have to be in a wheel chair for the rest of his life. Then he said that Daddy would never walk again; then, that he would walk, but never dance again. Anyway, everything was up in the air with the show. The costumes had been ordered, people were hired, the theater had been lined up for this show. One of the things that destroyed Daddy psychologically, was the plight of Charles Dillingham, the producer, a man Daddy had worked for for twenty-five years. Daddy kept saying, "What have I done to him? What have I done to him?" You see, the show *Three Cheers* had been written for a family. It had a double entendre, but a clean double entendre. All of a sudden, the casting problem was ended, because Will wired . . . but wait — let me get my book so I can read the exact words. Ah, here it is, August 22nd, 1928: "IF YOU DON'T WANT DOROTHY TO WAIT UNTIL YOU ARE ENTIRELY RECOVERED I WILL GO INTO THE SHOW WITH HER JUST TO SORT OF PLUG IT ALONG UNTIL YOU ARE ABLE TO REJOIN AND I WILL DO THE BEST I CAN WITH YOUR PART. DOROTHY CAN KEEP TELLING ME HOW YOU WOULD HAVE PLAYED IT." And it's signed, "WILL ROGERS." Now by this time, Will was a tremendous star and he was writing columns. Well, we called Mr. Dillingham, the producer, and he said, "This does it!" So Will came East and I met him at the station — that was September 13, 1928. The rest of the cast was already in rehearsal by the time he got to New York. The photographers had a field day, shooting us from all angles. We drove immediately to New London, Connecticut, to see my Dad. Will went in the room, with Dad swabbed in bandages and a cast from his chin to his toes. It was so electric. Will was completely overcome, but he didn't let Daddy know. Not until we were back in the car, going back to New York, did he let himself go. Well, the next day he came to rehearsal. The cast was just waiting for Will Rogers. This great show of friendship, this gesture, had swept New York and brought it to its feet, it made an entire city teary-eyed. I'll never forget when Will walked through that stage door, the whole company had been waiting for him, and now they all leaped to their feet and applauded and applauded and applauded. But that's not all of the story, there's more. Opening night in New York, I was in a terrible state. I had never appeared without my father before, and to think that he was in the hospital, and here I was, doing the show without him — I was just about ready to crack up. Mother was backstage with me, she had come down from New London to keep people away from me. You know, people who would have said such things as, "You are a brave little girl, keeping up the tradition of the family," or "If only your father were here tonight," or something like that which would have surely made me blow my top. So here I was, making up and being very tense. They had called "Overture!" Well, when that overture starts, there is no reprieve, you're on your way. Well, all of a sudden, the door burst open and in came Will, and he was crying, and he said, "Nobody can take your father's part, nobody can do it. What am I doing here?" And he threw his arms around me and put his head on my neck and he sobbed, pointing to the stage, "That's his music, that's his audience! What am I doing here?" Well, my mother thought, "The audience might just as well pack up and go home, because Dorothy will be no good after this." But the most marvelous thing happened for me psychologically. For the first time I was comforting somebody else. I was saying, "You can do it! They are waiting for you out there!" Here I was giving a pep talk, instead of being the "poor little thing that was all alone." It did the most marvelous thing for me, and we sailed through the show together.

BBS: *Surely you are not trying to tell me that the show went on just as it was written?*

DSC: Hah! That's another story, but I didn't know whether you'd be interested in that.

BBS: *Most certainly!*

DSC: Well, that was a funny story. All through rehearsal, Will was reading from the script. At the dress rehearsal in Springfield, Massachusetts — now this is prior to what I just told you, which was opening night in New York — he was still reading this thing. So I looked for Mr. Dillingham — I called him "Uncle Charley," because I had known him ever since I was a tiny child — and I said, "Uncle Charley, I think we ought to postpone this opening, because Will doesn't know his part." And Uncle Charley said, "Dorothy, I have news for you. Will is never going to know that part, because he's not going to do it." I said, "You mean he is going to leave?" And Dillingham said, "No, he's not going to leave, but he's got something up his sleeve, and I'd like to know what it is. And we are going to open because I want to know what this guy is going to do. Just remember this, this is going to be a type of show you've never seen in your life!" So that opening night in Springfield, we were all standing in the wings, waiting for Will to make his entrance. The audience gave him an ovation that you've never heard. Then this is how he started his first scene: he walked down to the audience, took the script out of his pocket, and said, "Now here it says that Fred is to do a flip-flop, a back somersault, a stiff fall, and an eccentric dance to open the show. Now I'm not going to do that! I'm going to talk about Hoover!" And he threw the script into the orchestra pit. Well, the audience just shrieked, they just shrieked. But I, I just stood there. My father's method had always been that every bit of business, every line, was rehearsed to the *nth* degree. And I thought, "Oh, my God! What's going to happen?" Well, Will proceeded to do a marvelous monologue about Hoover. And I stood in the wings and wondered when I'd go on. When, just as I was wondering whether I should change clothes, or go on, or stay there, or what, Will turned and saw me in the wings. He said, "Dorothy, honey, come here! Come on stage and meet your Daddy's friends." I came on, and he put his arm around me, and he talked to me for a while; I know we didn't do our scene at all. I don't know what we did. Will just talked to me, and he finally said, "Now you run and change your clothes for that number you're going to do with the leading man." The audience didn't even know there was a leading man, because I hadn't met him yet on stage. "You know," Will went on, "that nice young man back there that I seen; he's all dressed up; he's very handsome. Now you just go and change your clothes and do that song with the leading man, because, after that, I want to talk about Congress!" So I went off, and changed my clothes — and — the whole show was musical numbers and nobody knew why they were there, because there was no book that led up to them. All of a sudden, two perfect strangers, that hadn't met, would come out and do a love song. But the audience adored it. It was brilliant, it was topical — and it was what they wanted. It wasn't *Three Cheers*; it was a one-man show.

CC: But they gave three cheers for the show.

BBS: *Well, that was opening night. How was the next night?*

DSC: All together different. You see the show had run way, way, overtime. The stagehands were clapping their hands because they got overtime. So the next day we were all called to rehearsal, thinking that we would be out of the show. But Burnside, the director said, "Ladies and Gentlemen, in a situation of this kind, we know what to cut. The audience has told us what they want. Some of you are going to be hurt, but this is a completely different show than we had planned. But we want a long run, and if we go along with what the audience wants, we'll have a long run." We all got out our blue pencils and marked our scripts as the director made the changes: "Scene number so-and-so — out! Scene number so-and-so — out!" The whole show was just cut to musical numbers, and Will. And that's how we opened in New York, and they just loved it.

BBS: *Were two shows ever the same?*

DSC: They had the same format, the musical numbers came in about the same place, and we had a line of Tiller Girls; but Will was different every night.

BBS: *How long did the show run?*

DSC: We opened in October 1928, and Will was in it until June 1, 1929, because he had a motion picture commitment. He had to leave the show, and you just couldn't put anyone else in, and you couldn't go back to the old book. So we closed.

BBS: *Well, that was enough excitement for one show.*

DSC: There were other things. Doing what came natural to him, Will caused quite a stir, almost a riot. You see, not wearing makeup, he would leave immediately after the show. And there were always a number of beggars waiting at the stage door at that time. Now when I say beggars, I mean beggars. These were not the unfortunates who were out of work; these you would not find at stage doors. But these were people who made their living just begging. Most actors were liberal and gave them quarters, or at most fifty cents, Will would pass out dollar bills. Well, pretty soon our stage entrance on 46th Street was just mobbed. There were hundreds waiting for Will, and Will would just throw out those dollar bills, and drive off. I, of course, having to remove my makeup, and change clothes, came out later than Will. So when I came out, I gave them what change I had, and the beggars grumbled. They wanted me to give them what Will had given them. But, you see, I didn't know what Will gave and, therefore, didn't know why they were so hostile. Well, the crowd at the stage door grew nightly, until I finally had to have policemen help me get to the car. I have one more story about *Three Cheers*. Will had a habit of always tossing all the pennies in his change up on the shelf in his dressing room. Every time he got paid, or bought something, he would toss the pennies up on the shelf. At the end of the run in New York, his dresser, who had been Daddy's dresser, asked, "Mr. Rogers, you have a lot of pennies up there. Aren't you going to get them down?" And Will

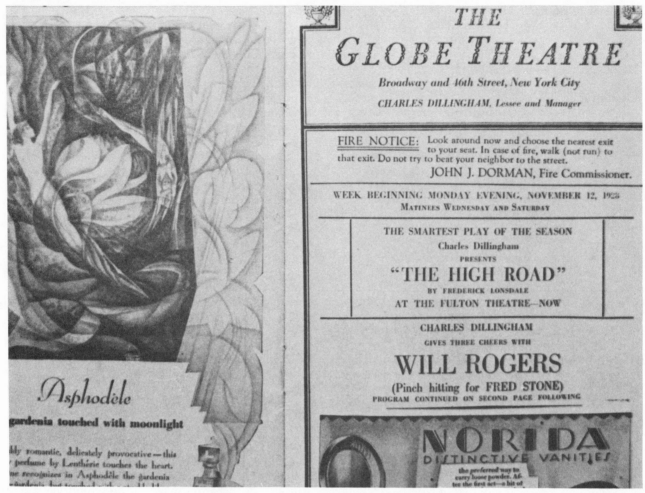

Globe Theatre program advertising Will's Three Cheers.

replied, "Me? I've been tossing 'em up there all year, you keep 'em." And do you know, there were over $250 worth of pennies up there?

BBS: *What happened after that?*

DSC: The next year Daddy came back on the stage, and in the new show I met Charles Collins. From the time they nearly amputated Daddy's legs, to the time he was back on Broadway, just a year and a half had elapsed.

BBS: *Did your Dad ever dance on stage again?*

DSC: Yes. He did remarkably well, but he didn't do all of the acrobatics that he used to do. The ankle had fused into one bone, having been crushed. He went to Hollywood and started to do dramatic parts. His first picture was *Alice Adams*, with Katharine Hepburn, this was 1935. It opened at the Radio City Music Hall in New York. Charley and I went to the opening; we were living in New York at the time. Daddy made quite a hit in it. After the picture was over, I started to cry like mad; of course the last scene was very moving. I stumbled out of the theater, crying, and we went home, and I said, "I am going to California immediately! Something terrible is happening to my father. I know that he needs me very, very much. I am going tomorrow!" I packed all night, and asked Charley to drive the car to California, and I'd take the train. And Charley went along with my plan. He was very much impressed with this traumatic premonition that I had. I got a little sleep that night, and the next morning I was trying to get my reservation on the train. They told me that they would call me back. A short while later, the telephone rang, and Charley thought that it was the reservation people. As I was busy, he picked up the phone. It was a broker friend of ours, and he said, "Charley, I'm so glad it was you who answered the phone. Something terrible has happened. It just came over the ticker tape, and you must know it before you read it in the papers. Will Rogers and Wiley Post have crashed near Point Barrow, Alaska, and they were both killed!" Charley came and broke the news to me, and right after that, the telephone rang again. It was Mrs. Rogers, whom we called Aunt Betty. She was up in Skowhegan, Maine, where Mary was in stock, and she asked me, "Would you please wait until I get down to New York with Mary, because I want you to go back on the train with me." I said that I would certainly wait for her. The poor woman was so beset by newspapermen and photographers and everything, and her grief was so dreadful, that she wanted to be alone. She called us again a little while later and said, "My train will stop," I forgot the name of the small town, but I think it was Stamford, Connecticut, "would you please be there and take us off? It will be an unscheduled stop." The next morning Charley and I got up at 5 o'clock to drive to Connecticut to meet the train. The station master, naturally knowing of the unscheduled stop, informed the police, so that Mrs. Rogers could have a police escort — something she didn't want. And that was how the newspaper people found out where Mrs. Rogers would leave the train. When we got to the station, everybody was taking pictures, and this poor, darling woman and Mary stumbled off the train; she was just ready to fall when Charley caught her. That's how Charley ended up on the front page of some tabloid, and, since no one knew who he was, the caption read "Jimmy Rogers meets his Mother." We finally got back to the car and had to drive all over the countryside, through woods and everything, until we finally lost the pursuing newspaper cars. Then we met another car, I think it was a cousin's, and they whisked her away. When we returned home, we lived in Forest Hills at the time, our front lawn was covered with reporters, demanding to know where Mrs. Rogers was. And we could truthfully say, we didn't know. One reporter even came into the house, pretending that he was a Western Union boy, trying to deliver a telegram.

BBS: *What were your Dad's last recollections of Will Rogers?*

DSC: I remember Daddy telling me that he had talked with Wiley Post, and that Wiley had told him that he was worried about this trip, that he didn't want to take the plane to Alaska. He told me that Will just wouldn't hear of anything else. He just wanted to take this plane, and that was it. But Daddy said, "Anyway, I'm glad it's Wiley Post, if it's going to be anybody, because he is the best pilot in the country. Mother said at the time, "If anything happens to Will Rogers, it will shake this country!" And she was in tears when he left.

CC: You know I have a hunch that Will Rogers had a philosophy that went through every facet of his life. You know, just his going on a trip and only taking his tiny bag with just a few things, then throwing away the dirty clothes and getting some more as he went along — he was unencumbered! And I think it was the same way with doing shows, paying his obligations, or anything. He did them as they came, and he was never personally tied down, or burdened by them.

DSC: There was just one more sad, touching thing, Aunt Betty told me after Will was gone. This worried her so much, almost more than anything — it grieved her so. You see, they had a little log cabin way off on the ranch in the ravine. When Will wanted to get away from everything, he and Betty would sneak off and spend the day, or a weekend there. When he went to his log cabin, nobody was supposed to intrude and bother him — it was his hideaway. And the evening before Will left on this trip to Alaska, he wanted Betty to stay with him at the log cabin. She was busy packing — she always packed for him — and she said, "When you come back, Will, we'll do that." You know, it grieved her ever after.

May 25, 1970

Lew Ayres

Bryan B. Sterling: *The reason I've come to see you is because of a motion picture you made with Will Rogers, called* State Fair. *Of course, that goes back quite a few years . . .*

Lew Ayres: 1933, I think.

BBS: *Do you remember anything about that picture, or is it just a memory, way in the back of your mind?*

LA: Oh no, I recall a good deal about the picture, because it was a big film at the time, and it was quite an experience. It was a film with a large cast of rather well-known players, more or less what you'd call vignette style. Will Rogers, of course, was there, and Janet Gaynor, Norman Foster, Louise Dresser, Sally Eilers, Frank Craven, Victor Jory. However, as far as Rogers, himself, is concerned, we had no actual scenes together. I didn't work with him, but I saw him many times around the set. Of course, there was a constant discussion of Rogers and his characteristics; he endeared himself a great deal. He was always cluttered with so many other portions of his public life. For instance, I remember, between each shot, he would immediately start on his newspaper column. He would have a stack of newspapers around him on the set, which he would read, making his own comments and notations. And for that he had to put on his glasses. I don't know when he learned his lines — of course he never learned them precisely, like some of us do. He learned them in a loose fashion, while they would try to get him to get himself ready for the next scene. He would rehearse only casually and would continue with his work at the time. At the last moment — of course there are so many delays in making a film, there is always the lighting problem, and the painting problem, and I don't blame him, he had many things on his mind — so at the last moment, they would finally get everything out of the way so they could go into a take, when, lo and behold, we would find out after we were halfway through, that he hadn't removed his glasses. Or he had a handful of pencils stuck in his pocket, which didn't match with the bucolic country character he was playing. There were many things that he did which made it difficult for the poor assistant director, but were very amusing to the rest of us.

BBS: *I can see that. I have heard many a time that Mr. Rogers didn't learn his lines at all, that the assistant director, or the director, would have to explain the scene just before the take, and that as far as dialogue was concerned, he would rewrite his own.*

LA: I think that was generally true, and some of us reacted with grave concern at any thought of working with someone like this. We were more or less bound by our limited capacity, not only to the sense of the scene, but, truthfully to the dialogue itself. It sometimes made it difficult on actors who worked with him. It took a particular kind of personality to respond to this loosely arranged manner of carrying on dialogue with him. Maybe his years in vaudeville were responsible. At that time we didn't have the real respect that came about later. This is an interesting point. In a sense, he was far ahead of his time. Not only as a human being, but as an actor, too. I see it now. You see, we are talking about something that took place in my life 37 years ago, and I am looking at it from another perspective. One of the reasons I didn't know him too well was, of course, the big age difference. I am now 62, so nearly 40 years ago would put me in my mid-twenties. He was considerably older and a most eminent man, so well known everywhere. Most of us stood in awe of him, but not as an actor. We stood in awe of him as a person of affluence and influence in the world. We recognized what he stood for — though not as much as history has proved. But in the acting sense, while I don't say that today's dramatization moves as far away from the actually written dialogue as Will Rogers was able to carry it, his relaxed attitude when you watch him today in those old films is like the most modern New York laboratory theater performance. There is nothing stilted, static about Will Rogers. He was alive and real. I wish today I had just his talent as a performer.

BBS: *Will Rogers, oddly enough, did not consider himself to be an actor. He would say that as long as a part fitted him, he could play it, but he didn't want any part where he would have to "act."*

LA: As time has gone on, many of us view acting differently. In older times, an actor was considered only such when he could portray many kinds of characterizations that were not necessarily anything like himself. That a man could assume the garb of a soldier of the king, next time play a beggar, or a young man, or an old man — that was more before motion pictures, which came up with the big close-up and revealing us to be what we really are. But in the theater, with makeup and lighting, we had a greater range. I now find that many of the so-called great personalities that had been recognized as "personality actors" — when we did not believe them to be great actors — I now maintain that that is good acting. The capacity of a man to communicate his personality — and we thought of Will Rogers as a personality — to communicate that to an audience is an art. It is an artist who does that. My evaluation of Will Rogers as an artist is that he was able, and willing, to reveal that within himself which he really was. So I consider him a fine actor, though apparently he would never have admitted it.

BBS: *Hasn't it been said that it is most difficult to be yourself? Yet in an acting era of over-large gestures, profiles and heaving bosoms, Will Rogers would scratch his ear, screw up his face, or play a whole scene with his back to the camera.*

LA: True. All the things that we thought were an actor's devices for the public, he never "monkeyed" with, except devices which were comfortable to him. If he scratched his ear, I guess it needed scratching.

Between takes, writing the column and roping.

BBS: *Would you say that it might have been easier for Will Rogers to "act natural," since he had travelled so much, met heads of state, been a successful public speaker, in fact, having faced almost any situation before?*

LA: That is true to some degree. But had he not had the self-confidence originally, he would never have been able to make it with the kings and presidents and officials. In other words, I think that that was an ingredient, a psychological advantage that he had right from the start. Of course, he added to that by his experiences along the way.

BBS: *Yet despite his successes, Will Rogers, whose career started as a roper, practiced religiously with the rope. He said that some day in this acting business, they would get wise to him, and he would have to return to roping.*

LA: It kept him in touch with the essential earthy part of his nature and his previous life. It made the world love him for not having renounced his heritage. He knew himself. This is really the aspect of a great philosophical insight, the capacity to know oneself. If you know yourself, and what your real values are, you are an adult. And Will Rogers certainly had this way ahead of us.

BBS: *Could this account for Will Rogers being so unlike anyone before, or since?*

LA: He was unique. Will Rogers had a way of slapping you, while he picked you up. That is a great art, and Rogers certainly was great. And it is all the more remarkable, a curious fact, that these rare gems of personality are so few and far between. Our popula-

tion has almost doubled since then, and out of this vast number wouldn't you think some similar personality would have emerged? But of the really great, and Rogers is certainly among them, there are so few. When you think of Rogers, don't you think of Lincoln? The similarity of background, the continuing wit, the ability to cut through sham and see the essence?

BBS: *Carl Sandburg, who was a friend of Rogers', was the only other one I have ever heard make the comparison. But let me ask you a question I have asked everyone who ever worked with Will Rogers. Was it difficult to get him to come on the set?*

LA: He had one comment that he made about films. It referred to the problems of film making, where there are always the minor details that are holding up the progress of the scene. Will Rogers himself sometimes was one of these problems, because he took, oh I don't know how long for lunch. We would have an hour for lunch, but he would be in the commissary, holding forth at one of the tables, as a raconteur and a socratic kind of character, too, questioning others, bringing them out. The poor assistant director would be at hand, trying to prod him into getting back on the set. And Will Rogers would just be saying, "I'll be right there in a moment, boys!" And his comment was, "No matter how late you are, you are never too late for pictures!" We, within the industry, often quote that, because there is quite a bit of truth in it.

December 31, 1970

139

Hal Roach, Sr.

Bryan B. Sterling: *Tell me about your association with Will Rogers from the time you two first met.*

Hal Roach: I met Will Rogers in New York, when he worked in the Follies, and we seemed to hit it off together, because I started in pictures as a cowboy — so we had a little something in common. I had been Superintendent of Freighting in the Mojave Desert, before I got into pictures; I was superintendent when I was 20 years old. But this is about Will Rogers, but I just wanted to point out that I was on horseback all the time. Anyhow, some time later, before talking pictures, we made a deal with Will to come to work for us — I think the salary was $2,500 a week, which at that time was a lot of money for anybody. My Irish Dad, who I don't think ever earned more than $10 a week before we got into the picture business, was treasurer of the company. One of his jobs was to give out the checks, and when anybody got over $5 a day, why, the old man thought it was absolutely ridiculous. So, as he handed out the checks, he would hand them out with a great deal of profanity, saying things like, "Here, you so-and-so, here is your lousy check that you're not entitled to!" Well, when Will came to work for us, his was the biggest check up to that time. Harold Lloyd, who was on a percentage, did not draw a very big check. But Dad thought, of course, that Harold was entitled to it, because Harold was our bellringer. Well, anyway, all of a sudden, Dad saw this check for $2,500. I could just imagine what he built up in his mind as to what he was going to say to Rogers, the first time he picked up his check. A week went by, and Rogers didn't come to get his check. Now Dad had two checks, each for $2,500, and he couldn't stand it. And a third week went by, and Will still didn't come in to pick up his check. Now the old man was about to have a nervous breakdown. I happened to be on the porch, near my Dad's office, as Will was walking by, and Dad walked over to him and said very humbly, "Please, Mr. Rogers, would you mind picking up these checks?" Instead of the profanity he had already set up — well — it never happened.

Will, of course, was brilliant. Now I have spent many years constructing comedy, but he could take a serious situation and turn it into a humorous one — perhaps with a little bite in it for some people. For example, after the end of the First World War, Arrowhead Springs was a hospital for veterans, and one year I agreed to put on a show for them at Christmas time. Will Rogers was to be the main attraction. Well, on the way up there, driving through Azusa, Will got pinched for speeding.

When Will got on stage, he talked for at least a half hour. The entire routine — and he had those veterans in stitches — was about his getting pinched. He used no other material at all. Now he was less than an hour from the hospital when he got pinched, so he had developed his monologue since then, and it couldn't have been funnier. To this day I can remember some of the gags.

When Will started working in Hollywood, he had a beautiful home in Beverly Hills, but instead of a front yard, he had a riding ring. They would rope calves, and goats, and do trick riding and roping there — usually on Sundays, because in those days, you worked six days a week. Then, if they had nothing else to do, they would get a baseball and play polo with it — from one end of the riding ring to the other. Well, I got interested in that, and although I am left-handed, I started riding some of Will's horses in this so-called polo game. It was a little rough, without any rules, and finally I couldn't stand it any longer, and bought myself my first horse. I began to like it so well, and I had a ranch at Arness Road, I built a larger field. It wasn't regulation size, just about half the size of a normal field, and Will Rogers and I and "Big Boy" Williams, and one other cowboy, would play two-handed polo. But here we would play with a regular polo ball. Will and I played a great deal of polo together.

BBS: *Will Rogers made 12 two-reelers for you. How did that work out?*

HR: We didn't do too well by Will, as far as the comedies were concerned, because he couldn't talk. We couldn't get the best part of Will Rogers on the screen. So he went back to the stage for a while. After he came out here for Fox, we were still very close friends, and that's when he bought the ranch. I had a house at the Uplifters, which was about as close as anybody was to where he lived, and we spent at least one evening a week together. My wife and Betty Rogers were very good friends. We were either at Will's house, or they were at ours. Will was a very good polo player in one way, but he was like a hound dog after a rabbit. The moment they threw the ball in, Will was after it as hard as he could go. The position he played on his team made very little difference to him, as long as he could get to the ball. He took polo very seriously. I remember one occasion, after he left Hollywood — it was in New York — and he was playing polo with Fred Post on Long Island. Fred Post was a fellow that sold polo ponies, a very nice man. I was visiting back East and they mounted me to play out there, on Long Island. And I remember so well, Skiddy von Stade, one of the top players of that day was on Will's side, and he criticized Will a couple of times, and finally Will said, "Skiddy, how many goals are you?" And Skiddy said, "I'm seven goals, Will. Why?" And Will said, "Anyone that's seven goals ought to know enough to tell a guy *before* he does something wrong, not after!"

One time, Eddie Mannix was in California. His business was to buy polo ponies in Texas for sale in both California and New York. Now, anytime Eddie was in Los Angeles — he was an old cowboy and a great friend of Will's — he would stay at Will's home. Well, this particular night, Mrs. Roach and I were there for dinner, and after dinner Will was writing his "Daily Telegram," but he wasn't satisfied with it. So he would write it and read it to us, and get our opinion, and then he'd go to rewrite it. Well, when Will was writing, he wore glasses. And, every time he would read the telegram, he would take those glasses

Will Rogers and Hal Roach, Sr., compare polo mallets.

off, and nervously rub them with his thumb while he was talking — you know, dirtying the glasses. Betty would quietly reach over, take the glasses, wipe them clean and then hand them back to Will. He wrote about three telegrams; each time this same thing would happen. Finally, when Betty reached again for the glasses, Eddie said. "Betty, why don't you just wash his thumb?" Now you better shut that tape recorder off for a moment and let me think of some more stories.

HR: Is the tape rolling? OK. Will loved brown Mexican beans. One day he told Betty, "Betty, I want those Mexican beans every night." So the first night Betty had a rather modest little dish of beans prepared, and Will said, "Betty, that's not what I want. I love them, I want a lot of these beans!" Well, the next day, there was a bowl containing at least four quarts of beans sitting in front of Will. And for the next month, a bowl with four quarts of beans was in front of Will every night until he got so damn sick and tired of Mexican beans, that he had to call it quits.

Will did a great deal of flying. What a lot of people don't know is that Will got airsick when the weather was rough. But he would still fly. At that time I had my own plane and a very fine pilot, Jimmy Dixon, whom Will liked very much. Will liked to fly with this plane of mine, because Jimmy would try and get up high enough to get out of the rough air. But here is the amazing thing. Will Rogers would call an air service first and ask them, "How much will it cost me to fly to Oklahoma, and back?" And they would give

him the cost. Then he would come into my office, lay down a check for the amount they had quoted him, and he'd say, "Do you mind if I take Jimmy to Oklahoma?" And I would say, "No. But Will, you don't have to . . ." But he was insistent, "I want to go; if you don't want my check, forget the whole thing and I'll rent a plane!" He would never use that plane that he didn't pay for it. One time, Will and I, and Eric Pedley, the famous polo player, were going to Mexico to ask the Mexican team to come to Los Angeles to play polo. So I said to Will, "I'm going to pay for the plane, the gasoline and everything. If you want to pay the other expenses, that's fine!" Will tried to interrupt me, "I want to pay . . ." But I insisted, "No! It's going to be my way or I won't go!" I was using his tactics. So Will finally had to agree. Well, we entered Mexico through Mexicali. The first thing Will did when we landed was run to the bank. He came back with sacks of *pesos* for Eric, Jimmy and me — one sackful each. It was heavy, each one weighed about five pounds. And that was our spending money. We couldn't even buy a pack of cigarettes ourselves.

We went into the bar at the local hotel, and they featured a Bacardi rum. Well, Will bought a Bacardi cocktail for everybody in the bar, and we were sitting with three or four polo players, and Will said, "Eh! that's a good drink!" Now Will wasn't a drinker and knew nothing about drinks, but he kept saying, "That's a good drink. I like that!" The waiter came over and said that the drinks were compliments of Mr. Bacardi. Well, Will had never heard of Bacardi,

Hal Roach, Sr., with production staff, circa 1922.

and he said, "Never mind the compliments, how much are the drinks?" The waiter tried to explain that Mr. Bacardi had bought the drinks for everybody. So Will said, "Well, then I'll buy a drink for everybody!" Finally Mr. Bacardi came over in protest, but Will said, "I never heard of you before and I'm buying for this party; I'm buying all the drinks, and you have nothing to do with it." So we had another round of Bacardis that Will bought.

We were to play polo there on Sunday. Joaquim Amaro was then the head of the War Department of Mexico, and Calles was President. So Will went to say hello to President Calles. Now Will could say things to people that nobody else could, and he said, "I've got it all figured out, Mr. President. I know who the principal people in Mexico are. The principal people are the English. The second principal people are the French. The third principal people are the Americans, and the fourth are the Mexicans!" Now he told this to the President. And while Will said this — he was a restless guy anyway — instead of sitting down, he was standing up, and he had a pocket full of these silver *pesos*, and he was jingling them in his pocket. So President Calles said to him, "Will, I wouldn't rattle those *pesos* if I were you, because in Mexico they can steal your socks without taking your shoes off!"

Now, this fellow Amaro had only one eye, but he loved to play polo. He had about 50 horses, all of different grades of polo ponies, and he played about the worst game of polo you ever saw. Of course Will thought that he and Eric and I would be on one team,

with maybe one Mexican to make up the full team against a Mexican team. But Will insisted that Amaro play in the game. And when Amaro finally agreed to play, he wanted Will on his side. So they had two Mexicans, Amaro and Will. On our side was Eric Pedley, who was worth ten goals on any kind of horse; myself, and I was pretty good in front of Eric because I knew his game; and we had two Mexican players, probably from the Army. But since Amaro played, nobody dared to run into him. So, any time Amaro got the ball, everybody stopped until he had hit it. At least 50 percent of the people in the stands were from the States, to watch Will Rogers play. Well, all Will Rogers did — it was a good thing that Amaro couldn't speak English — because all Will did was bawl the devil out of him during the whole game. I remember so well; the ball would be up there, and Amaro was close to it. Pedley was back of me, yelling, "Get the ball!" and I'd say, "The hell, I will!" I wasn't going to go to jail in Mexico for bumping their top military man off his horse. Anyway, we had a very good time. But Will sure took his polo seriously; he worked hard at it. OK, shut it off again!

HR: Are you ready?

BBS: *All set, you can start any time.*

HR: Another amusing story is the story with Max Fleischmann. Max was the head of the Fleischmann company, you know, Fleischmann yeast, Standard Brands, and so on. One of the richest men in the United States. Max was crazy about Will Rogers. Any

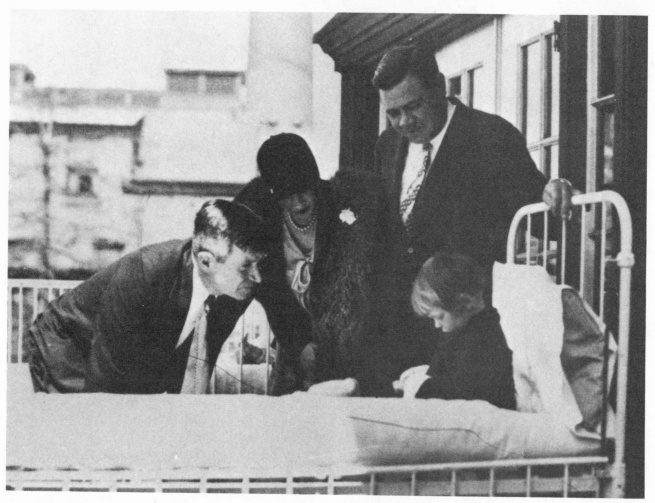

Will and Babe Ruth visiting a children's hospital in Boston.

time that Will was in Santa Barbara, Fleischmann would be right next to him. Now at that time there was a very fine stallion called "Senator." Every horse that he produced was a good polo pony. A fellow named Brooks, who lived in Denver, had shipped five or six of Senator's offsprings into Santa Barbara for the season. There was one particular small horse. It was too small for me, a little husky thing, but a very good polo pony. I was playing that afternoon, and Will said, "Hal, I like that horse. It would be a great horse for my boys, and I'd like to buy it." The price on that horse was $2,000. Will suggested that I ride the horse so that he could watch it work. "But," Will cautioned me, "don't tell anybody that I want the horse; tell 'em you want it." So I rode the horse for a period. It was great but too small for me. I had to reach way down on the mallet in order to play the horse, but it played beautifully. When I came back, Rogers and Fleischmann were standing together. So Will said, "Ride it once more, for another period." So I did. When I came back to Will I told him, "It worked just as well the second period, you can't tire it out." So Will said, "Tell Brooks you'll buy it." So I went to tell Brooks. I told him I'd be over the next morning at 8 o'clock with the $2,000.

Well, at 8 o'clock the next morning I went over to Brooks' place, and he told me, "I'm very sorry, but Mr. Fleischmann bought the horse last night for $2,500. When I reported this to Will, he was angry. He jumped in his car and off he went, back to Los Angeles. That afternoon at the game Max Fleischmann kept asking, "Where is Will?" So I told him, "Will went home." Max wanted to know why. I explained, "Will bought a horse yesterday afternoon for $2,000, and you bought it after he left for $2,500." Well, Max got excited. "I thought *you* bought the horse!" "No, Max," I told him. "I wasn't buying it for myself. I was buying it for Will!" Max was upset. "What'll I do? What'll I do?" he kept asking. "I thought you wanted the horse." I looked at him, "Oh, you'd do me out of a horse for $500, but not Will, eh?" Anyway, the only thing Max could think of was to hire a trailer right away, and he sent the horse to Will as a present.

Well, the horse arrived at Will's ranch, and Will sent it right back. When the horse arrived at Max's, he sent it back to Will. That poor horse made about six trips from Santa Barbara to Los Angeles. Every time Max would send the horse to Will, Will would send it right back. Finally Max called me in desperation, "What do you think I ought to do?" So I went over to Will and I told him, "Look, the horse is worth $2,500. Why don't you send Max a check for $2,500 which is what he paid for the horse. That way you're not taking a gift, and you'll have the horse." Will thought that was a good idea. So the next time the horse arrived, he kept the horse and sent the check.

Well, now the check kept going back and forth. Whatever happened after that, I don't know. The last I ever heard was that the check was still going from Will to Max and from Max to Will.

BBS: *I have heard a story that in July 1935, you were invited to take a polo team to Hawaii, but you did not invite Will Rogers.*

HR: In the first place, we would have rather had Will than anybody else. But I never dreamed that he would want to go away for four weeks. Yet when he heard about the trip, he came up to me and expressed his desire to go. I said, "My God, Will, why didn't you let me know?" He sort of criticized me for not inviting him. I told him, "The Hawaiian people invited us to come over and play polo, and I've been having the damndest time trying to get a team together — I had no idea you'd want to go." Will said, "Oh Glory, I would have liked to go." So I said, "Well, you're in!" He looked down for a moment, then he said, "I promised Post that I'd go on a trip with him." I asked him, "Well, can't you change that and come with us?" So Will said, "Let me think about it."

A day or so later he told me, "I don't think it's right for me to call this trip off; Wiley's got it all set up." So I said, "If by any chance you change your mind, please let me know."

It's such a shame. He would have loved the trip. We had a marvelous time over there. If I had had any idea that he would have gone, I mean, in the early stages of the planning — you see, we were going to be gone a month, and I didn't think he'd want to be away for that long. . . .

We were in Honolulu when I received the cable that he had been killed.

January 2, 1971

Irene Rich

Irene Rich: I remember hearing the news that Will Rogers was gone. It was the day of my broadcast. I was devastated. I went to the studio early, and I heard them rehearse the sound effects for the program that day. It was an airplane crash. Can you imagine how I felt? I said, "You can't do this! You can't do this to the people, and I can't do it to myself!" So they wanted to know what we could do. I suggested that we'd do next week's program. And that's what we did. Then, at the end of the program, I cut out the commercial entirely and inserted the little letter, the part where he talks about death, and what he thought of death, and the darling way he said, "And if you walk down the lane, and you see a little old lady, tell her you saw her son; and if you see a little boy. . . ." Oh, it was heart breaking. When I got home that night, all the newspapers had sent reporters, all asking, "Where did you get that letter?" And the next morning, in his usual column, they had a black border around it, and they quoted that letter.

Bryan B. Sterling: *That particular quote is from the foreword to* Trails Plowed Under, *a book about Will Rogers' close friend, Charles Russell. Mr. Rogers wrote that foreword, and I understand that it most closely expresses his philosophy.*

IR: You know, he was quite profound. All this great comedy, and all this about being a hick from whatnot, he was none of that. Except, perhaps, when he first came out here. I remember when he first came to our house for dinner. He always had a broken rib or a smashed something from playing polo, or being dragged by a roped calf. And this day he had his arm in a sling, and he had a sweater on, no coat. And as we went in, dinner had just been announced, I asked him, "Do you think you'll be able to eat like that?" He answered, "If you don't mind, M'am." He thought I meant with the sweater on, but I meant with his arm in the sling. He was a simple man, not pretentious.

BBS: *Your first picture with Will Rogers was* Water, Water, Everywhere.

IR: Yes, and I have some pictures from that film; that was August 1919. You know I was in fourteen films with Will Rogers. Some of them were made for Goldwyn, those were in the silent days. Then later, we were together in some of the Fox films. Let me show you some of the pictures I have. Here are some from *The Strange Boarder*.

BBS: *That is Jimmy, Will Rogers' younger son.*

IR: Yes, and do you see here, I'm holding little Jimmy in my arms? Well, when the scene was being taken, with me facing the camera and Jimmy in my arms, at right angle to it, his little hand behind my back was inside my dress, going up and down my spine. Now don't think I didn't have a hard time doing that scene. I still remember little Jimmy. He was such a sweet, cuddly little kid.

BBS: *This is such an unusual photo album, these are all candid snapshots, taken long before the usual movie stills.*

IR: Here is one of Will! Did anyone ever tell you how Will concentrated on his little column? How he would sit with his typewriter between his knees, and he'd sit there, and he'd chew his glasses, till the wing would be all chewed down, and only a little stub would be left? And then he would start chewing on the other side!

BBS: *I understand that acting with him was not the easiest thing.*

IR: He didn't stick to the script; he always improved upon it. And you know, you had to be ready for it; you just had to play with him, that's all.

BBS: *Well how did you pick up your cues?*

IR: You just ad-libbed and followed along and did the best you could. I never had any trouble with him. 'Course in the silent pictures you could say anything, as long as you had the proper expression. But in the sound films, the thing that was so hard, was that you didn't want to laugh, of course. So you just had to hold it in and wait till the scene was over. And the moment the director yelled "Cut!" the whole place, carpenters, electricians, grips, everybody would scream with laughter.

BBS: *Several of his fellow actors have said that Will Rogers was really an excellent actor, even though they didn't think so at the time.*

IR: That's right! He was completely himself. He said, "I don't know anything about this acting business. All I can do is be myself, and if they don't like me, it's just too bad for me."

BBS: *Tell me, what kind of an atmosphere did you have when you went on location?*

IR: You see, that was the thing. They would get a story, then they would talk over what they would do, "We'll get old Irene, and then we'll go up in the mountains, and do the film." They would gather the whole cast, everybody; maybe it would take a couple of carloads on the train, but we would all go. We would live in a hotel, but it was just like one big, happy family — everybody was happy, everybody liked each other. It's not like that today.

BBS: *Let's talk about your sound films with Will Rogers.*

IR: The first one was *They Had to See Paris*. Do you know what date that was?

BBS: *It must have been in 1929, but I have no exact date.*

IR: Let me look in my little black diary. Ah, there it is, June 1929. Frank Borzage was the director. You see here, in May 1929, I was in vaudeville. I appeared in Yonkers, in Newark; I was in Brooklyn, in Boston, and at the Palace in New York. Then, in June, from the second to the fifth, I was at the RKO in New York, then at the RKO in Philadelphia, then to Baltimore, and after that I jumped out to the Coast, and did this film with Will Rogers. That ran, let's see, through June, July and into August. Then I went back and picked up my vaudeville tour. Then look! In Feb-

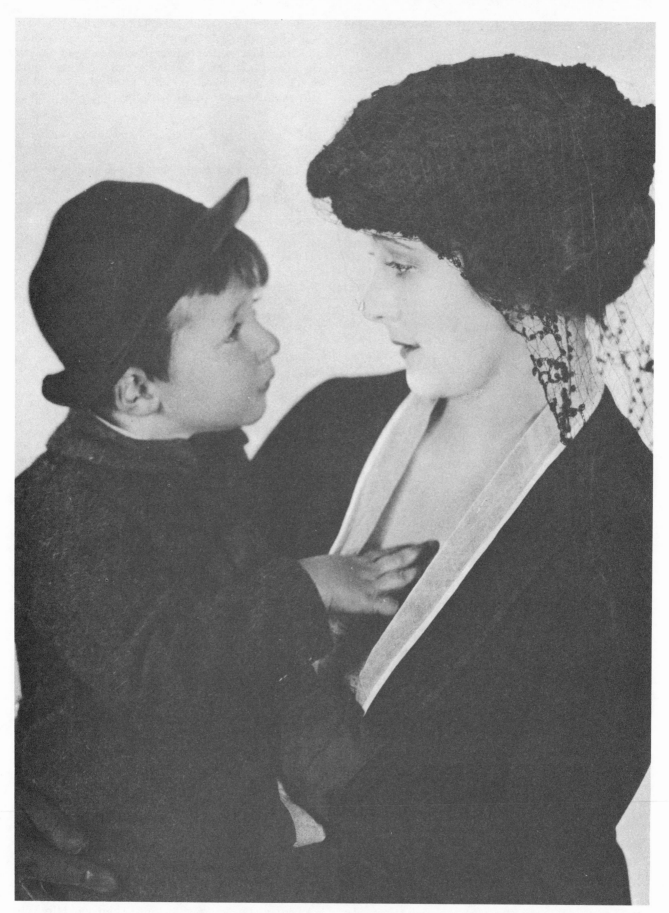

Irene Rich with an armful of young Jimmy Rogers.

Irene Rich between Will and Jimmy, circa 1920.

ruary, I stopped the tour again and did *So This Is London*. Let's see, it lasted all through February, March, April, up to the 27th of April. By this time I was getting $3,500 a week; that was a lot better than the $5 per day I got as an extra when I first started.

BBS: *Your next picture with Will Rogers was* Down to Earth.

IR: That started in April 1932 — April 14th. Isn't this little book wonderful? You know I played Will's wife so often, that some people thought we were really married. One time, crossing the Atlantic, Will was asked to make a little speech and after he had addressed the passengers, he was asked questions. One woman asked him to tell about Irene Rich. And Will quipped, "Oh, you mean my reel wife." The woman that asked the question later wrote me about it, and I thought it cute.

BBS: *Even though you made 14 films with Will Rogers, you probably saw him only rarely on the set, since he was always busy.*

IR: Now this may sound conceited for me to say, but it was told me that he would never sit and have lunch with the gang, except on the films that I was on. Mrs. Clarence Badger, the director's wife, told me that. She said, "Well, we'll have Will with us again at lunch, now that Irene's here." I think he sort of felt at home with me. I'm sure he never felt self-conscious. He'd just sit down and talk, just like one of the gang. And everybody adored him. There was never anything personal about it. The whole thing was just family — no gossip, no anything.

BBS: *Speaking about gossip, Louella Parsons used to write*

about Will Rogers occasionally, but she never said anything to hurt him.

IR: How could she? About him?

BBS: *In fact, she wrote him a marvelous letter. Will Rogers had addressed a convention of newspaperwomen in New York. Miss Parsons was one of the officers of that organization, and in her thank you letter, she said, "If there is ever anything you want me to do, just ask me; if you want to run for President, I know all of our ladies will vote for you."*

IR: That was nice of her, but I was just thinking that I haven't told you any jokes.

BBS: *I am not looking for jokes, perhaps an anecdote, or two, about your work, or Mr. Rogers' activities.*

IR: Well, there was one thing Will did in one picture we did together that was positively awful. I don't remember the name of the film, but I know it was silent. Will played the part of a woodsman, or something like that, and we had shot part of the film. He came in one morning after having his long hair cut the night before. Here he had gone through a door with long hair and was about to come out the other side with short hair. They had to paste on part of a wig on the back of his head. Everybody was just so upset. Then there was one other thing. He wouldn't let anybody put makeup on him. Well, it got so that he needed some, and he had a little bag with a powder puff in it, and he'd go way out behind a bush to put it on. He wouldn't let anybody see him do it. He had to put on just a little dab of powder, but no other makeup.

January 3, 1971

Evelyn Venable
Mohr and
Hal Mohr

Bryan B. Sterling: *Miss Venable, you appeared in two Will Rogers' films.*

Evelyn Venable Mohr: Yes, *David Harum* and *County Chairman*.

BBS: *Mr. Mohr, you were the director of cinematography on three Will Rogers' films.*

Hal Mohr: That's right, *David Harum*, that's the one Evelyn and I met on, *State Fair* and *County Chairman*.

BBS: *In those days life was easier in the studios, wasn't it?*

EVM: It was an awful lot of fun. There wasn't the terrible pressure of schedules. And of course, Will always took his time, whenever he wanted to.

HM: There is an expression I remember very well, that Will always used around 4 o'clock in the afternoon. He would say, "Mr. Cameraman, what time is it?" And when he was told that it was around 4 o'clock, he would shout out "Santa Monica Canyon!" and off he'd go.

BBS: *Didn't he also write his column on the set?*

HM: He had a roadster that he drove, I don't remember what it was, and he took that car wherever he went, even on location. He had his little typewriter in the back of it, and between takes and set-ups, he would sit there and peck at that typewriter, writing his daily column. Very often he would call Evelyn, or me, or both of us over, or whoever happened to be handy, and read it to us for reactions. He knew us well enough to know that we weren't conning him. If we liked it, we said so, and if we didn't like it too well, he'd rewrite it.

BBS: *I have heard that in the mornings he was quite preoccupied, until the column had been sent off.*

HM: That's right; he'd do scenes, of course, but the moment the take was finished, he was off to his little roadster which was parked nearby, and he'd get to work on the column again.

BBS: *What would he do in the afternoon between takes?*

HM: Oh, he would kid around and egg us on so we'd get through, so he could get back to Santa Monica Canyon. I think he just lived to get back to that canyon.

EVM: I don't blame him.

BBS: *Did Mr. Rogers have any preference as to camera angles, or a favorite side he wanted photographed?*

HM: No, Will didn't care how he looked. His choice of his staff and his crew was as to his personal feelings towards them. If he liked them as individuals, he enjoyed working with them. If he didn't like them as individuals, he wanted to get off the set and get out of there. It was my good fortune, and Evelyn's good fortune, that we worked with happy crews on the pictures we did with him. The director was James Cruze, the love of our life. He was, I think, the greatest man that ever lived in our industry. Too bad we don't have a few more of him. He directed *David*

Harum. And John Blystone, who was a lovely person, and Henry King did *State Fair*.

BBS: *All these films are still in existence. In fact,* County Chairman *was just recently on TV. Micky Rooney was in it, he was then a small boy.*

HM: The only two people for me that were in those films, were Evelyn Venable and Will Rogers. You know, I remember we were on location up at Sonora. Naturally, everywhere Rogers would go, the Chambers of Commerce, the Boards of Education, the various Women's Clubs would descend on him, trying to prevail upon him to come and speak to their organizations. So he finally said, "I'll put on a show for you. I'll do it at the auditorium of the high school, and you can all come to that." So Evelyn and I went with him, as well as a couple of other people from the cast. And he was up there, on that stage, for about two and a half hours, a steady solo show, except that he introduced the cast. It was a free show, but he worked just as hard as he ever did in the Follies; he was just magnificent.

BBS: *Were you under contract to Fox, Miss Venable?*

EVM: I was under contract to Paramount, and Fox borrowed me for *David Harum*, and about a year later, for *County Chairman*. As a matter of fact, they borrowed me in between for *The Little Colonel*, with Shirley Temple — Hal and I eloped during that one!

HM: Evelyn was a bit of a problem. She was known as the "Kissless Girl," as you may recall . . . or you may not recall. . . .

EVM: I would just as lief, nobody would recall!

HM: I think it's worthy of being told. Evelyn's father was a highly moral man, an educator, as indeed there are many generations of educators in her background. Well, the publicity department of the studio got a hold of that, and they started some whimsical story about the fact that, according to Evelyn's contract, she couldn't be kissed.

EVM: Isn't that silly! In every picture I was thoroughly kissed, and yet that story took hold, and a lot of people remember that more than anything else.

HM: So because of that, the studio was almost bound to cast her in that kind of picture. In a sense, she was typed as the virtuous, 19th-century ingenue. So when Evelyn was suddenly married, Louella Parsons had something in her unique way to say about it.

EVM: She had several things to say, none of them anything like what Will Rogers would have said.

HM: Will did everything in good taste. It seems a shame that a man like Will couldn't be perpetuated forever. He would have been terrific medicine for this period. I think today's kids would have listened to him. I think everybody would have listened.

EVM: He had some answers to offer, instead of just criticisms. He would have been just as great today.

HM: Will could get along with anybody. I remember driving out on location with him. It must have been

for *State Fair*. We drove out to the Mojave Desert, and we stopped for breakfast at Mojave, the entire motorcade stopped. Mojave was a rail junction with a large complement of hobos. As we were stopped, Will wandered over to the freight yards, and there were a bunch of 'bos. And he just sat down with them and talked with these fellows for over an hour, while the whole motorcade waited to proceed on location. He got all the money he could from everybody — Will never carried any money himself — and he distributed the money amongst these fellows, and went on his merry way. He was that kind of fellow.

BBS: *How was he to work with?*

EVM: Just darling! Just one thing — and I am sure you have heard this from other actors — he didn't follow the script.

HM: You never got your cues.

EVM: Exactly! You had to be on your toes. You had to dovetail what you were supposed to say into what he actually had said. You had to do that to make sense

and follow the story line. It was fun, because it gave a good deal of freshness to the scenes. But it was a little bit nerve racking, too.

BBS: *Did he ever break you up?*

EVM: Many times! But he broke himself up, too. Sometimes he'd say something totally irrelevant, something funny that had just occurred to him. But that was what was nice about pictures then; there wasn't the horrible, horrible pressure because of costs.

HM: Before the assembly line.

EVM: He kept along with the thread of the story, to whatever extent suited him at the moment.

HM: His ad-libs were improvements on the script. But the only actor that Will really had any difficulty with — well, it wasn't difficulty — he used to drive Will completely mad, was Stepin Fetchit. There was no antipathy there on Will's part, except that Step threw him, just the way Will would throw the rest of the cast. Let's say Step would have a line to say:

Will and Evelyn Venable in David Harum, *1934.*

153

"Well, how are you today?" So Step would go, "Weeeell, eh hmmmmm ehhhh hoooooowwww aaaaaare . . ." and would take forever to do it, and Will would stand there, with egg on his face, waiting for Step to get through with it.

BBS: *Did Mr. Rogers have any idiosyncrasies?*

HM: I do remember Will doing things, like knocking on wood when he went into a scene, or when he came out of a scene he thought was OK.

EVM: I remember when he liked a scene as it was played, he'd yell "Print it!" and he wouldn't do it again. He liked it just as it had been played.

BBS: *This sort of thing couldn't have been too easy on a director.*

EVM: I imagine it was a little difficult on a certain type of director; that's one of the reasons we liked Jim Cruze.

HM: And Will loved Jim Cruze too, because Jim was so sure of what he wanted, and, occasionally Jim would let Will do what he wanted, knowing that Will knew what to do. For example, Will hated to do scenes over again, and we had a night scene coming up in Inglewood. I think it was in *David Harum*. Now Jim Cruze was notorious for driving the production units insane, because he was always ahead of schedule. They couldn't keep up with him, making the sets fast enough. We'd break for lunch, for example, and Jim Cruze would say to me, "Stall for about 20 minutes when we get back, or we'll run out of work." So I would stall around on my lighting, which was unusual. We were always through with the day's work around 2:30 or 3 o'clock in the afternoon. The production office went insane. So, as I said, we had this one long night sequence to do out in Inglewood, at the railroad station. Will is supposed to come up on the train, get off at the station in a rainstorm and be met by Stepin Fetchit with a wagon. He gets into the wagon; they have a couple of lines of dialogue, and then they drive off. In preparation for this, they had dinner ordered for us, and midnight lunches, and all that sort of thing. The only reason I tell this story is because it's the sort of thing Will loved. We finished the daylight work about 3 o'clock in the afternoon, and we told Will to be at the station as soon as it got dark, and we'd be ready to go. In the meantime, we went out to Inglewood in the afternoon and walked through the scene at the train. We got it all set up, got it lit, got the rain pipes in place. I had two cameras on the thing, one to get the long shot of the train pulling on up, and one to get the close shot, shooting across at Step. So, just as it got dusk, we started the rain. Will was on the train; Step was in position with the wagon, and the train pulled up. Now mind you, this is before it was dark — and that was the only take of the scene. Will got in the wagon, they pulled away, and Jim Cruze yelled, "Keep going, Will!" and we all were home in time for dinner. Now Will loved that sort of picture making. He adored Jim for that reason.

BBS: *I see you have an autographed picture of Will Rogers hanging on the wall. What is the inscription?*

EVM: It says, "From the old matchmaker, with affection and good wishes to Evelyn and Hal, from Will Rogers." He was kind of interested in the fact that we met on *David Harum*, and then a year later, we did *County Chairman* just immediately before we were married.

HM: Of course, Will was not actually the matchmaker, he liked to call himself that; he felt responsible in a way, but I think it was chemistry beyond Rogers, or anybody else. But something of Will Rogers rubbed off on everybody. Most of the people who were around Will were pretty decent people, but some of his philosophy would rub off on you. Now Will and I didn't agree politically, but there was so much about the man that you had to admire, that you unconsciously tried to emulate a lot of his thinking.

Director of cinematography, Hal Mohr.

January 4, 1971

Patricia

Ziegfeld

Stephenson

Bryan B. Sterling: *Will Rogers thought of you almost as one of his own children.*

Patricia Ziegfeld Stephenson: He was such fun. The first year we came to California, he just did everything he could to make us like the place — and we certainly did. We used to go up to the ranch.

BBS: *What year was that?*

PZS: Late 1929, or early 1930, shortly after the stock market crash. Daddy came out to do *Whoopee* for Sam Goldwyn. When we came out here, we rented Marion Davies' guest house at the beach, which was very near the ranch. I was up there almost every day to ride with a girl friend, and Will Rogers gave us each a horse we could ride any time we wanted to. And, of course, he was there, except when he travelled.

BBS: *Were you close to his daughter Mary?*

PZS: We were friends. When we first moved here, Mary was just at the age when she started to date and go out, and I was just a little behind. She was wearing high heels, and I wasn't, and I bugged mother about it.

BBS: *Did Will Rogers ever come to your house?*

PZS: Oh, yes. The Rogers came — Will loved to swim. I don't think anyone ever thinks of him as a swimmer. We had a pool at the house and Will would dive. You see, there was no pool at the ranch. They did have a pool when they lived in Beverly Hills. Will loved to clown in the water, race out on the diving board, plunge into the water — always that marvelous twinkle in his eyes. There was something special in those china-blue eyes.

BBS: *When you came to California, had you already met Will Rogers in the East?*

PZS: I had met Mr. Rogers. He used to come down to Palm Beach occasionally when he was going through. And I had met him backstage, when he was in the Follies. But I had never met Mrs. Rogers before, or Bill, Mary and Jim. It wasn't until we got out to California that we all got together. Aunt Betty was very shy and didn't go 'round too much.

BBS: *Yet she was really the manager in the family, wasn't she?*

PZS: Yes, but she had a very quiet way about her as she held the reins.

BBS: *Did Mrs. Rogers handle the finances?*

PZS: I guess so, though Will was pretty smart. He did buy a lot of real estate that was in the right spot at the right time. He always said to my father, "Put your money in land, Flo. Put your money in land!"

BBS: *Tell me about your visits to the ranch.*

PZS: He was such a warm person. I always felt at ease with him. He was always kidding you; he was such fun. He would always say, "C'mon, let's do some roping!" or, "Let's go and catch a steer!" And he was such a dear after Daddy died. He took Mother and me up to the ranch, and we spent about a week up there. Then the Olympics were that year in Los Angeles, and he gave us tickets. We went every day to the games. Mother adored Will. Next to my father, he was her favorite.

BBS: *You know, of course, that Will Rogers always gave your father credit for discovering him. He said, "If it hadn't been for Mr. Ziegfeld, I would be today 12 miles North of Claremore, Oklahoma, slopping the hogs, and plowing for corn."*

PZS: Daddy perhaps broadened his act by pointing out the things that were of greater entertainment value. Otherwise, perhaps, he might have been known as the greatest of ropers.

BBS: *Is it true that there never was a contract between your father and Will Rogers?*

PZS: As far as I know, there never was — they never had any written agreement, just a handshake. They were great friends, and I do not ever remember them having any problems. If they did, they ironed them out very quickly, because they had a mutual admiration society going.

BBS: *Were you ever at the ranch when Charles Lindbergh and Anne Morrow were there?*

PZS: No. But Howard Hughes used to come up and see Mary. He would land his little plane on the polo field. He was always around, and I was always around. He was great fun and would always pop in. I remember one time, we were going East, and he met the train at some out-of-the-way place. He was a very shy young man. But they always had the most interesting people up at the ranch.

BBS: *Is this the trowel used at the dedication of the Ziegfeld Theatre?*

PZS: Yes, it needs resilvering.

BBS: *What year was that?*

PZS: It says on the trowel, "December 9, 1926." Mother and I used it. Will Rogers was there, and he saw that I was not very charmed with the whole procedure. It was cold, and there wasn't much going on, so he said, "Here, Patricia, have a piece of gum." So I was chewing the gum merrily, and my mother caught me, "What are you doing with that gum in your mouth?" I thought it would be perfectly all right if I said that Mr. Rogers had given it to me. But it wasn't. She said, "Spit it out!" But I tucked it up on the roof of my mouth, because it was sort of a sacred piece of gum, because Will Rogers had given it to me.

January 4, 1971

Form 1227 B

CLASS OF SERVICE DESIRED	
TELEGRAM	
DAY LETTER	
NIGHT MESSAGE	
NIGHT LETTER	

Patrons should mark an X opposite the class of service desired; OTHERWISE THE MESSAGE WILL BE TRANSMITTED AS A FULL-RATE TELEGRAM

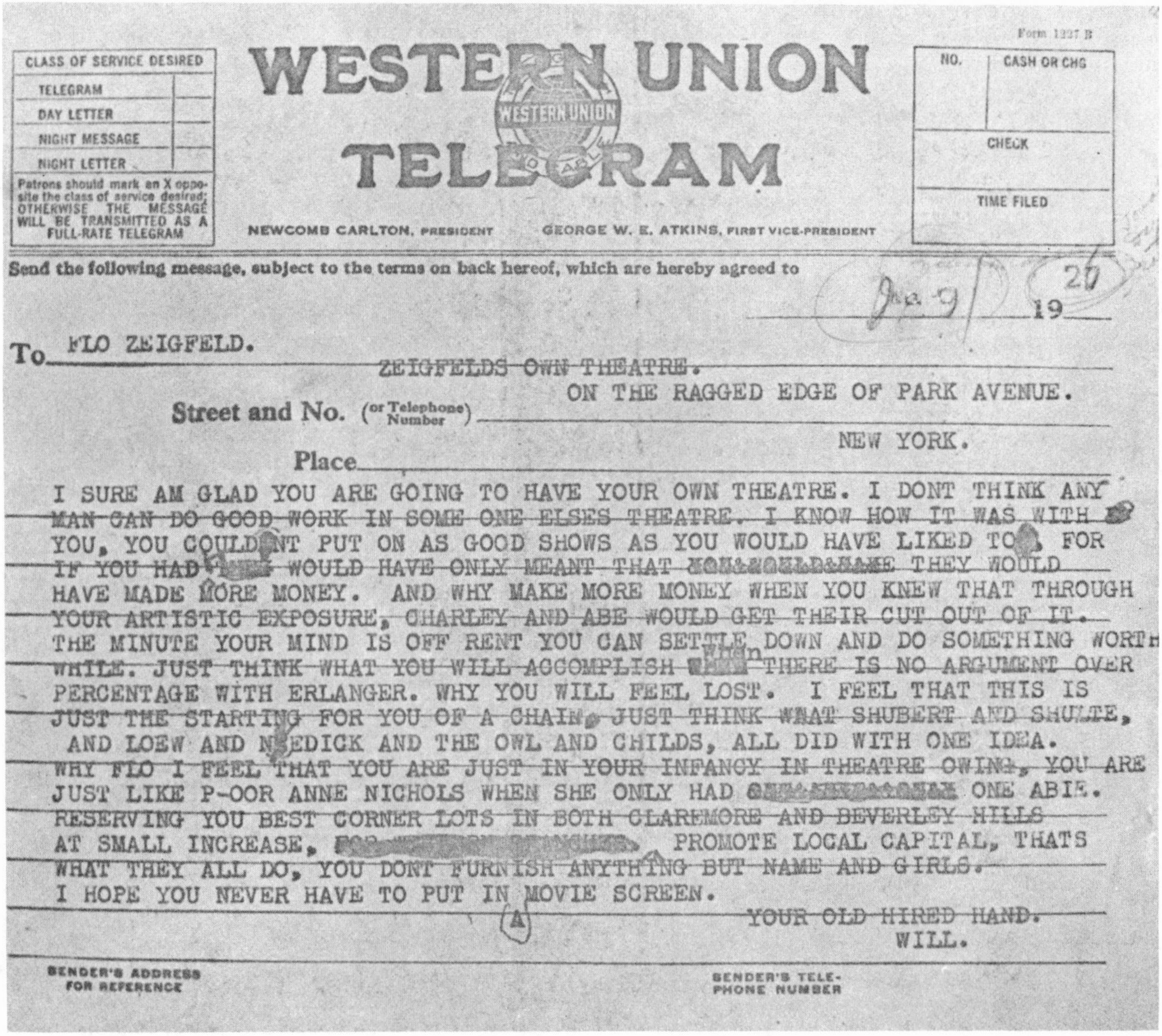

WESTERN UNION TELEGRAM

NEWCOMB CARLTON, PRESIDENT GEORGE W. E. ATKINS, FIRST VICE-PRESIDENT

NO.	CASH OR CHG
CHECK	
TIME FILED	

Send the following message, subject to the terms on back hereof, which are hereby agreed to

Dec 9 1920

To FLO ZEIGFELD.
ZEIGFELDS OWN THEATRE.
Street and No. (or Telephone Number) ON THE RAGGED EDGE OF PARK AVENUE.
Place NEW YORK.

I SURE AM GLAD YOU ARE GOING TO HAVE YOUR OWN THEATRE. I DONT THINK ANY MAN CAN DO GOOD WORK IN SOME ONE ELSES THEATRE. I KNOW HOW IT WAS WITH YOU, YOU COULDNT PUT ON AS GOOD SHOWS AS YOU WOULD HAVE LIKED TO, FOR IF YOU HAD [illegible] WOULD HAVE ONLY MEANT THAT [illegible] THEY WOULD HAVE MADE MORE MONEY. AND WHY MAKE MORE MONEY WHEN YOU KNEW THAT THROUGH YOUR ARTISTIC EXPOSURE, CHARLEY AND ABE WOULD GET THEIR CUT OUT OF IT. THE MINUTE YOUR MIND IS OFF RENT YOU CAN SETTLE DOWN AND DO SOMETHING WORTH WHILE. JUST THINK WHAT YOU WILL ACCOMPLISH when THERE IS NO ARGUMENT OVER PERCENTAGE WITH ERLANGER. WHY YOU WILL FEEL LOST. I FEEL THAT THIS IS JUST THE STARTING FOR YOU OF A CHAIN, JUST THINK WHAT SHUBERT AND SHULTE, AND LOEW AND NEDICK AND THE OWL AND CHILDS, ALL DID WITH ONE IDEA. WHY FLO I FEEL THAT YOU ARE JUST IN YOUR INFANCY IN THEATRE OWING, YOU ARE JUST LIKE P-OOR ANNE NICHOLS WHEN SHE ONLY HAD [illegible] ONE ABIE. RESERVING YOU BEST CORNER LOTS IN BOTH CLAREMORE AND BEVERLEY HILLS AT SMALL INCREASE, [illegible]. PROMOTE LOCAL CAPITAL, THATS WHAT THEY ALL DO, YOU DONT FURNISH ANYTHING BUT NAME AND GIRLS. I HOPE YOU NEVER HAVE TO PUT IN MOVIE SCREEN.

YOUR OLD HIRED HAND.
WILL.

SENDER'S ADDRESS FOR REFERENCE

SENDER'S TELEPHONE NUMBER

(Left to right) Patricia Ziegfeld, Will, Billie Burke (Mrs. Florenz Ziegfeld), 1933.

Myrna Loy

Myrna Loy: I started at Warner Brothers around 1925, shortly before talking pictures. At first I played Orientals, then wicked ladies. I wasn't really a star, but I was costarred then. You know, there is a style of leading ladies, there still is, but not perhaps as much as there was at that time. At that time, I didn't fit into that category, that style of virginal leading lady. Leading ladies were all virginal, like Dolores Costello. I, with my slanty eyes and my sense of humor — which was unforgiveable — seemed to fit into the category of "doubtful ladies." I guess that's why I seemed right for Morgan Le Fey, the wicked queen in *A Connecticut Yankee*.

Bryan B. Sterling: *When you were first told about A* Connecticut Yankee, *and that Will Rogers would be in it, did it in any way affect your thinking?*

ML: I was thrilled, of course! Also, I knew the material, and there was a quality of the fantastic about it that appealed to me very much. I was very pleased.

BBS: *Do you recall anything about Will Rogers on the set?*

ML: I remember him on the set, in the commissary. I remember him outside, in his automobile, when he would whistle as I went by. He was a shy man; his head was down; I think he was especially shy with women. Of course, I was pretty young in those days, scared and very shy myself. I remember that he used to like to tease me about my freckles and red hair. I remember once hearing that sharp whistle, and then a "Yahooo!" and I looked around, and there he was,

passing in the car. Then, of course, I remember distinctly one of the scenes we were playing. I don't recall exactly what I was supposed to be up to, but apparently I was trying to lead him astray. That's where they used the "blushing." The film was in black and white, but they decided to tint his face, so obviously I was making passes at him. But he was charming, an attractive man, really wonderful. Unfortunately, I didn't know him very well. I was only in a small segment of the picture. Therefore, I wasn't there very long, and I didn't have many scenes with him. I recall vividly the scene where I condemn him. I guess it must have been pretty awful, from the standpoint of an actress; I don't think it was very good.

BBS: *Speaking of the "blushing scene," it says here:* "Queen Morgan Le Fey becomes enamoured of Sir Boss, and her protestations of affection and admiration result in Sir Boss's suddenly blushing a violent red."

ML: Aha! So there it is. Then that would be all the more reason, when he wouldn't do what she wanted him to do — she got mad at him and condemned him to death. I would like to see the film again, but I have given up. I was told that it had been burned.

BBS: *That's what we all thought. But 20th-Century Fox found a copy in a vault in Australia, and they now have a complete set of Will Rogers' sound films.*

ML: Then there is a chance to see it.

April 6, 1971

Sterling
Holloway

Bryan B. Sterling: *You were under contract to Fox Studio?*

Sterling Holloway: The only contract I ever signed was to do Will Rogers pictures.

BBS: *Did Mr. Rogers select you?*

SH: I don't know whether he did, or not. But all I ever did at Fox was Will Rogers pictures. And I had never signed any other contract before; I didn't want to be tied down.

BBS: *I would say that he selected you, because he liked working with certain people.*

SH: He called me "The boy." He would say, "All right, put the camera on the boy! I got to go and write my column!" And then, about 4:30, he would say, "OK. Now comes the window shot!" Which meant that he quit. Hot or cold, around 4:30 he wouldn't do another thing. And why he called it the "window shot," I really don't know, unless you just looked out the window and saw him going home.

BBS: *Tell me, was he temperamental?*

SH: Not at all! Not a bit. He was like a child in a lot of ways. I know when he was doing his column, his squib, he would come and read it to me on the set. He'd say, "Look, I just did this for tomorrow." And he'd be so pleased when it worked, when you liked it, when he got a laugh from you.

BBS: *If you didn't like it, would he rewrite it?*

SH: I don't remember ever not liking one. I stood in great awe of him.

BBS: *Do you recall the film* Doubting Thomas?

SH: That was originally *The Torch Bearers.*

BBS: *You appeared in it with Miss Billie Burke.*

SH: The strange thing about that film was that there were mostly stage actors, people who really knew what they were doing. Of course, Will Rogers was from the stage, too, but he was not an actor, as such. And this cast just acted all around him, and it seemed that he was just there. But when the film was shown on the screen, none of the others meant anything. You couldn't take your eyes off Will Rogers. He was just such a great personality, and he was a great entertainer. It really amazed me, because you thought he was just shuffling through the part — that it really wasn't going to count — but it sure did. And how!

BBS: *I have heard it said that Will Rogers was slow to respond to the director's call.*

SH: Yes, he used to say, "Make 'em call you three times!"

BBS: *You also appeared with Will Rogers in* Life Begins At Forty.

SH: I think it was in that picture, we were doing a scene, and I was the hired boy, or whatever, and we had to go out and shoot at a blue jay that was troublesome up in a tree. The prop man handed the gun to Will Rogers, and he gave it to me, saying, "Let the boy do it!" Finally I said, "I don't know what to do here. You will have to show me. I've never handled a gun in my life." He said, "Neither have I." Now here was the picture of the Westerner, who didn't know what to do with a gun. And in that same picture, he had a fishing scene and had to bait the hook, and again, he said, "What do we do? I've never caught a fish in my life."

BBS: *Will Rogers didn't believe in shooting animals, or fishing, either.*

SH: I was doing another scene with him once. I had to carry a chicken down the street; it was a crowded street, and the chicken was flapping its wings and kicking hard. Will Rogers looked at me and said, "You know, you're holding it the wrong way. You know, if you hold that chicken the right way, you won't have any trouble." So I asked him, "What is the right way?" And Will Rogers said innocently, "I haven't any idea."

BBS: *Did Will Rogers know his lines when he came on the set?*

SH: No, he didn't. He would say, "What's the sense of this scene here now?" And he would just get an idea of it.

BBS: *Then actually the lines were his own?*

SH: Mostly.

BBS: *Wasn't this hard on the other actors?*

SH: It wasn't for me. It fascinated me, and I loved it and I played right along with it, which is maybe the reason I was in a few of his films. And I can guarantee that whatever he did was better, because it was strictly Will Rogers and that's what they wanted, and everybody loved it. It was always a happy set, and actors were always trying to get on a Will Rogers picture. It was, as they say, "no sweat." I remember he would come to me and say, "Now, in this scene I will say so-and-so, and when I do, you ask me 'why?'" He would just set up a special gag in a scene. So we played the scene, and he would say what he had arranged, and I'd be surprised and "But why?" and he would have an excellent comeback ready for it. But he wouldn't rehearse them, he didn't like to give them away. He liked to please everybody — he was strictly a showman, an entertainer. He was an intuitive performer; he knew exactly what was right. No director really ever could tell him how to do something. He knew the "how," always.

BBS: *Isn't it strange to think that there was a time when a mature man and a little girl, Shirley Temple, were Fox's biggest stars?*

SH: I remember Shirley well. She would come over to our set a lot, when we were working. I can just see her in a little white coat with a white ermine collar, and Will Rogers saying, "That's my girl!" I think I met Shirley at the Rogers ranch once, and we went for a long walk together.

BBS: *I understand that Will Rogers was very liberal with his money, and that if anyone needed money, all they had to do was ask him.*

SH: I heard that, and I know that he took care of different people on the set, you know, the grips, and so on, if he heard that some wife was in a hospital, or something like that.

BBS: *Did you ever see him nap on the set?*

SH: I don't think so. One time I saw him sitting and somebody asked, "Is he sleeping?" And somebody else said, "Are you kidding? That man's mind is going a mile a minute."

December 31, 1971

David Butler

Bryan B. Sterling: *You directed five pictures with Will Rogers.*

David Butler: That's right: *Business and Pleasure, Down to Earth, A Connecticut Yankee, Handy Andy* and *Doubting Thomas.*

BBS: *You must know his working habits pretty well.*

DB: He would usually peck out his column before lunch, then come on the set and read it to everybody. Before noon he would concentrate a little more on the column than on the work.

BBS: *Do you remember that Mr. Rogers used to improvise his lines.*

DB: He had quite a time with his lines. He would branch off. You see, he learned them, but they weren't written in his language. He improved his lines. He was remarkable that way.

BBS: *Wouldn't that throw off his fellow actors?*

DB: They knew what to expect when they started with him — no cues. But you could just throw a close-up in, and start over again. We had two cameras, anyway, so when he got too long-winded, we'd just cut in. But he never liked retakes. He just wanted to do the scene, and that was that. He wanted to get back home again. He was a peculiar guy that way. He always wanted to get off at 4:30, but if I'd ask him to stay longer, he would. He was a nice guy and would do anything to help. We always made the pictures on time with him; we never went over. I never saw him moody. Some days he would clown a lot, and other days he would just go about his business. But he was always talking, from morning till night. He would never stop — he talked to everybody.

BBS: *During his years at Fox, he was always among the top five money-makers, and in 1934, he was number one.*

DB: Yes, his pictures always made money, and they didn't cost too much to make. The film *Connecticut Yankee* did, because it was a costume picture, but that made a lot of money. They played that in every language — Japanese, Chinese, and everything else. In fact we saw the rushes of Will speaking Japanese. They'd get a company speaking Japanese, a company speaking Spanish, a German company, and they would dub it right here. It was *very* funny. Will and I saw the Japanese version while the company was doing it. Will nearly died laughing — it made everybody laugh.

BBS: *Miss Myrna Loy mentioned that you tinted part of* Connecticut Yankee.

DB: That was my idea. You see, they had no color, and she kissed Will, and he had to blush. The only way they could do it was to have a little Japanese girl tint every single frame progressively darker pink. This little girl had to do that on every print we sent out.

BBS: *In the silent version of* Connecticut Yankee, *the rescuing army used motorcycles. What made you use small automobiles?*

DB: I came up with the idea of using "Baby Austins." They told me I could never get them, but I did. I got them through the agency, and we paid them $25 a day, and gave them back to the agency which deducted that from the price. But I don't think they were worth a quarter by the time we finished with them. I had the USC [University of Southern California] football team in them. My God, what they did to those cars and costumes!

BBS: *Do you know that you directed more sound films with Will Rogers than any other director?*

DB: The funny part of it is that the pictures that kept Fox Studio alive were the films of Will Rogers and Shirley Temple. Not because of me, don't misunderstand me. But Will Rogers wanted me to direct him; Shirley wanted me to direct her; and then Will Rogers wanted me again. So I was between the two of them all the time. Which made it a very wonderful career for me, because they were both wonderful people.

BBS: *Do you recall the day the news came of Will Rogers' death?*

DB: I'll never forget that morning as long as I live. Some fellow from the newspapers woke me up and asked me for a statement. And I said, "About what?" When he told me, I threw the phone right up in the air. I couldn't believe it.

January 6, 1972

Henry King

Henry King: In July 1930, I went with Fox, and the first assignment I had before signing a full contract was a special contract just to do a picture with Will Rogers. That was the Frank Bacon show *Lightnin'*. You see, Frank Bacon, who had written the show, played it for over 20 years all over the country, and Rogers was thinking in terms of the way Frank Bacon had played it. And Rogers said that he could never imitate Bacon. So I told him, "Suppose we just let it be Will Rogers playing that part."

Bryan B. Sterling: *How would you best describe Mr. Rogers?*

HK: You know the line, "I never met a man I didn't like"; well, that was the thing he stood by. That was the way he lived. And you couldn't help liking him. He had a great personality. And even though he was shy, he had the ability to get to you, and for you to understand him.

BBS: *You also directed Mr. Rogers in* State Fair.

HK: I went to Des Moines, Iowa, to the State Fair to buy three hogs. One that won first prize, called "Blue Boy" in the film, and I bought two understudies — just in case anything happened to Blue Boy. I tried to keep this rather quiet until I could telephone the studio to tell them that I had bought these hogs and to get the publicity department to break the story. But the *Des Moines Register* was too smart for me. The next morning they had the story on the front page, with pictures of Will Rogers and the hog.

BBS: *These hogs were obviously not specially trained, not like the usual film animals. Weren't you worried about having Will Rogers handle such animals?*

HK: Of course you'd never know what to expect of any of these boars, but the thing that relieved me completely was an incident I observed. Rogers didn't go to lunch at noon, when we stopped. I went to the restaurant and did the things a director has to do, you know, a lot of little details, preparing for the afternoon's work. Well, when I came back onto the set, looking for Will, I passed Blue Boy's pen, and there he was. Blue Boy was asleep, and so was Will — sound asleep, using Blue Boy for a pillow. From that time on I never worried about Blue Boy hurting Will. When we woke Will, he said, "I think Blue Boy likes me." Now I would never have done that, but Rogers would slap him on the back, and rub him, and sit on him, or lean against him or walk around him. He had absolutely no fear of animals.

BBS: *In general, how would you describe your experience of working with Will Rogers.*

HK: Will was a lot of help on a picture. He was unpredictable. When you rehearsed through the scenes, he would stumble over lines and walk all around, and then something came to him in the middle of a scene, and he'd just say it. But it would so fit, it would be so in character with what he was doing, that there was never any discord — it was always the real thing. That was the thing that some actors became confused

with. Now you take Louise Dresser. When she worked with him, she got so accustomed to this, the two of them went on in little ad-libbed conversations of their own — still about the story. I would sit back, holding my sides to keep from laughing. In fact, two or three times I almost spoiled the scene myself. For instance, in *State Fair* we had a sideshow at the carnival that goes along with a state fair, that had these dancing girls. Now I wanted a scene where these girls would just pass through, with just a couple of little remarks, one to the other. Will Rogers looked at the girl, and she looked at him — well, he made a monologue, and she was the straight man, feeding him lines in a scene which ran for six or seven minutes, which is a long time on film. It was a great joy to work with him. Especially after you have worked in films for years, where you become so pedantic about this and that and the other, and then you find this man so completely relaxed at all times. Except on one occasion. That was in *Lightnin'*. There was one thing that disturbed him terribly. He didn't know whether to speak to me directly, but I knew he was disturbed about something. I didn't find out what bothered him until we got back to the studio from location. You see, the locale of the film is a divorce colony, Calneva, where all these people go for their divorce — you know, the six weeks' residence in Nevada. So when we got up there, we met a number of people that Rogers knew, and a number of people that I knew, as we say, "doing time." They told us what they did to amuse themselves, and how they spent their waiting time. So I said, "Let's put them in the picture!" They were mostly all women — a man who went up there for a divorce was looked down upon. So I arranged these women in bathing suits, spread out all over for atmosphere. And, as I said, I knew something was irking Rogers, but I didn't know what. Well, when he came back to Hollywood, he went to see Winnie Sheehan, the head of Fox Studio, and he said he hoped that Henry King wasn't going to show these girls lying around in these swimming suits — we didn't have bikinis in those days. Rogers said that he had never been in a picture that had half-dressed women.

BBS: *In the film you don't show any of these scenes. Mr. Rogers must have made his point. You do refer to them in dialogue, but they are not seen.*

HK: There are one or two scenes where we do show them, stretched out in the background, but not in the foreground.

BBS: *But I have seen a number of publicity stills which show a whole line of these bathing beauties.*

HK: Naturally! You turn a cameraman loose, and you know he's going to put something on that film. He's not going to let it go blank.

BBS: *I have repeatedly heard that it was difficult to get him to come on the set.*

HK: He was very punctual. But the trouble with Rogers was that he wrote that column. He had to

have that column out before noon. And he would come to me and he'd say, "I have to have a few minutes; you're not going to need me, are you?" And I'd tell him, "No, Will, that's fine." Well later, when we would call him — you see, if he got the idea of what he was going to write about, and he started to write, why, you couldn't pry him loose till he had finished that little column. Then, of course, the great delight was that he always wondered if his column was any good. So we had to be his audience. I'll never forget what Janet Gaynor said one time. We were working out here, just this side of Riverside, and Janet Gaynor came to me one day and said, "Isn't this wonderful? Just imagine, people all over the country will read this column tomorrow. And we are here and hear him read it first, before anyone ever sees it!"

BBS: *Did you ever see him rewrite a column?*

HK: I never saw him do that. His mind was so quick; he knew what to write. To show you how quick his mind was, let me tell you a story. A prominent man from San Francisco had a home at Tahoe, and he gave a dinner for us at his house. There were Louise Dresser, Joel McCrea, Rogers, Helen Cohan, George M. Cohan's daughter, and I, — oh, about 15 or 16 in all. Now everywhere, everyone always wanted to hear Will Rogers speak. Of course for us, being around him, it was sort of contagious; you wanted to hear him and you couldn't get enough. So at this dinner, they insisted on Rogers making a speech. Well, Rogers suggested that everyone talk a little, and he kept saying, "How about you!" till everybody said something. You had better say something, or he would have kidded the life out of you. He just kept urging everyone around that table, "Now you better say your piece, nobody came here just to hear me talk." Finally it got around to him; he was the last. And what he had done was that out of all the people around the table he had accumulated enough ideas in his mind to make a marvelous continuity — his mind worked as quickly as that! If he had a scene to do, you'd see him off to one side, talking to himself — you know, jab, jab, jab — then finally he'd say, "I've got it now!" That mind was always working. Or take an amusing scene we got a lot of fun out of in *State Fair*, when he was supposed to be concerned about Blue Boy. This was the day of the judging, and Blue Boy hadn't been feeling well. You may remember that we had them living in the camp at the State Fair. They were about to have breakfast and were worrying about Blue Boy as they sat down at the breakfast table. Norman Foster was playing the son; Louise Dresser was the mother; Janet Gaynor was playing the daughter; then Will says Grace, and ends up with, "Bless - us - oh - Lord - I - wonder - how - Blue - Boy - is - doing-now?" You know, all in one breath. It just broke all of us up.

BBS: *Was Will Rogers usually on time in the mornings?*

HK: In the morning the son-of-a-gun would always meet you on the set. He'd be there ahead of you, walking around, snooping around the set for props.

He loved props. If there was a scene he had, sometimes he would say, "This darn script! You don't expect me to take these words too serious, do you?" "No," I'd tell him. "They are all in fun." But if he could find a pair of scissors, he could find more things to do with them. He used his props like all good actors. And I tell you, whether he was a good actor, or not, he sure knew how to use props.

BBS: *How would you describe his acting talent?*

HK: Well, take a three-year-old child. It obviously doesn't know anything about acting schools; yet they are the greatest actors in the world. That's exactly the way Will Rogers was. He just had an instinct, and he just followed that instinct that prompted him every minute through everything he did. That is to me the highest and greatest form of acting there is. So much has been said and written about acting, yet Rogers was probably the beginning of the school "Don't try to act; be it!"

BBS: *Did you ever play polo with Will Rogers?*

HK: No, I never did. I used to be quite a rider, but I never had time to go in for polo. But I did see them play a great deal; Zanuck used to· play with Rogers, and Jack Warner, Hal Roach used to be a good polo player; so was Frank Borzage. Of course Will Rogers' polo was totally different. He'd get the ball playing, and he'd start yelling, slapping the horse with his hat, and riding like a Comanche.

BBS: *Did you ever see Mr. Rogers take a drink?*

HK: Never in my life. We would go over to the Cal-Neva Lodge. Will loved to play roulette. We'd go over there for dinner, because they had very good food. And Will and Betty and I, sometimes Joel McCrea would go along, sometimes Winnie Sheehan, when he came up for a couple of days; well, anyway, we would go over there and Will would play roulette. Now Rogers never lost any money; maybe he'd win a few dollars. He didn't play for very much; it was just the fun of playing. Now this was during prohibition, and the manager of Cal-Neva was so grateful for Rogers coming over there — that was the big attraction for him — that every night, when I would leave there, as I put my coat on, it would be heavy like lead, and there, in my coat pocket, would be a new bottle of Scotch!

BBS: *So very little has been written about Mrs. Rogers. Did you get to know her?*

HK: She was one of the nicest, sweetest women — lovely, and the ideal wife for Will Rogers. I knew her quite well; she was a remarkable person. And Rogers was a great family man. He would bring Jimmy to the studio, sometimes Mary would come out. You know, he had what he called his "fund raising suit." He said, "I just put on my blue serge and a black tie!" And that was his way of dressing up. That's what he'd wear when he went to these dinners and benefits, and he was asked to appear at many benefits. But here is a story he told me himself — and you were asking about Mrs. Rogers. He was invited to a special dinner, almost like a command performance. Naturally he was asked to address the guests. When he was finished, he gave 'em a bill for $500! And they said, "Why, Will, you were our guest! This was just a little social gathering!" And Will said, "No, it wasn't. I was a paid speaker! If it had been a social gathering, my wife would have been invited!" Now whether he took the $500 or not, I really don't know. But I do know that if he went someplace and his wife was with him, he would tell stories and entertain. But he didn't want to do it when she was not there.

BBS: *You also shared your interest in flying with Will Rogers.*

HK: You know, Rogers had a peculiarity about airplanes. He didn't care much about being a pilot, but he liked to fly. And if you said you were a pilot, that was fine; he'd get right in there with you. He trusted everyone. He told me about his trip to China and Russia, to Harbin and to Peking, and clear on into India. He told about a Chinese pilot with a trimotor Ford plane. He said that they flew so low, that he was sure the Chinese must have been thinking he ran, "not a plane, but a lawn mower!" Rogers said, "I've flown low before, but during this flight I was closer to China than I was to the sky! I think our wheels were touching the ground all the way!"

BBS: *As a highly experienced pilot yourself, what opinion have you formed about the accident?*

HK: Wiley Post was putting his airplane together out at a little hangar at the south side of Lockheed Airport. It's been added to now, and you can't recognize it. I kept an airplane out there for forty years, so I know the airport very well. Will Rogers used to go out there and sit on the fence, while Wiley Post was working on the plane, putting it together. Now you talk about a conglomeration! This was an Orion fuselage, with Sirius wings, and Pratt Whitney loaned him the engine for the trip. The engine was twice as big as the airplane was built for; it had half again as much horsepower. Post changed the Orion wings because they had retractable gear, and the Sirius wings had fixed gear. That way he could put floats on it, or skis. He had floats on it when they had the accident. Whenever Rogers had any time off, he'd run out to Burbank, and he'd sit there on the fence and crack jokes with Wiley, while Wiley was under the airplane or inside the airplane. I used to go out there with him and see what was going on. Now Post was another great character, but there was a certain closeness between those two; there was something about them, just like twin brothers. And Rogers would have this line of chatter of his, and he'd sit there and keep Wiley Post laughing, and him working all the time. Once in a while Rogers would help him a little with something; he wouldn't know what he was doing, except hold something for Post. And that's the way that airplane was put together.

BBS: *That plane was nose-heavy, as I am sure you know.*

HK: Post had to get Will to sit as far back as possible to get it up, and to get it down. The theory is now that that was in part responsible for the crash. Joe Crosson, who flew the bodies back, had a theory of what happened after they landed in that little, shallow inlet. Wiley Post was like those early fliers who believed that an airplane could do anything they wanted it to do. They had carburetors then; they didn't have fuel injection, like they do now. Rogers and Post stopped at this inlet just long enough to have some ice form in the carburetor. Then, to get out of the shallow water, Post just raised her up steeply; the engine coughed, stalled and jackknifed, and dove right back down. It just shows what can happen if you begin to think that you have control all the time. It's fine if nothing happens, but . . . I used to fly test flights for the Air Force, after General Westover was killed out here, checking on carburetor icing. I would say that there are more monuments in aviation erected on account of carburetor ice, in that period, than for any other reason.

BBS: *It also shows that the plane wasn't well enough balanced to glide.*

HK: Any airplane, when you pull it up in a complete stall like that, and then chop the power, is going to jackknife.

BBS: *I was also told that Wiley Post was advised not to fly that day, August 15, 1935. That the weather was too treacherous. But that he replied that all he had to see was the take-off and the landing sites; that he could fly to Point Barrow above the clouds.*

HK: Well, he came down all right, but he was afraid that he would overshoot it. And they told him that he was still 15 miles from Point Barrow. I remember so well the first time I saw Betty Rogers after the accident. She had come to this restaurant and was having lunch. I walked over, and she reached up and put her hand up to me, and I was not able to utter a single word. She had a sort of smile, yet you knew what was behind it. Neither of us said anything. I must have stood there for two or three minutes. And neither of us ever said one word. I couldn't, or I would have made a baby out of myself. Just looking at that woman, knowing what was on her mind, was one of the most moving moments I ever experienced in my life.

January 14, 1972

John Ford

Bryan B. Sterling: *You made three motion pictures with Mr. Rogers,* Dr. Bull, Judge Priest *and* Steamboat 'Round the Bend.

John Ford: That's correct.

BBS: *Well, the only story I have so far about* Dr. Bull *is the one told me by Andy Devine, who said that Will Rogers introduced him on that set to his future wife. And they are both still happily married.*

JF: She is a fine girl, and they have grown children. What is that you are wearing there? An American flag?

BBS: *That's a pin of the state of Oklahoma. I have spent so much time there, that I feel like a native son.*

JF: Will remained a native son all his life.

BBS: *He was always the small town boy, wasn't he?*

JF: Just a small town Oklahoma boy. That's all he talked about — well, among other things; he talked all the time, but he always brought up the topic of Claremore and Ponca City.

BBS: *The character of* Judge Priest *fitted right in with that background. Was that shot on location?*

JF: No, we did it right in the studio.

BBS: *In those days, how long would it take to make a picture?*

JF: On the largest pictures it would take four to five weeks. And they weren't expensive pictures at all, but they all did very well. In fact, my favorite picture of all times is *Judge Priest*.

BBS: *It was number two on the honor roll of best pictures for that year. But let me ask you about* Dr. Bull, *which was the first film you two made together.*

JF: It was a little out of the ordinary for Will, but it was a very successful picture. You know, the thing was written as a drama, and rather heavy, and we just knocked that aside and injected comedy overtones. So that made it all right. We made it into a humorous picture, but the script that came to us was pretty heavy.

BBS: *Will Rogers didn't stick to the written dialogue anyway, did he?*

JF: Oh no! Never! Nobody could write for Will. He'd read his script and say, "What does that mean?" And I'd say, "Well, that's rather a tough question. I don't know what it means exactly." Then we would finally figure out what it meant, and I'd say to him, "Say it in your own words!" And he'd go away, muttering to himself, getting his lines ready, and when he came back, he'd make his speech in typical Rogers fashion, which was better than any writer could write for him. Because no writer could write for Will.

BBS: *Wasn't it a little tough on his fellow actors?*

JF: Oh, no! no! no! We had good people, and Will always gave 'em a cue. It wasn't tough on them at all.

BBS: *Didn't they have to ad-lib a little at the same time?*

JF: Oh yes, they ad-libbed a little bit, too — and Will would ad-lib back with them. We'd let them ad-lib a little bit, so it made sense, but he'd always give them a cue. He was very professional, Will was; as an actor, you know — very professional. I had only one request of him. Once I said, "Look, I'm a late sleeper. I have to get up and stand in a shower bath for ten minutes, a cold shower. Then I have a cup of coffee, and dash down here, and I'm always a little late. But I'm down here at 8:30." Will said, "I'm an early riser, you know, my cowboy training." So I told him, "Well, will you hang out in your dressing room until I get on the set! You're making a bum out of me!" But he didn't. He wanted to visit with the grips and the cameraman and the rest of the cast, and whiz around and chat and talk, making jokes. I'd sneak on the set and he'd spot me, "Ah, there he is! The late sleeper!"

BBS: *You mentioned that you suggested he wait in his dressing room. As far as you know, did he ever use that fancy bungalow Fox had built for him?*

JF: No! I don't think he even knew where it was. He never went near it. I don't think he even knew he had a dressing room. He just sat on the set, either writing his column, and when he finished that, he'd be talking to whoever was near. When he wasn't in a scene, you know, he'd sit down with a pencil and paper and start writing his daily column. And then he'd read it to me, and asked me to criticize it. And I told him, "I can't criticize what you're writing. You're writing about topical things. I never look at a newspaper, with the exception of the sports pages. But it sounds awfully good to me; it sounds very funny, very timely and to the point. As far as politics are concerned, I know nothing about them." But he was a delight to work with. It got so that I could read a scene and I'd say, "Will, this doesn't look right. You better say this in your own words." And he'd come back and say it perfectly in his own words. We never stuck to the written script. There was nobody that could write for Will. Lamar Trotti, God rest his soul, he could write closer than anybody for Will.

BBS: *You said that Mr. Rogers was easy to work with. If you asked him to do something, he'd do it? Or did he ever display any temperament?*

JF: We didn't work like that. We'd talk the scene over, and I'd say, "To me this is a useless scene. I don't think it belongs in the story; it just holds the story up." And Will would say, "I agree with you. Why do it, if it's just going to be cut out?" So I would say, "Let's go to another scene." Will liked to work. He liked pictures. But as far as temperament is concerned, my God, you just as soon have temperament from St. Peter!

BBS: *I understand that Mr. Rogers wouldn't even read the script, or prepare himself, but come on the set and ask you, "What's this next scene all about?"*

JF: Yes. We talked it over, and he'd ask, "Do I have any lines?" and I'd say, "I'm afraid so." And he'd say, "Well, let me look at them." And I'd say, "Go out, read 'em your own way, change 'em, take a pencil, write something. This is hogwash! It's from an Oxford graduate. Go on, write it your own way!" And what he came up with was so much better than what was written in the script. But I don't think he ever read a script at home.

BBS: *Ad-libbing so much, wouldn't each retake be different?*

JF: With Will? We never had any retakes. And he never watched any rushes. When he finished a day's work, he'd get in his car, go home and start roping calves.

BBS: *About 4:30, would he sing out "Santa Monica Canyon!" to let the director know that he was ready to go home?*

JF: I never knew him to do that, for the simple reason that I would let him go at 4 o'clock. Well, he worked very hard, and I worked hard, so around 4 o'clock I'd say to him in bad Spanish, *"Andamo la casa!"*

January 17, 1972

Alice
Roosevelt
Longworth

Alice Roosevelt Longworth: Do you come from a large family? I am one of six.

Bryan B. Sterling: *Sorry, I am one of one.*

ARL: Actually, I am the only child by my father's first marriage. You know my horrid little brothers inquired from their nurse, "Sister doesn't have a mother, what did she do? How could she feed?" "Oh," said the old nurse, "she had a wet nurse." Whereupon these horrid little brothers would sing, "Sissy had a sweat nurse! Sissy had a sweat nurse!" You know, they were fascinated to tell about the oddity that I am. There are all sorts of things that are funny about families like that.

BBS: *You called them your "horrid" little brothers — but you don't really . . .*

ARL: No, of course not! I was just laughing about them. They are all very good boys.

BBS: *You are famous as "the rebel."*

ARL: I was in revolt all the time. I was pretty awful.

BBS: *Weren't you one of the first women to smoke in public?*

ARL: I did all those things, deliberately defying my parents.

BBS: *Isn't that the way most young people are?*

ARL: Yes, they are. But they made a fuss about my doing it!

BBS: *You were on very good terms with Franklin Roosevelt.*

ARL: I liked Franklin. I enjoyed Franklin. He couldn't have been more fun. But it was dreadfully trying, when you consider that there were no people like those wonderful Republican Roosevelts who lived at Sagamore Hill, and suddenly the Democratic Roosevelt nemesis came down the Hudson River. It couldn't have been funnier. They all took it seriously, rather my side of the family did. I could have had a heavenly time, but it would have been disloyal if I had had such fun with Franklin. But you want to talk about Will.

BBS: *I have several notes here. At a birthday party for FDR, which must have been in January 1934 — his birthday was the 30th of January . . .*

ARL: Yes.

BBS: *Will Rogers wrote that you were wearing a rather unusual pair of gold earrings. Those earrings had the shape of coal scuttles. Mr. Rogers thought that the reason you wore those gold earrings to the White House was strictly for laughs. Because they were gold, you wanted to see whether your fifth cousin was going to confiscate them.*

ARL: I never had coal-scuttle-shaped earrings. I don't know what he means. I love gold earrings, and of course, I would tease Franklin. You know that we went off gold at that time and you were supposed to turn in all the gold. I found every old gold necklace — I rooted out everything I had in the way of gold; in my time they wore those necklaces made of gold beads — and I wore them to tease Franklin. We had fun about it. But you see, I couldn't go on being seen at the White House, on account of political things. It was terribly hard on my darling Ted, my eldest brother — they are all younger than I. My father, how like parents, wanting the sons to follow in his footsteps. Nothing could be worse! Of course, Ted did follow. He went to the war, Assistant Secretary of the Navy; he ran for Governor and was defeated by Alfred Smith. So that broke things up. He obviously adored my father —we all were tremendously under the influence of our father. It was great fun, but I was in revolt all the time. But you can see, it wouldn't have been fair to Ted.

BBS: *And furthermore, you had to keep some distance, because you were considered one of the leaders of the Republican Party.*

ARL: Oh, no!

BBS: *Will Rogers said that everyone came to you for advice, and that you were the most knowledgeable person in Washington.*

ARL: Oh, indeed, I knew what was going on, but I think it was all exaggerated.

BBS: *Do you still keep up with all the insides of politics?*

ARL: Now I just have to read about it. But I have a taste for it. My earliest recollection about politics is waiting to hear the returns on the first McKinley election in 1896. I recall the buggy coming up the drive with the latest returns.

BBS: *Will Rogers had the greatest admiration for you.*

ARL: I had an affection for him, and I think he had an affection for me. And Mrs. Rogers was awfully nice too.

BBS: *One time, in 1922, you, Mr. Longworth, and Mrs. Rogers, went to a White House reception. This was during the Harding Administration. Mr. Rogers wrote that as long as you were there, the evening was a success.*

ARL: Oh, we used to have a good time. But when you have a good time, you don't remember all the details, you know. There were many occasions when I would see Will. Often he would be at one end of the room, and I would be at the other end, and we would wave "Hi" to one another.

BBS: *I recall having read that the first time you met Will Rogers was aboard the German ship "Imperator."*

ARL: My brother Kermit was married in 1914, and he and his bride were coming back from Europe. As I recall, when the ship landed, war had been declared. That was the first time we met. Then I saw him in New York, in the Follies, and he waved to me from the stage. I sat in a box and I waved back. And Betty, his wife, she was a dear; she was exactly right for him. Will was always sheer fun, incapable of bad taste, incapable of an error of any sort in his relations to people.

BBS: *I have long wondered what this reference meant. In December 1926, Will Rogers wrote about a party of 160 guests, which you and Mr. Longworth also attended. He wrote, "Miss Alice looked wonderful, as usual . . ."*

ARL: Bless his heart.

BBS: *". . . and Nick wore his hair brushed straight back. I had never seen him with it fixed that way."*

ARL: How lovely! This is delightful! Oh, how like Will! You see, Nick was completely bald!

BBS: *Will Rogers said that he used to drop into Mr. Longworth's office with Mr. Tilson, the Republican majority leader at the time, and they used to sit and visit with him . . .*

ARL: . . . and have a drink . . . a drink, is putting it mildly. Wait, what was it they used to call it? They had a facetious name for it. "Incipient drunkards" is what they called themselves.

BBS: *Did Mr. Rogers drink?*

ARL: Never! He never drank, yet there was an enormous amount of drinking going on then.

BBS: *Yes, Will Rogers wrote, "Look at Congress! It votes dry and drinks wet!"*

ARL: Absolutely! By the way, where do you live?

BBS: *New York City.*

ARL: I have loved New York ever since I was a child.

BBS: *Your father was Police Commissioner of New York City, wasn't he?*

ARL: Yes, and after that he came down here to Washington as Undersecretary of the Navy.

BBS: *Will Rogers loved your father.*

ARL: Oh, yes. I think that was primarily because my father was out West, and having that experience, there was some common bond there.

BBS: *Perhaps that was one of the reasons. But Will Rogers had the highest regard for your father, and he said so many* times. *But tell me, you wrote the book* Crowded Hours *in 1933.*

ARL: Yes, I had to make money. Nick died, and there were debts, and I had to do something to pay them. Although I had to sell the thing when the market was very low. So then, I, gritting my teeth, turning up my nose, making faces, cashed in on my notorious past under another name. So I was able to make, whatever it was, marvelous by those standards, between $75,000 and $100,000 on this book, which seemed very much to me — and it was, then.

BBS: *What are you writing now?*

ARL: Absolutely nothing. The stuff that is being written today is fatuous.

BBS: *That's why I think you should write your story, not somebody else.*

ARL: I do keep notes. But let us speak about Will. What tribe of Indians did he belong to?

BBS: *The Cherokees.*

ARL: Will used to talk about Indians. He just loved them.

BBS: *In those days there was an entirely different feeling towards Indians.*

ARL: It has been only in the last years that the Indian has been recognized as one of the most abused of people, and there it was their land in the first place. It's really amazing!

BBS: *In our show, Will Rogers says, "In Claremore, Oklahoma, they just built the first Indian hospital in the country. Now let's see, Columbus discovered America about 400 years ago, and it took us 400 years to build a hospital for the Indians. Just think of what us Indians have to look forward to in the next 400 years. They might even build us a cemetery!"*

ARL: Hah! That's just like him! What an extraordinary character he was, and you know, everyone had affection for him — affection in the truest sense of the word.

April 16, 1974

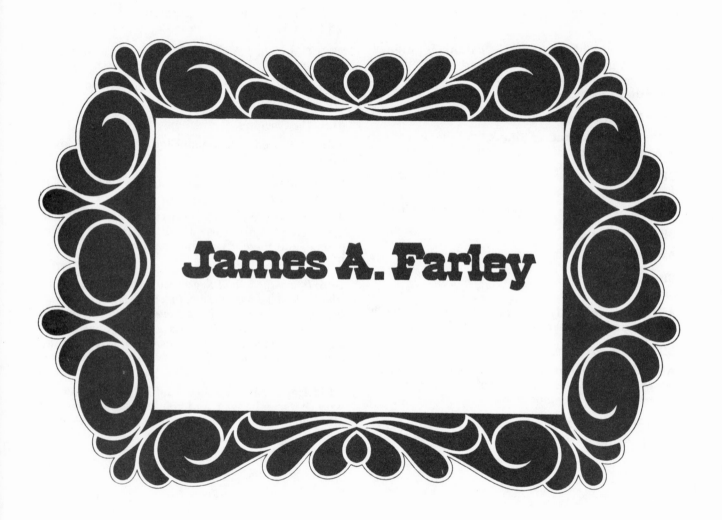

James A. Farley

Bryan B. Sterling: *My questions will concern Will Rogers and any association you might have had. As you know, he did have numerous personal contacts with President Franklin D. Roosevelt.*

James A. Farley: That is right.

BBS: *In fact, he stayed with Mr. Roosevelt at the White House overnight.*

JAF: That's one night more than I ever stopped there under Mr. Roosevelt. That's interesting, isn't it. I had dozens of luncheons with him. I used to lunch with him every so often, and many dinners, but I never slept a night in the White House then. That isn't any criticism, but people wouldn't believe that. The only time I ever slept in the White House was during the Atlantic City Convention, when President Johnson sent for me. Speaking of the White House, they say that Will Rogers abhorred getting into a dress suit. Now I never saw him in anything but a dark suit. Even when he went to the White House for dinner,

he would wear a black tie, when everybody else would wear white tie and tails — which was more or less obligatory. He knew better, but he wouldn't change. Now I know I saw him in the Follies wearing a full dress suit, but not to the White House. Do you know anything about his reason?

BBS: *I know what Will Rogers wrote about that. He said: "I drag out the old blue serge suit, double breasted, that has fooled many a one, if you don't watch it too close, into thinking maybe it's a quarter-breed tuxedo. Course, the soft shirt and collar looks kinder negligee, but the black bow tie, and the old blue serge, looking black by lamp light, why, it looks within the requirements of 'dress formal.' " But tell me, do you recall President Roosevelt's evaluation of Will Rogers?*

JAF: He had an extremely high opinion — everybody did who knew Will and enjoyed his writings. Whether you liked Will, or not — and I know Mr. Roosevelt did like him, he liked him very much, and everything that was ever said by Will about Mr.

Roosevelt, whether it was all good or not, he appreciated. No doubt about that.

BBS: *I understand that one Sunday night, Will Rogers had his regular broadcast, and President Roosevelt was to deliver one of his fireside chats later that evening, but he listened to Will Rogers first.*

JAF: I am sure he did. He would do that; he would listen to Will — everybody else did. Or most people who read the *New York Times*, the first thing they did was to look for his observation that day. Regardless whether it was good or bad for us, there was always a laugh in it.

BBS: *I always felt that President Roosevelt and Will Rogers made a great pair.*

JAF: No doubt about that.

BBS: *Mr. Rogers often explained some of the policies Mr. Roosevelt tried to initiate.*

JAF: He certainly could do that in his own clever way. And he would take the wind out of the sails of some of these pontifical fellows who thought they were important. You know, I saw Will when Mr. Roosevelt spoke in the Hollywood Bowl, on that first trip he made West during the campaign of '32. Will Rogers was in a box with Mr. Hearst and Marion Davies, and some other people. But I left that night before Mr. Roosevelt spoke, because I was taking a night train back to New York. You see, I didn't fly in those days. So on the way out, I passed that box, and Will stopped me and introduced me to Mr. Hearst. That was the only time I ever met Mr. Hearst.

BBS: *That was the occasion when Will Rogers introduced FDR to the crowd. He called him Franklin and said, "This introduction may not have been very flowery, but remember, you are only a candidate. Come back when you are President, and I will do better. I am wasting no oratory on a mere prospect."*

JAF: You know, I had forgotten that.

BBS: *At one time, while you were Postmaster General, Will Rogers kiddingly suggested that "Jim Farley thought up this current craze of chain letters to increase the revenue of the U.S. Post Office."*

JAF: I didn't think it up, of course, and Will knew it. If he wanted to write a friendly line, I had no objection to it. I thought it was all right. But I remember that, because many people wrote me after that appeared, some of them kidding me, and some of them wrote very serious letters.

BBS: *He was just kidding about it.*

JAF: Of course he was. In fact he gave me an autographed photograph on which he had written: "To Jim Farley, a politician and a gentleman — a rare combination, Will Rogers." It disappeared out of my office one night, and I never found out what happened. It may turn up some day someplace.

BBS: *Did you ever meet Will Rogers in Oklahoma?*

JAF: No, but I saw Will once with Amon Carter, down in Texas. Now Amon was a most powerful man in Fort Worth. He did a lot of good for Texas, but especially for Fort Worth. He used to say, Fort Worth was where the West begins. As I said, I was down there in Dallas. They were giving me some kind of a dinner; either Ma or Pa Ferguson, I don't remember which one, was Governor at the time. And Will brought Amon over to Dallas. Amon wouldn't go into the ballroom — he didn't like the Dallas crowd. Amon Carter sat just outside the ballroom, right at the door, and the door was open. Now everybody there knew that Amon Carter was outside and wouldn't come in. So when Will got up to speak, he began, "I have a friend . . ." Now I don't want to attempt to imitate Will, but he told how he had this friend, and how this friend finally consented to come over to this village, or town — whichever way he referred to Dallas. And he went on like this for quite a while about this friend that didn't want to come into the ballroom. And Amon never did show up inside. He had just made up his mind — it was a strange thing — but that was Amon's attitude.

BBS: *Do you recall the last time you spoke with Will Rogers?*

JAF: I was in Los Angeles, and I saw in the papers that Will was planning to leave for Alaska, either that day or the next. So I called him up and chatted with him. It was a very friendly chat and he told me how much he appreciated my call, and I wished him well. You can imagine how shocked I was when I heard he had been killed. It seemed like only hours since I spoke to him. He was a great person. It was a tragedy that he lost his life in the way he did, and when he did. He had many more years to live, to make a contribution to this country.

October 30, 1975

Charles V. McAdam

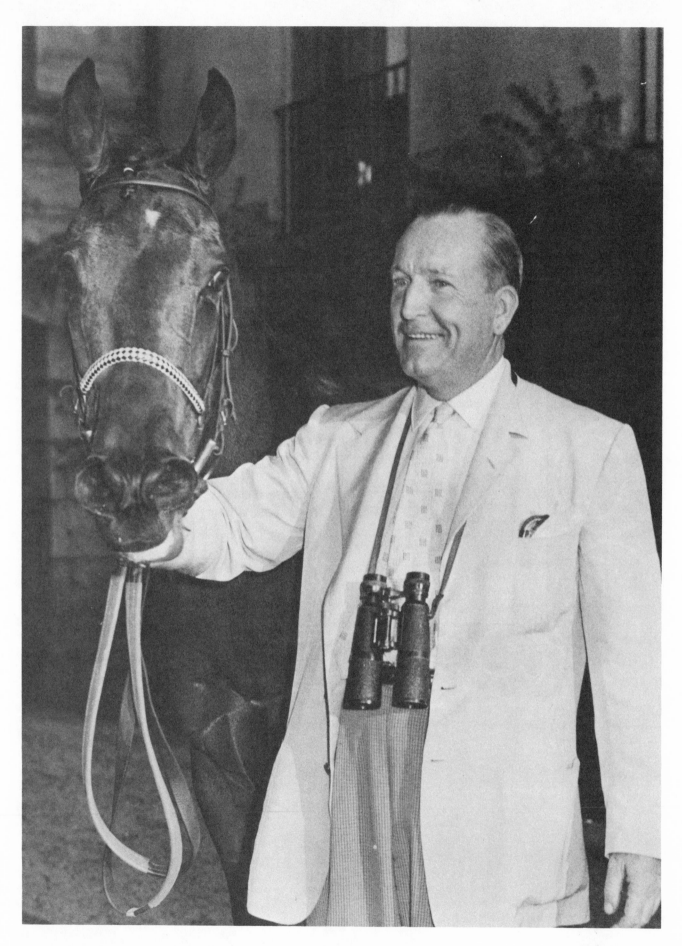

Bryan B. Sterling: *You were one of the cofounders of the McNaught Newspaper Syndicate?*

Charles V. McAdam: Yes, I cofounded the syndicate with V. V. McNitt. I don't want to belittle my cofounder, but I am always shocked when I read stuff about the syndicate and I'm not in the picture.

BBS: *When did you form the syndicate?*

CVM: We started January 3rd, 1922.

BBS: *If you started in 1922, then Will Rogers' weekly articles, which began in December 1922, must have been one of your earliest syndications.*

CVM: Yes, Rube Goldberg was in our syndicate, and he said to McNitt and me, "Come to a luncheon with me and you'll hear a guy I think you'll like!" So we went to the luncheon. Rube knew Rogers well, and he introduced us. After we heard Will address that luncheon crowd, we chewed it over and decided that we needed humor in the syndicate. We started Will at $500 a week. Then, after he had been with us a couple of years, he came up to the office one day. We were in the *New York Times* building at 42nd Street and Broadway; we had the 22nd floor at that time. He was appearing at the Ziegfeld Theatre, right across the street. Anyway, he came in and shut the door. "Charlie," he said. "I want to talk to you. Two of your competitors want me to come with them, and they've offered me $800 a week. But you fellows are pretty good." So I said, "I tell you what I'll do with you. Suppose I make it a thousand a week?" He said, "You're nuts. I love you and I'll never leave you." And he never did. I just shook hands with him — never had a contract. Can you imagine that nowadays? Just a handshake!? And on the wall in my office hangs an autographed picture of Will, with this inscription: "With best wishes of ample sales, Will Rogers." After that he always wanted to see me. He called me "the liberal fellow" — McNitt was a Scotsman; I'm Irish. Oh, he'd come in from the Follies, and like a cowboy by the campfire, he'd sit crosslegged on top of my desk, and he'd say, "Get the girls in here! I want to see how this will sound tonight. The governor of Maryland is coming, and the mayor of Pittsburgh." He used to be alerted as to who would be in the audience. So he would try it out on the girls, and everybody listened. Of course the men did, too. You might say that was his work-out before he got on stage.

BBS: *You said that he started at $500 a week, how high did he go?*

CVM: I got him up to $2500 a week, at the time of his death. And he had no office, no secretary.

BBS: *He even wrote his own letters.*

CVM: If someone wrote him a letter, he would use the back of it to send in his column; he'd use the back of bills, anything. And his grammar! I had an editor, Charley Driscoll, all through his career with us, and one day he said to Will, "Mr. Rogers, you use the word 'ain't' all the time. Now I am the editor, and

that is incorrect!" You know what Will Rogers said? He said, "Listen, Driscoll. I know a lot of people that don't say 'ain't' that ain't eatin'!"

BBS: *To the best of your recollection how many papers took Will Rogers' column, and how did they get supplied with the column overnight? It must have cost a fortune in wire charges.*

CVM: This is the way it went out. It went out by wire, to say, the *Cleveland Plain Dealer*, which was a morning paper. Then the various papers throughout the state would simply clip it out of the Cleveland paper, and save toll. We would send it to Cleveland, night press rate, collect. Or any paper near Kansas City would clip it from the *Kansas City Star*. You see, they would pay us for the column, but they didn't have to pay any wire charges. In answer to your other question, I would say well over 400 newspapers took the column. The *New York Times* wouldn't let us sell it anywhere around New York. They took a territory way up to Syracuse.

BBS: *I have heard that you sometimes had business discussions right on the street.*

CVM: I'd be out, coming from lunch, or something, and he'd see me, and he'd holler "Hey!" across the street. He would sit on a fire hydrant, wrap his legs around it, and we'd talk about the syndicate. Soon a big crowd would be all around us, and I'd suggest, "Let's go up to your dressing room, we're drawing flies."

BBS: *Will Rogers didn't smoke and . . .*

CVM: He chewed little bits of string, or he'd pick a rubber band out of my little thing here on the desk, and chew that, not chewing gum. You know, one time, late on a Saturday, he decided to go to Europe. I asked him, "Do you have enough clothes?" And he said, "I'll go down on Seventh Avenue; they're open Sundays. I'll get a suit for fifty bucks, that'll do. I don't need two suits!" That's the way he was. Or listen to this! Rube Goldberg's cartoons were cancelled the week before, and when I met Will, he asked me, "I don't see Rube Goldberg's cartoon in the *New York Journal*. What's happened?" I said, "Well, I hate to tell you, but the Hearst organization cancelled Goldberg in their entire list of papers." And Rogers said, "You know, Charlie, I never want to be a great success. The road down is terrible." Now get this, this is Rogers talking, and here he was, on top of the world. You know, one time Betty said to me, "I wish that Will would give up films and all that stuff, and just work for you."

BBS: *Do you remember the last time you saw him?*

CVM: Well, I tell you, just before he was going on this trip with Wiley Post, I went to the Waldorf Astoria Towers, where Mrs. Rogers was, and I said, "Betty, isn't there something you can do to keep him from taking this hazardous trip? Now to begin with," I said, "I don't want to fly unless there are two pilots, and I certainly wouldn't want to fly with a guy with one eye." And she said, "Well, Charlie, you like to play golf, some people like to play bridge, some people collect stamps, my husband doesn't care where he's going, as long as he's flying. Do you know he would get on a plane at Glendale and fly to Albuquerque, just to have a game of polo, and then fly back?" I thought she'd say, "I'll do what I can and see if I can't stop him." But I guess she couldn't.

BBS: *Mrs. Rogers, herself, was not too keen on flying.*

CVM: You are forcing me to say what I shouldn't say. There wasn't anything left for Will Rogers to accomplish. He had everything; he couldn't go any further. He took chances he didn't have to take. I remember, I was fishing at Lake Mahopac, where I had a home. And outside my home, I had a cowbell. And they would ring that cowbell if somebody wanted me on the telephone. Well, that day I was fishing with one of my kids, and suddenly that cowbell rang and kept going and going and going and going. I came in off the lake as fast as I could, and when I answered the phone, I said, "When was Rogers killed?" And my office said, "How did you know?" I said, "The way that cowbell kept ringing, I knew it was an emergency." So I get in the car — 52 miles from my office — and I start for New York. I don't know how fast I was going, when a motorcycle cop stops me. He says, "Where the hell do you think you're going?" And I said, "Well, officer, I just got the news that Will Rogers was killed." He said, "WHAT!? You don't mean it? Don't fool me! Oh, that's a terrible thing. You better go on, but don't kill yourself. Now go on!" That's the way they thought of Will Rogers. That guy was unique.

June 11, 1972

Biographies

LEW AYRES, b. Minneapolis, Minn. Began show business career touring Mexico with own orchestra, played with Henry Halstead's orchestra. Screen debut in 1929. Served as medical corpsman and assistant chaplain in W.W.II. Films include: *All Quiet on the Western Front, Dr. Kildare* series, *Dark Mirror, Johnny Belinda, The Carpetbaggers, Advise and Consent, Altars of the World* (producer).

DAVID BUTLER, b. San Francisco, Cal. Actor, director. Began career as stage manager and actor in Los Angeles for Oliver Morosco. Most famous film of acting career: *Seventh Heaven*. Directed, i.a., *Lullaby of Broadway, Where's Charley?, By The Light Of The Silvery Moon, Calamity Jane*; for TV: "Wagon Train," "Leave It To Beaver," Three Bob Hope Specials, "Seven Little Foys."

CHARLES COLLINS, b. Indian Territory (Oklahoma) in a "half-dugout"; organized dance band and studied dancing. American shows include *Artists and Models; Say When; Hooray for What; Ripples; Smiling Faces; Lightnin'*. In London appeared in *Stop Press; That's a Good Girl; Coo-ee; The Co-Optimist*. Films: *The Dancing Pirate; Swing Hostess*. Also TV appearances.

DOROTHY STONE COLLINS, b. Brooklyn, N.Y., June 3, 1905, d. September 24, 1974. Stage debut with her father, Fred Stone, in *Stepping Stones*. Other productions include *Criss Cross; Three Cheers*, with Will Rogers; *Gay Divorcee*, with Fred Astaire; *Hooray for What*, with Ed Wynn; *Show Girl*, for Zieg-feld; *Ripples; Smiling Faces*. m. Charles Collins, September 24, 1931, in London, while appearing at the Palladium.

JAMES A. FARLEY, b. Grassy Point, N.Y., May 30, 1888, d. June 9, 1976. Democratic political leader, Democratic National Committee Chairman, successfully managed Franklin Delano Roosevelt's presidential campaigns 1932 and 1936. United States Postmaster General (1933–1936 and 1937–1940). Presidential advisor and confidant, known as Mr. Democrat.

JOHN FORD, b. Portland, Me., 1894, d. 1973. Academy awards for best director: 1936, 1940, 1941, 1952. Films include: *Arrowsmith, Hurricane, Drums along the Mohawk, Grapes of Wrath, Tobacco Road, How Green Was My Valley, Quiet Man, Mr. Roberts, The Last Hurrah, The Man Who Shot Liberty Valance.*

STERLING HOLLOWAY, b. Cedartown, Ga. Started career on stage in New York City, i.a., four yearly editions of "Garrick Gaieties," also vaudeville, night clubs, radio. Films include: *Walk in the Sun, Death Valley, Alice in Wonderland, Jungle Book* (voice). Numerous TV credits.

HENRY KING, b. Christiansburg, Va. Actor, writer, director. Began career touring in stock company, vaudeville, burlesque, circus. New York stage debut in *Top O'the Morning*. Directed, i.a., *Stella Dallas, Winning of Barbara Worth, Lloyds of London, In Old Chicago, Alexander's Ragtime Band, Wilson, Twelve O'Clock High, The Sun Also Rises.*

ALICE ROOSEVELT LONGWORTH, b. New York, N.Y. First child of Theodore Roosevelt, 26th President. Mother, Alice Hathaway Lee, died after giving birth. "Princess Alice" became famous for her escapades and rapier sharp wit. Brilliant hostess, most influential in Republican circles. In 1906 married Nicholas Longworth in White House ceremony. (Nicholas Longworth, b. Nov. 5, 1869; d. Apr. 9, 1931. U.S. Representative 1903–1013, 1915–1931; Speaker of the House, 1925–1931.)

MYRNA LOY, b. Helena, Mont. Started career on stage, continued in Hollywood. Voted among top ten money-making stars in Motion Picture Herald Fame Poll, 1937, 1938. Films include: *Desert Song, Black Watch, Arrowsmith, Vanity Fair, The Thin Man* series, *Test Pilot, Best Years of Our Lives.*

CHARLES V. McADAM, b. New York, N.Y. Began life in crime ridden "Hell's Kitchen" and worked his way up to presidency of McNaught Newspaper Syndicate, which he cofounded. At one time syndicated: O. O. McIntire, Rube Goldberg, Dale Carnegie, Abigail van Buren (Dear Abby), Alfred E. Smith, Leonard Lyons, Eleanor Roosevelt, Carroll Righter, Irvin S. Cobb, Bob Hope, Billy Rose, Paul Gallico, Walter Winchell and others. President Eisenhower's advisor and golf partner.

JOEL McCREA, b. Los Angeles, Cal. Started in amateur dramatics, then went into films. Pictures include: *Foreign Correspondent, Sullivan's Travels, Virginian, Four Faces West, Stars in My Crown, Ride the High Country, Mustang Country.* Member: Cowboy Hall of Fame.

EVELYN VENABLE MOHR, b. Cincinnati, Ohio. Started stage career with Walter Hampden in *Dear Brutus, Cyrano de Bergerac, Hamlet.* Films include: *Cradle Song, Death Takes a Holiday, The Little Colonel, Alice Adams, Star for a Night, Happy-Go-Lucky, My Old Kentucky Home, The Frontiersman.*

HAL MOHR, b. San Francisco, Cal., Aug. 2, 1894, d. May 10, 1974. Film pioneer, inventor and innovator, began career as independent film producer, director and cameraman, then came to Hollywood. Cinematographer of over 100 films, including *The Jazz Singer* (first sound film, 1927), *Outward Bound, Front Page, Captain Blood, Green Pastures, Destry Rides Again, Watch On The Rhine, Another Part of the Forest, Rancho Notorious, The Four Poster, Member of the Wedding, The Wild One, The Last Voyage.* TV: "I Married Joan," "Bob Cummings Show," "Barbara Stanwyck Show," "Father of the Bride." Winner of two Academy Awards for best cinematography: *A Midsummer Night's Dream* (1935), *Phantom of the Opera* (1943). Governor of Academy of Motion Picture Arts and Sciences; President, American Society of Cinematographers.

IRENE RICH, b. Buffalo, N.Y. Started in films as extra, also vaudeville, night clubs, radio, starring for several years in own series. Films include: *Lady Windemere's Fan, Craig's Wife, Mortal Storm, That Certain Age, This Time for Keeps, Joan of Arc.*

HAL ROACH, b. Elmira, N.Y. Director, writer, producer. Started film career as stock cowboy, met Harold Lloyd and together made picture, which they sold for $850. Hal Roach Studios developed, concentrating primarily on comedy shorts such as Harold Lloyd, Our Gang, Stan Laurel and Oliver Hardy.

PATRICIA ZIEGFELD STEPHENSON, b. New York, N.Y. Only child of Florenz Ziegfeld, Jr., America's most splendent producer and showman, and Billie Burke, star of stage and motion pictures. Author of *The Ziegfelds' Girl, Confessions of an Abnormally Happy Childhood.*

PEGGY WOOD, b. Brooklyn, N.Y. Actress, singer, author. Starred in musicals *Maytime, Bittersweet* (London). Legitimate theater, i.a., *Candida, Merchant of Venice, Ol' Acquaintance, Blithe Spirit.* Films include: *Story of Ruth, Sound of Music.* TV: "Mama." Books: *Splendid Gypsy, How Young You Look, Star Wagon, Arts and Flowers.*

Index